# REFORGING AMERICA

THE WORKS OF LOTHROP STODDARD

VOLUME ONE

Revisions and Additions Copyright © 2025 by Liberty Bell Publications LLC

ISBN: 978-1-59364-034-7 Softcover

ISBN: 978-1-59364-036-1 Hardcover

All Rights Reserved. No revised or added part of this book may be reproduced in any manner without the express written consent of the publisher, except in the case of brief excerpts in critical reviews or articles. All inquiries should be addressed to:

Liberty Bell Publications
655 Sandifer Road
York, SC 29745
1-803-818-5407
dmartyo@protonmail.com

Liberty Bell Publications® is a registered trademark of Liberty Bell Publications LLC, a South Carolina Limited Liability Company.

Printed in the United States of America

# Editor's Note

> Those who cannot remember the past are condemned to repeat it.
> —George Santayana, *The Life of Reason* (1905)

Liberty Bell Publications is reprinting this controversial book from 1927 as the first volume in a new series entitled *The Works of Lothrop Stoddard*. It is a thorough study of the forging, or building, of America from its discovery and founding, through the migrations of the various peoples who came here over the centuries and the struggle to maintain the character, culture and beliefs of those founders, in order to have a cohesive and united people as time went on. This study is prescient to issues, both good and bad, which America faces today. The unprecedented and seeming failure to assimilate these incoming immigrants, forebodes issues which are becoming obvious and remain to be resolved by future generations. Stoddard explains the methods used to deal with many of these issues during the eighteenth and nineteenth centuties. Some thought that many of the issues were resolved and others thought that they were nothing to be concerned about. A hundred years later, we find ourselves still struggling with these issues and finding, some say, that they are worse now than ever and, perhaps, unfixable.

We have corrected grammatical errors that were found, including punctuation and obsolete spelling where possible. We have deleted hyphens in words that were hyphenated in 1927 but no longer are. No correction has altered or changed the author's intent or meaning.

We plan on publishing the other works of the author as time permits.

Please send any corrections or ideas to the publisher.

Liberty Bell Publications

# REFORGING AMERICA

THE STORY OF OUR NATIONHOOD

BY

LOTHROP STODDARD, A.M., Ph.D.

(Harvard)

CHARLES SCRIBNER'S SONS

NEW YORK · LONDON

1927

## BY LOTHROP STODDARD

REFORGING AMERICA

SCIENTIFIC HUMANISM

SOCIAL CLASSES IN POST-WAR EUROPE

RACIAL REALITIES IN EUROPE

THE REVOLT AGAINST CIVILIZATION

THE NEW WORLD OF ISLAM

THE RISING TIDE OF COLOR AGAINST
   WHITE WORLD-SUPREMACY

## CHARLES SCRIBNER'S SONS

REFORGING AMERICA

COPYRIGHT, 1927, BY

CHARLES SCRIBNER'S SONS

*Printed in the United States of America*

TO
MY SON

# PREFACE

To us Americans of today there has been vouchsafed what is at once a high duty and a high privilege. For we are able to share in the greatest enterprise since Independence—the reforging of America.

Clear and strong athwart the tumult of our present discords sounds the call to national unity. Firm and staunch is the national will to become again what we once were—a truly like-minded people.

This book essays the story of American nationhood. It tells how, on the deep foundations of the long colonial past, there arose a splendid young nation. It goes on to tell how the bright promise of our early days was darkened by the disaster of the Civil War and by the blight of alien factors. Lastly, this book tells how, after more than half a century of deepening confusion which threatened to destroy our ideals, our culture, our very nationhood itself, we awoke to the peril and are today engaged in the inspiring task of fulfilling the early promise of American life.

The problems of national reconstruction are many. The closing of the gates to mass immigration is merely a first step. Alien elements in our population must be assimilated. Political and cultural dissensions should be harmonized.

Above all, our great Negro problem must be realistically and constructively dealt with. The dilemma of color, at once the most chronic and the most acute of American issues, has long been regarded with despairing pessimism. In these pages we have suggested at least a tentative solution which we have termed bi-racialism: The Key to Social Peace.

The task before us is thus long and arduous. But the heart of the American people is sound, its courage is high, and its eyes are opened to the challenge of the times. With knowledge and vision, we may have faith that we shall overcome our present difficulties and shall continue to tread the upward path toward a greater and better America.

LOTHROP STODDARD.

Brookline, Massachusetts,
March 3, 1927.

# CONTENTS

| CHAPTER | | PAGE |
|---|---|---|
| I. | THE FOUNDATIONS OF OLD AMERICA | 1 |
| II. | THE BEGINNING OF NATIONAL LIFE | 11 |
| III | THE FIRST FORGING OF AMERICA | 25 |
| IV. | THE SCHISM OF THE CIVIL WAR | 35 |
| V. | THE SHATTERING OF OLD AMERICA | 43 |
| VI. | THE ALIEN FLOOD | 57 |
| VII. | ON THE ROAD TO RUIN | 83 |
| VIII. | THE GREAT AWAKENING | 107 |
| IX. | THE CLOSING OF THE GATES | 117 |
| X. | THE WILL TO NATIONAL UNITY | 137 |
| XI. | THE DILEMMA OF COLOR | 155 |
| XII. | BIRACIALISM: THE KEY TO SOCIAL PEACE | 173 |
| XIII. | THE SCOPE OF THE TASK BEFORE US | 197 |
| XIV. | REFORGING AMERICA | 217 |
| CITED WORKS | | 229 |
| INDEX | | 231 |

# CHAPTER I

# THE FOUNDATIONS OF OLD AMERICA

Strong and deep are America's foundations. Long and staunch was their laying—as befits that which should endure. From the first settlement at Jamestown to the Declaration of Independence (1607 to 1776), more time elapsed than has passed from Independence till the present day. That long colonial period of almost two centuries, which preceded the beginning of national life, must never be forgotten. It is the basic fact in American history.

America arose from the coming of a picked stock to a splendid and virgin land. The heart of a continent unsurpassed in climate, soil, and natural resources lay empty to the advent of civilized man. The few, red-skinned aborigines who roamed its vast forests and illimitable plains had set no real mark upon the country and were foredoomed to melt away. What the future was to be thus depended upon the character of the European newcomers. America was a clean slate on which its possessors could write virtually at will.

Under these circumstances the nature of the firstcomers was a matter of paramount importance. Fortunately, America's beginnings were made under highly favorable auspices. Practically all of the first colonists along the Atlantic seaboard were of the same general type. To be sure, there were some national differences. The two primary blocks of English settlement in Virginia and New England were at first sundered by Dutch and Swedish footholds along the lower Hudson and Delaware. Furthermore, the English colonists brought with them homeland divergencies displayed in contrasts like those between Puritan New England, Cavalier Virginia, Catholic Maryland, and Quaker Pennsylvania. However, none of these differences were insuperable. The Dutch and Swedes were racially so akin to their English neighbors that when their small settlements were annexed by the dominant English power, no lasting grievance was felt and no political feud perpetuated. Contrast what might have happened if real antagonists like Frenchmen or Spaniards had intruded! Then, indeed, the Atlantic seaboard would have witnessed ferocious colonial wars. But the French settled far away in the Canadian north, while the Spaniards remained in the remote south. Indeed, such hostile pressure as the French and Spaniards did eventually exert served the useful purpose of giving the young colonies common enemies, thereby making them tend to forget their domestic bickerings before the menace of foreign foes. Thus, long before the year 1700, it was clear that the Atlantic seaboard of North America (the nucleus of the future United States) was to be settled by a population essentially one in blood and outlook and welded into an embryonic unity by the predominance of English speech, institutions, and ideals.

This early English predominance is another point of capital importance. Not only was the Atlantic seaboard inhabited from the first by closely allied North European stocks, but it was also from the very outset saturated with Anglo-Saxon civilization. The Anglo-Saxon stamp was so deeply impressed upon this virgin land that the other cultural elements were either entirely absorbed or relegated to mere local significance. Thus the influx of large non-British elements like the Palatine Germans and the French Huguenots during the later colonial period never really disturbed the Anglo-Saxon mold into which America was cast from the very beginning—and which she has always basically retained. The widespread belief that colonial America was a hodge-podge of races and cultures is as erroneous as is the twin notion that modern America is a heterogeneous mass, still "in the making," and with no predominant blood, culture, or ideals. Both these false notions represent mainly the emotional protests of dissatisfied, unassimilated elements.

A glance at early population data is enough to dispel the idea of a polyglot colonial America. To begin with, the colonists were so prolific that the early settlers (who were, of course, mainly English) got a long head start over later arrivals. For example, the 20,000 Puritans who landed in New England between the years 1620 and 1640 had, by the beginning of the next century, increased fourfold to something like 80,000. Both New England and Virginia (together with Maryland), the two earliest centers of English colonization, remained "English" in the strict sense of the word right down to the Revolution. A few Scotch-Irish and French Huguenots represent virtually all the newcomers to New England during the later colonial period, while in Virginia and Maryland there is hardly a trace of anything save English immigration.

The middle colonies (New York, New Jersey, and Pennsylvania) and the far South (the Carolinas and Georgia) received the bulk of the non-English elements, albeit even these were mainly from other parts of the British Isles and were thus of "British," if not of "English," stock. The most numerous of these elements was the "Scotch-Irish," who arrived during the eighteenth century. These people, mostly of Lowland Scotch origin, had been settled by the British Crown in Ulster as a Protestant loyalist garrison to hold the disaffected native Irish in check. The decline of its industrial prosperity brought hard times to Ulster and caused a mass migration to America. Whole villages and towns came over, headed by their ministers, and settled thickly in Pennsylvania, New York, and the Southern colonies. Nearly 200,000 Scotch-Irish had entered America before the Revolution. In the later colonial period another Scotch migration, this time of Scotch Highlanders, took place. The merciless "flailing of the Clans" after Culloden made them restless and brought more than 20,000 Highlanders to America, mostly to New York or the far South. To Pennsylvania likewise came a considerable body of Welsh. These, together with a sprinkling of Celtic Irish and a small but steady stream of Lowland Scots, made up the tale of British migration to colonial America. It must, of course, be remembered that England continued to send a heavy influx to all parts of the colonies except self-contained New England, down to the Revolution.

Of the non-British elements in colonial America, the oldest were, of course, the Swedes and Dutch. Unsupported from home, the small Swedish settlement was soon absorbed by its Dutch and English neighbors. The more numerous Dutch, however, preserved their identity and set an ethnic and cultural imprint upon the Hudson River valley and adjacent districts, which still persists. Curiously enough, New Amsterdam, from the first, foreshadowed its future as the great cosmopolitan city of New York. Established, not like its neighbors from religious or political motives, but frankly for trade and commerce, New Amsterdam soon became a strikingly polyglot port town. During Dutch days no less than eighteen different languages were spoken on Manhattan Island, the population containing such then-exotic elements as a contingent of Italians and a community of Spanish and Portuguese Jews. English rule modified the situation somewhat, yet New Amsterdam (renamed "New York") continued throughout colonial times to be the only really cosmopolitan spot in America. In New York Colony and in New Jersey, the Dutch element steadily grew by natural increase until at the Revolution it numbered from 50,000 to 60,000.

The only really numerous non-British element in colonial America was the Germans. The German influx began with the founding of Pennsylvania, toward the end of the seventeenth century. Invited by William Penn, persecuted German Protestants entered Pennsylvania in a stream that soon swelled to notable proportions. These refugees came, not merely from what is now Germany, but also from parts of Austria and Switzerland. Fully

60,000 entered Pennsylvania alone during the colonial period, settling so compactly that they retained their ethnic and cultural identity and today survive as the so-called "Pennsylvania Dutch." Other lesser streams of German immigration turned to the South, to New York, and to New Jersey. The total number of German-speaking immigrants to colonial America was probably from 90,000 to 100,000.

The only other noteworthy non-British element in colonial America was the French Huguenots. They totaled at the most 10,000, but their significance was quite out of proportion to their numbers. Largely persons of education and good breeding who had left their homeland solely for conscience's sake, the Huguenots scattered widely over the colonies and everywhere made their mark in American life. Unlike the Germans, the French Huguenots assimilated rapidly and were soon absolutely incorporated into the cultural fabric of Anglo-Saxon America.

From the figures above quoted, we are able to form a fairly close estimate of the national origins of the colonial population. Since the total White population at the outbreak of the Revolution in 1775 was about 2,000,000, we find that fully 1,500,000 were of straight English blood, with perhaps 300,000 of other British stock and somewhat less than 200,000 of non-British elements. In other words, more than 90 percent of the White population was of British origin, the non-British elements totaling not much over 8 percent.

And what was true of national was equally true of racial origins. The colonial population was overwhelmingly of North European, or as it is generally termed, "Nordic," stock. The English, Scotch, Dutch, and Swedes were alike Nordic race-brethren and were thus temperamentally predisposed to harmonious understanding and complete fusion. Even the French Huguenots were mainly of Nordic blood. The only considerable non-Nordic element was found among the Germans. Apparently about one-half of the German immigrants during the colonial period were of Central European "Alpine" stock. This probably accounts in large measure for the aloofness and slow assimilation of the "Pennsylvania Dutch."

Even more striking than national and racial similarity was the high level of vigor and ability possessed by the population of colonial America. The colonial population was, in very truth, a "chosen people," rigidly selected by a whole series of ordeals that killed off the weak and worthless and left the fit to sire the Americans of the morrow.

To begin with, the colonists were largely religious refugees—men and women of unusual character who had exiled themselves for conscience's sake, seeking in a new land the fulfillment of their ideals. This was particularly true of the New England Puritans. As one of them phrased it, "God sifted a whole nation that He might send choice grain into the wilderness." Many of the Puritans were men of standing, learning, and high culture, who left comfortable homes and assured careers for the hardships and dangers of a pioneer life in a bleak and untamed land. The same was eminently true of the French Huguenots. In fact, it is these two stocks that, in relation to their numbers, have contributed the largest proportion of eminent men to American life.

Even those colonists who sought America from less idealistic motives tended to be persons of exceptional courage and enterprise. In these days of mighty ocean liners, we can scarcely conceive what crossing the Atlantic meant in colonial times. The average voyage was from six weeks to two months; the ships were small and often old and ill-found; the food and water were bad; sanitary conditions were unspeakable. Under such conditions the crowded immigrant ships were scourged with typhus, smallpox, scurvy, and other dread diseases, so that sometimes one-half or even three-fourths of the passengers died before the vessel sighted land. These conditions were well-known in Europe and sufficed to daunt weak and cowardly souls. What wonder that English convicts, given the choice of transportation or the gallows, often prayed to be hanged!

Many thousand convicts were, however, shipped to America and constituted the seamy side of immigration in colonial days. During the later colonial period, the British government systematically dumped its criminals upon America. The colonies bitterly resented the practice, but all attempts at restriction were overruled by the Crown. This was, in fact, one of the many colonial grievances that led to the Revolution. The Southern colonies were the worst sufferers, and the descendants of these human dregs constitute the majority of the "poor Whites," "sandhillers," "hillbillies," and other degenerate communities so often met with in the barren districts of the South.

Yet here, again, the stern conditions of colonial existence tended to weed out the weak and vicious, so that they bred relatively few of their kind to vex succeeding generations. Life in an untamed wilderness was hard. No sooner had the colonists landed than hardship and disease took another fearful toll. The harsh New England winter and the fever-haunted swamps of the South alike slew the unacclimatized newcomers wholesale. For example, nearly three-fourths of the *Mayflower* Pilgrims who landed at Plymouth, Massachusetts, were under the sod before the first year was over, while at Jamestown, Virginia, 900 persons landed, but only 150 remained at the end of the third year.

And, behind the specters of cold, disease, and famine leered the painted visage of the savage, ready with tomahawk and scalping knife to dispatch the careless and the unwary. The entire process of colonial settlement was, in fact, one continued, drastic cycle of eugenic selection. Only the racially fit usually came, and the few unfit who did come were mostly weeded out by the exacting requirements of early American life. More and more, the native-born colonial population became a stock remarkable for courage, initiative, and forceful vitality. America's human foundations had indeed been laid solidly and well!

Such, in brief, was the make-up of the 2,000,000 White inhabitants of the American colonies on the eve of the Revolution. Remember that these colonial population figures are no mere matters of historic interest. On the contrary, they are of vital importance for our own times. This is so because of the tremendous potential increase of the colonial stock. Planted on the fringe of an empty continent of incalculable possibilities, the colonists, once acclimated, bred with amazing rapidity. Furthermore, from the Revolution until well into the nineteenth century, few newcomers landed in America. This meant that the pioneer peopling of America, right across the continent to the Pacific Coast, was done almost exclusively by the colonial stock, which thus became the vital basis of nearly every part of the United States. The far-reaching significance of this is surely clear. We have already seen how the early colonists got a long lead over those who arrived in later colonial times. Well, in just the same way, the colonial stock as a whole got a corresponding lead over subsequent immigrants and thus acquired a primacy—political, economic, cultural, and otherwise—of basic importance in the development of American national life.

What this means in terms of mere numbers alone becomes evident when we examine a few of the statistical studies made on the basis of the most recent census—that of 1920. The almost incredible potentialities latent in the early colonial stock, especially in its more virile and expansive elements, are shown by the instance of the *Mayflower* Pilgrims. It has been estimated that the 51 survivors of the Plymouth settlement of the year 1620 had increased by the year 1920 to no less than 85,000 persons. The millions of "Yankee stock" spread clear across America spring from the 20,000 Puritans who landed in New England between the years 1620 and 1640. Lastly, considering the colonial stock as a whole, we find that it increased from about 2,000,000 at the end of the colonial period (1775) to almost 50,000,000 at the present day. In other words, the old colonial stock represents nearly one-half of all the White blood in present-day America.[1]

In our survey of the American people in colonial times, we have purposely omitted one element—the Negroes. Of course, numerically speaking, the Negroes had, by the later colonial period, become a considerable fraction of the population, numbering, as they did, nearly 500,000 at the outbreak of the Revolution. But the Negroes then formed a servile caste, fenced off from the White majority by a strict color line, and had no direct influence upon the times. The Negro was destined to be the cause of our worst disaster (the Civil War), and he is today the gravest of our national problems. But all that was far in the future. On the eve of the Revolution, the Negro was a negligible factor. Thus the Negro need not detain us when surveying America's colonial background. We will, therefore, defer considering his beginnings in America until he emerges as an important factor in the course of events.

Returning to our survey of the White colonial population, we may ask: what was the temper, and what were the tendencies, displayed by this hardy and vigorous folk that had taken root on the eastern fringe of the great American wilderness? At first glance it might seem as though the colonial Americans could not as yet be called in any sense a "people." Divided politically into thirteen colonies strung along the Atlantic seaboard for a thousand miles, from cold New England to semi-tropical Carolina and Georgia, the American colonists were sundered by obvious divergencies in aims and interests. Yet, beneath these divergencies, stronger and deeper trends were working for unity. We have already seen that the colonial Americans were virtually all of one blood; that they were steeped in a common culture and tradition; that they were governed by the same basic laws and institutions; and that they acknowledged an undivided allegiance and a common loyalty. The vast majority of colonial Americans considered themselves as overseas Englishmen. They prided themselves on their English speech, culture, and political liberties, and they felt themselves in the larger sense one with that distant motherland back across the ocean, which even the colonial-born of five or six generations always referred to as "Home."

Such were the bonds of union that the colonists had brought with them from the Old World. But the New World contributed others as well. First: the unifying pressure of the wilderness. Primeval America, with its vast forests, its brooding solitudes, and its sense of illimitable mystery, smote the first-comers from trim, well-ordered England with a sense of fear—almost

1. The Census Bureau estimates that 49.9 percent of the White blood in America is of the old stock. By the 1920 census this amounted to 47,330,000. Since the White population is today slightly over 100,000,000, the old stock should be conservatively estimated at approximately 50,000,000.

of terror. They were so few, and the new land was so huge and so untamed, that they instinctively kept in touch for fellowship and coordinated action.

Second: the pressure of the Indian. Primeval America was not quite empty. Its gloomy forests were haunted by ferocious and implacable beings. The North American Indian was the most formidable savage ever encountered by the colonizing European. The Redskin was a born warrior. From time immemorial the sparse Indian population, divided into many tribes, had waged fierce internecine war and had thereby developed a remarkable system of military tactics admirably suited to the country. Too few and too disunited to expel the White invaders, the Indians nevertheless slowed down the White advance and rendered it a difficult and dangerous undertaking. Every gain had to be consolidated, and every new district had to be cleared and settled before the frontier could once more be pushed forward. In all this the Indian really (albeit unwittingly) aided the formation of American unity by keeping the colonial nucleus relatively compact and preventing the White intruders from spreading out too thin, as might have occurred if the continent had been uninhabited. Furthermore, Indian opposition gave the colonists a common objective, imparted a sense of common loyalty, and put a continuous fighting edge on the colonial temper, which were all helpful in the evolution toward unity and nationhood.

These same qualities were at the same time being stimulated in even greater measure by a third unifying factor—the pressure of European rivals. The English colonists along the Atlantic seaboard were not the only Europeans in North America. The Spaniards had long preceded them in the far South, while the French established themselves, first in the Canadian North and later at the mouth of the Mississippi. The Spaniard meant little to the English colonists. Save for a few half-hearted raids on the Carolinas and Georgia, the Spaniard never attempted to harass the English in America. The Frenchman, on the contrary, was a great and ever-present peril. Intent on nothing short of the mastery of the continent, the French tirelessly explored the great American hinterland, connected their footholds in Canada and on the lower Mississippi, and threatened to strangle the English in the narrow strip of land between the Appalachian mountains and the sea. Furthermore, the French succeeded in stirring up the Indians against the English, making the Redmen more dangerous than before. The upshot was an interminable struggle of implacable ferocity. Both sides instinctively realized that it was a duel to the death. The homelands might suspend their rivalries from time to time, but there was no real peace in America. For almost one hundred and fifty years the grim struggle went on, until at last the vision of the elder Pitt rallied England to strike a decisive blow for empire. At Quebec the thrust struck home, and "New France" went down in hopeless defeat. By the peace of 1763, Britain and her colonies became joint masters of America.

The year 1763 marks the logical end of the "colonial" period. France having been eliminated, what were to be the relations between the triumphant overseas English and the motherland? Certainly, things could not remain as they were. The old easygoing days of filial dependence and maternal benevolent indifference were over. Pitt had awakened Britain to America. And Britain, having spent much blood and treasure, was minded to make something out of the imperial prize she had just won. Not only did British Cabinet Ministers devise taxes to make the colonists pay for part of the recent war debts, but British officials likewise began to draw up far-reaching plans for the development and exploitation of Canada and the new western lands.

And all without consulting the colonists or even ascertaining the state of colonial opinion. Dangerous business, this! For the colonists were in a mood that required careful handling. The destruction of the hereditary foe had lifted a great weight from their shoulders. No longer in need of British protection, the colonists gazed exultantly out over a continent that they had helped to win. One more common tie now bound them together; one more step toward unity had been taken. The last supreme struggle against the French had welded them as never before. During the dark days of 1754, an intercolonial congress had met, and Benjamin Franklin had proposed to transform this into a permanent Colonial Council—a proposal hastily vetoed by the Home Government, which had instantly taken alarm.

Six generations of American birth and American environment; over one hundred and fifty years of uninterrupted molding by all the factors that we have described above had done their work. The trend was obviously toward unity, toward the emergence of what could rightfully be called an "American people." Already the two oldest sections of colonial America, New England and Virginia, had developed a clear-cut self-consciousness and a genuine local patriotism. The middle colonies and the far South were less welded and less articulate; yet even they were, relatively speaking, old and well-established communities.

The foundations of colonial America—that older America that evolved so long and so solidly before it was transformed by the storm of the Revolution—had indeed been well laid. A united America was coming. The only question was: what sort of an America was it to be? Would it form part of a great Anglo-Saxon Confederation spanning the ocean, or would it set up an independent national life?

Such was the alternative. Unfortunately, few persons either in America or Britain saw the issue with anything like clarity. The sweeping vision of the elder Pitt (now become Lord Chatham) came nearest to seeing the situation as our informed hindsight views it today. Among Americans, perhaps Franklin had the keenest prescience of what was on the cards. But, aside from a few far-sighted minds, there was on both sides of the water little but narrow vision, legalistic quibbling, obstinate insistence upon "rights," anger, and prejudice in place of constructive thought, and above all—drift. So matters went from bad to worse for a full decade, until the shots on Lexington Green and at Concord Bridge precipitated the Anglo-Saxon Civil War, which was to end in political schism and the birth of an independent America.

# CHAPTER II

# THE BEGINNING OF NATIONAL LIFE

No event in our history is so persistently misunderstood by us Americans as is the Revolution. That the very starting point of our national life is so grossly misapprehended may seem a singular paradox. Yet such is undoubtedly the case. Most Americans take the Revolution for granted as a perfectly natural thing. That the American nation was born in convulsions seems to the average American as inevitable as were the birth pangs that attended his own individual entry into the world. Furthermore, the present-day American thinks precious little about the Revolution anyway, regarding it as a bit of almost ancient history that has no practical connection with our own times.

Now this is an extremely unfortunate attitude, for it is wholly untrue. In the first place, the American Revolution was neither natural nor inevitable. Understand: I am speaking of *the Revolutionary War*, not of the political separation of the colonies from Great Britain. Given the particular circumstances and the general conditions of the time, political separation seems to have been almost (though not quite) unavoidable. But surely, we should clearly distinguish between the fact of separation and the manner in which it was brought about. There was no *inherent* reason why the political connection between the colonies and the motherland should not have been either dissolved peaceably, as was customary in ancient Greece, or at most severed after a virtually bloodless quarrel, as was the case with Portugal and its colony of Brazil. That the two branches of the English folk (as it then was) should have grappled in a supremely bitter internecine war was surely not a normal event, to be expected as part of the natural order of things!

Equally erroneous, and even more unfortunate, is the notion that the Revolution is a mere archaic episode of no practical importance for our own times. As a matter of fact, the upheaval of the Revolution has profoundly affected the whole course of American history, from the beginning right down to the present day. More than any other one factor, it has molded our political and social thinking, has shaped both our foreign and domestic policies, and is largely responsible alike for our subsequent triumphs and disasters. Indeed, unless we understand the full significance of the Revolution, we cannot deal adequately with many of our present-day problems—especially with those pressing problems of national reconstruction to which this book is devoted.

Let us, then, analyze the Revolutionary epoch, seeking its deeper significance and ultimate consequences. In the previous chapter we observed that the expulsion of France from America logically ends the "colonial" period and ushers in a phase of acute readjustment in the relations between colonies and motherland. The colonies had many grounds for dissatisfaction, some recent, others of long standing. For instance, we have seen how the colonies had vainly protested against the Home Government's policy of dumping its criminals upon America, and we have also noted British alarm at Franklin's proposal to endow the colonies with an advisory council—the possible forerunner of a colonial parliament.

These two British vetoes of colonial aspirations well illustrate the basic British attitude toward colonial America. England regarded her American colonies as "possessions," to be treated indulgently perhaps, yet always in strict subordination to her own interests. Anything approaching equal consideration, anything like mutual reciprocity, was quite beyond the traditional British point of view. Britain's attitude is best illustrated by the commercial relations then existing with the colonies. The idea was that the colonies should send home their raw products and that in exchange they should take from Britain everything they required, whether produced in Britain or in foreign countries. All foreign trade was forbidden to the colonies. Furthermore, manufacturing within the colonies was also prohibited. The colonies were to be kept as a closed preserve for British manufacturers, merchants, and shipowners. Even things that the colonists disliked were forced upon them if there was a British profit to be made. For example, there had always been a strong colonial opposition to the importation of Negro slaves, and some of the colonies had tried hard to stop the practice. But the slave trade was a lucrative perquisite of the merchants and shipowners of the English port of Bristol. Colonial protests were therefore disregarded, and the Negroes, like the convicts, were dumped wholesale on America. This was bitterly resented by many far-sighted colonists, who had a glimpse of the terrible problem that was thus being created. In the original draft of the Declaration of Independence, this formed one of the counts in the indictment justifying the severance of the British political connection. Now, let us understand that this British attitude toward the colonies was the attitude of virtually all Englishmen, even of such outstanding champions of the colonists as Burke and Chatham. Did not Chatham, with all his vision, once assert that the colonies should not be allowed to manufacture so much as a nail or a horseshoe?

It is a pity that in considering the Revolution, so much emphasis is laid upon the particular incidents that occurred and the formal arguments put forward. These are not the things that really mattered. So prodigious an explosion as the shattering of the Anglo-Saxon world was not caused by revenue stamps or a tax on tea. If those imposts had never been dreamed of, far graver issues, such as the British plans for the exploitation of the Ohio Valley and of Canada, would have surged to the fore. The crisis was, of course, precipitated by a stubborn king and by short-sighted cabinet ministers anxious to get some revenue out of America, but a crisis would have arisen somehow within a very few years.

The trouble was not George III, nor his henchmen, nor the hotheads of the Boston coffeehouses; the real trouble lay in a profound difference between the American and British points of view. The Americans were a virile, determined folk, conscious of their strength, flushed with victory, chafing at outgrown restraints, and resolved on a great future. The British simply had no conception of all this—and if the American attitude had been clearly mirrored before their eyes, it would have stirred most of them to wrathful indignation. Even today the average stay-at-home Englishman condescends to "Colonials" from the British Dominions as to persons not quite his equals. At the time of the Revolution, that feeling was one of mild contempt. Bluff old Doctor Samuel Johnson probably voiced the prevalent British feeling of his time when he termed the American colonists: "a race of convicts, who ought to be content with anything we allow them short of hanging."

Given such profound differences of temper and outlook, could the relations between colonies and motherland have been so readjusted as to maintain a harmonious political union? Theoretically it was perhaps possible. Humanly speaking, it was not. The only way to have really satisfied American aspirations would have been the recognition of the colonists as full-fledged overseas Englishmen and the grant to the united colonies of something akin to the "Dominion" status today enjoyed by the self-governing parts of the British Empire. Indeed, even a Dominion status would probably not have sufficed for long, because the American colonies on the eve of the Revolution were relatively much more populous and powerful than any of the Dominions are at the present day. We must remember that in 1775 the American colonies had 2,000,000 White inhabitants, to say nothing of 500,000 Negroes, whereas the population of England itself was then barely 7,000,000. We know that the American population was growing at a faster rate than that of England, and we can be almost certain that if the Revolutionary War had not taken place, it would have grown even faster than it subsequently did. We may be sure, therefore, that a united, peaceful, and prosperous "British America," presumably including not only the thirteen colonies but likewise Canada and Florida,[1] would have made such prodigious strides that within a generation it would have been claiming something like full partnership in the management of the Empire.

Now we ask: could the Doctor Johnsons, could even the Burkes and Chathams, have so utterly transformed their temper and outlook as to have come round to any such radically novel point of view? It is scarcely believable. We may, therefore, conclude that political readjustment was impossible and that the separation of the American colonies was inevitable.

An independent America was thus certain. *But was the revolutionary upheaval that actually occurred also inevitable?* The answer is emphatically: *No!* Despite their grievances, the colonists felt no hatred of the motherland, no conscious desire, even, for independence. On the contrary, they considered themselves Englishmen, and they merely claimed what they believed to be their inalienable rights as men of English blood and heirs of the English tradition of ordered liberty. Franklin stated the American position admirably when he was examined before the House of Commons in 1766, at the time of the Stamp Act agitation. Franklin declared emphatically that no one in the colonies, "drunk or sober," had ever contemplated independence. But Franklin went on to warn the House that the Americans would maintain their attitude, that nothing could change their opinions, and that unless Britain was prepared to grant their pleas, the only alternative was to reduce the colonies by force.

But the use of force meant war—an Anglo-Saxon Civil War, and this instantly aroused a large and influential section of British public opinion to alarmed protest. Leading men like Chatham, Burke, and others considered it a monstrous and unnatural contingency, to be averted at almost any cost. And on the American side, as we have seen, there was as yet no hatred of England, no conscious desire for independence, and no intention of taking up arms except as a last resort.

Here, surely, were not the makings of the bloody and desperate struggle that was actually to occur. Why, then, was the trouble not peaceably adjusted? Or why, even after the first shots at Lexington and Concord, did not

---

1. Florida was ceded to England by Spain by the peace treaties of 1763. Spain, however, recovered it from England after the American Revolution, ceding it to the United States early in the next century.

the influential British peace party force an early termination of hostilities, which would have left few bitter memories? A dispassionate observer of the situation as it then was would have probably predicted one or the other of these alternatives—not what did take place.

What caused the Revolutionary War—what transformed the Americans from colonists seeking their rights as Englishmen into haters of England bent on absolute independence—was the malevolent and brutal policy of George III and his ministers. King George, despite his boast of being a true-born Briton, was not really an Englishman. The descendant of despotic German princes, he was himself a despotic German prince—being not only the constitutional king of England but also the absolute elector of Hanover. This tended to harden his arbitrary nature and to inflame his anger at opposition. George apparently thought of the American colonists much as he did of his German subjects—as people to be kept in strict obedience. When the colonists broke into open revolt, he proposed to deal with the Americans after Lexington as his own great-uncle, "The Butcher" Cumberland, had dealt with the Scotch Highlanders after Culloden. Rallying behind him the aroused patriotism of the British majority, George balked the efforts of the peace party and undertook the crushing of rebellious America.

The plans of George and his ministers were as atrocious as they were fatal to the success of their own cause. They planned to subdue America largely by using foreigners and savages! Combing Europe for mercenaries, they first tried to get a horde of Russians, but the Czarina Catherine disdainfully refused to let out her subjects for any such purpose. The British government therefore hired some 30,000 Germans from Hesse, albeit Frederick the Great, King of Prussia, showed his contempt by charging a cattle tax for their passage through his dominions. The Hessians ultimately reached the New World, and their name is still a hateful byword in many parts of America.

Yet the Hessians were lambs beside the savages. Long before the Hessians arrived, the British authorities were systematically playing the old French game of setting the Indians on the colonists. The game worked, and the whole frontier, from New York to Georgia, went up in blood and flame, to the usual accompaniments of fiendish torture, rape, and cannibalism. In some instances, British agents actually paid the Indians bounties for rebel scalps—men, women, or children. Lastly, the British actually toyed with the idea of arming the slaves—a project which, if carried out, would have plunged the Southern colonies into the unspeakable horrors of servile war. Fortunately, this plan came to naught.

These and other acts of the British government showed the colonists what they were in for. Is it any wonder that after more than a year of all this, the revolted colonists ceased to consider themselves as Englishmen, and that on the Fourth of July 1776, they issued the Declaration of Independence, repudiating the British connection forever? The wonder is that they waited so long. Nothing better attests to the strength of the ties binding the two branches of the English folk than the reluctance with which they were severed. Throughout a year of warfare, the colonists proclaimed themselves to be fighting solely for the redress of grievances and the just rights of Englishmen. It was the British government rather than the colonists who made the breach irreparable.

Yet more striking proof of the strong bonds between the colonies and England is revealed by the large number of persons who, despite everything, clung to the motherland. The colonists were far from unanimous in repudiating British allegiance. At the beginning of the Revolution, at least one-third of the population was clearly loyal. Though the policy of the British Government converted many of them to the Patriot cause, the bulk of these "Loyalists" remained true to their convictions and themselves took up arms to aid the British forces in putting down the rebellion. The presence of this large group of Loyalists, or "Tories," as the Patriots dubbed them, adds the final touch of tragedy to the struggle that ensued. From our long perspective of independent national life, we are apt to think of the Revolution almost as a foreign war, waged by a united people against an alien invader. But of course, it was nothing of the sort. The Revolution was really a civil war of a most unusual and deplorable character. It was a *twofold* civil war—first, as between the two branches of the English folk; second, as between the overseas English themselves. It is this latter aspect that lent the war its incredible bitterness. No colony was without its Loyalists, and in some regions every town, every village, and almost every family was cleft asunder. The Loyalist strongholds were New York and the far South. In New York nearly one-half of the population were Loyalists, and the colony furnished nearly 25,000 fighting Tories to the British forces. In Georgia and South Carolina, the Loyalists seem to have been actually in the majority, and these colonies likewise gave thousands of soldiers to the British cause. As the war went on, the feud between Loyalists and Patriots grew more implacable. Harried and persecuted by the Patriots, the Loyalists revenged themselves in the districts under British control or, fleeing to the frontier, joined the Indians and vied with the savages in cruelty. Often when Patriots and Loyalists met in battle, no mercy was shown on either side. On one or two notable occasions, while the British regulars were freely granted quarter, their Tory auxiliaries were summarily brained or bayonetted.

After eight long years the war ended, and the United States of America took its place among the nations of the earth. Independence had been won, but the winning had left deep scars. The newborn nation was exhausted and financially bankrupt. The people were restless and embittered. Even before peace was signed, a decision had been taken which, however natural, was to be a heavy loss to American race life. This was the expulsion of the Loyalists. The Loyalists knew what was in store for them, and wherever possible they left with their British friends. Fully 30,000 Loyalists sailed away with the British fleet from New York alone, and other multitudes quitted the Southern ports or made their way overland to Canada. The total Loyalist emigration has been estimated at from 60,000 to 70,000. These people were, on the whole, a superior group. Not only did they include many men of prominence and high achievement in colonial America, but they were, by the very nature of the case, persons with the courage and steadfastness to fight and suffer for an ideal. They soon proved the stuff that was in them. Some returned to the homeland; others went to the British West Indies; the bulk of them (about 50,000) settled in Canada. There they made splendid pioneers. The "United Empire Loyalists," as they appropriately called themselves, made Canada British and founded its present prosperity. Their descendants are today the finest element in the Canadian population.

The departure of such a group was a heavy loss to American race life. Since the colonial stock has increased over twenty-fold, the descendants of the Loyalists, had they remained, would today number at least 1,500,000 and would meanwhile have been giving America many men and women of conscience and ability throughout its national history. The expulsion of the Loyalists was the first serious racial loss that America had suffered. Hitherto it had been receiving superior elements and had parted with practically none. If we add to the Loyalists the many thousands of picked men killed on both sides in the eight years of fighting, we can form some idea of the human costs of the Revolutionary War to America.

The expulsion of the Loyalists is the best proof of the almost incredible passions aroused by the Revolution. Americans were destined to fight another civil war—the Civil War of 1861-65. Yet that later struggle, though long and terrible, did not give rise to the implacable and vengeful spirit displayed during and after the Revolution. The Civil War was followed by no general confiscation of property, no wholesale expulsion of the defeated, such as drove the Loyalists, beggared and attainted, from America. Had a proscription of the Southern Confederates and their Northern sympathizers, the "Copperheads," occurred on the same relative scale as that of the Loyalists, the Civil War exiles would have numbered nearly 1,000,000. The temper of the victorious North was certainly bitter, and many of its "Reconstruction" measures were deplorable; yet in comparison to the Revolution, the aftermath of the Civil War was mild indeed. No punitive confiscation occurred, no general proscription was ordered, and not a single American was exiled.[2]

So volcanic an upheaval as the Revolutionary War was bound to exert a profound and enduring influence upon the American national consciousness. That is the real significance of the Revolution. The Revolution's material effects were serious enough at the start, retarding stability and prosperity for more than a generation. Yet in a young country of a virile population and limitless natural resources, these were mere temporary difficulties that were soon entirely outgrown. The mental and spiritual effects of the Revolution, on the other hand, have influenced American ideals and policies throughout our history. Let us, then, observe some of the ways in which the Revolution has affected our national life, for good—and for ill.

Right here, however, let us once more emphasize the distinction that we have already made between the fact of independence and the manner in which it was achieved. The political separation from England, being both natural and inevitable, was almost wholly for America's good. Since, under the then existing circumstances, a harmonious Anglo-Saxon Confederation was impossible, any continuance of the "colonial" status would have spelled chronic friction and would have produced a cramping, narrowing effect upon American life. The attainment of independent nationhood acted like a splendid elixir, stimulating thought, quickening the spirit, and clarifying the vision. The epoch of our national birth is truly a *great* age, and the "Fathers of Our Country" were not only great men but men whose great talents were supremely inspired by the challenge of their time.

To imagine that this inspiration was caused solely, or even mainly, by the Revolutionary War is, however, a mistake. The war, of course, intensified the challenge of the times. A life-and-death struggle, with a rebel's doom and the dishonorable subjection of their Native land as the price of defeat, naturally nerved the Patriot leaders to heroic extremes of thought and action. Yet it also tended to becloud even their judgment with passion,

---

[2]. A few prominent Southerners went abroad after the war, and certain small groups of ex-Confederates attempted to form settlements in Mexico and elsewhere. But these were, of course, voluntary exiles. Furthermore, most of them ultimately returned to America.

CHAPTER II    BEGINNING OF NATIONAL LIFE    19

and it compelled them to forced decisions, which sometimes proved unfortunate. Supposing that war had been averted, the process of separation from England and the tasks of building a new nation would have afforded problems arduous and exciting enough to have stimulated the best energies of America's ablest men. Here again we may confidently affirm that, while the natural and inevitable coming of independence was an unmixed good, the by no means inevitable upheaval of the Revolution, like most unnatural events, bore within itself the germs of future misfortunes.

America's revolutionary origin certainly imparted disruptive tendencies to its early political life. The birth of the nation in violent revolution rather than through constitutional evolution inevitably gave a moral sanction to schism, rebellion, and civil strife, which was to furnish ominous precedents to future American malcontents. The Revolution gave moral justification to the various threats of secession, North[3] as well as South, which finally culminated in the Civil War. Like the Revolutionary War, the Civil War was by no means inevitable. If the United States had had a more normal origin, the finespun constitutional arguments of Calhoun, however logical, would have lacked the emotional reinforcement of the Revolutionary past, and, lacking that emotional appeal, the Civil War might well have been averted. Even today it is interesting to observe how our extreme radicals prime their subversive preaching with good old revolutionary texts. Should a radical upheaval ever take place in America, would not the victorious "Reds" have in the fate of the Loyalists a splendid precedent for a wholesale confiscation of property and the general proscription of their opponents? Again, may not much of our popular impatience and tendency to lawlessness have their origin in the terrible passions and the breakdown of social controls that occurred during the Revolutionary period? When we compare our history with that of Canada or Australia (likewise young commonwealths with similar frontier problems), does it not seem that, in the breach of the Revolution, we may have left behind somewhat of the old English traditions of evolutionary progress and ordered liberty?

Certainly, much of their English heritage was, consciously and unconsciously, discarded by our Revolutionary forefathers. The sharp sword of war severed more than political ties; many idealistic and spiritual bonds were sundered as well. We have stressed the tragic episodes and fierce passions of the Revolutionary epoch, not to revive bitter memories, but to show that

---

3. It is curious to note that the earliest serious talk of possible secession from the Union occurred in New England, which was bitterly opposed to the policy of the Federal Government during the War of 1812. This seditious feeling culminated in the so-called Hartford Convention of late 1814. But the end of the war shortly afterward quieted New England's grievances, and it soon became one of the strongholds of Unionism.

the Revolution was as great an upheaval in the realms of thought and emotion as it was on the material plane. Imagine the tremendous overturn of old beliefs and viewpoints that was involved. Picture Washington asserting at the beginning of the war that he abhorred the idea of independence, yet within a year transforming into its standard-bearer! To a steadfast, constant soul like Washington's, the emotional wrench of so sudden a shift of fundamental loyalties must have been prodigious indeed.

We are therefore not surprised to find the Revolution followed by a general revulsion against things British—a revulsion strengthened by the bad relations with England, which continued for a generation and culminated in the War of 1812. Manners and customs recalling the colonial past and dependence on Britain were eschewed. Gentlemen discarded British fashions. The silk coat, the satin breeches, and the powdered wig went out of style, and republican simplicity became the order of the day. Democratic and egalitarian tendencies steadily gained ground, stimulated by the French Revolution and hastened by the rapid growth of the ultra-democratic pioneering West.

This anti-British bias profoundly influenced the intellectual and idealistic concepts of American nationality. Colonial America was so thoroughly English that, had independence been unaccompanied by the passions of the Revolution, the new nation would almost certainly have desired to develop on a definitely Anglo-Saxon basis. The emotional chasm of the Revolution prevented this. Of course, the emancipated colonists had no intention of renouncing their English speech or the fundamentals of their Anglo-Saxon culture and institutions; indeed, they could not have done so, even if they had so desired. Nevertheless, their national aspirations trended away from the old Anglo-Saxon basis toward a new basis founded on theoretical and cosmopolitan ideals.

This novel trend was bound up with the spread of French radical thought in America. Even before the Revolution, French ideas had begun to influence a few minds, including such leading men as Thomas Jefferson and Patrick Henry. The vital aid that France gave the Americans in the Revolutionary War enormously enhanced the popularity of what were then known as "French principles." Their old ideals shaken, the Americans (as men always do under such circumstances) were longing for something to take their place, and the new ideas were seized upon with avidity.

Now what were these imported ideas? They were those proclaimed by Rousseau, Diderot, and the other members of the French "Encyclopedist" school. Their basic tenet was a firm belief in the unbounded virtue of abstract principles. One of the leaders of the French Revolution put the matter in a nutshell when he cried, "With six principles I could regenerate mankind!" The logical inferences from such a belief are the natural equality of all men, the absence of inborn differences between either individuals or races, and the infinite power of laws, institutions, and other environmental factors to mold human beings, regardless of their origin or antecedents.

Such ideas chimed in admirably with America's post-revolutionary mood. Engaged in the task of building a new nation, our forefathers welcomed philosophical arguments that emphasized the uniqueness of American nationality and its independence from the colonial past. Jefferson stated that the American soil had evolved a new race of men, while Tom Paine asserted, "We have it in our power to begin the world over again. A situation similar to the present has not happened since the days of Noah. The birthday of a new world is at hand."

Of course, we should not overemphasize the immediate effects of this attitude. With characteristic Anglo-Saxon common sense, our forebears did not, like the more logical French, attempt to carry these abstract principles to their ultimate conclusion. The Jacobin rulers of Revolutionary France did really try to "regenerate" the world in fanatical obedience to their theories. The Americans, on the contrary, kept theory and practice in more or less distinct mental compartments and did not hesitate to sacrifice logic to workability. That masterpiece of political architecture, the American Constitution, is an eminently practical document based on a clear-headed grasp of realities. In fact, America's entire legal and institutional framework was erected on the solid foundations of tested experience. The past was not scrapped merely because it was the past; neither were political novelties adopted just because they were new or had an alluring appeal.

Notwithstanding their popularity, therefore, the immediate effect of French ideas on America was more apparent than real. Despite the Revolutionary breach, the new nation remained fundamentally Anglo-Saxon in its institutions, its culture, its modes of thought, and the temper of its people, who had changed their allegiance but not their blood.

Later on, however, the ideas of the Encyclopedists were to produce momentous consequences. The handling of our two gravest problems—the Negro and immigration—was powerfully affected by the idealistic attitude adopted at the beginning of our national existence. A good instance of this is the changed popular interpretation of that much-discussed phrase in the Declaration of Independence: "All men are created equal." When those words were penned, they carried only a limited, political significance.

What the revolted colonists had in mind was merely the assertion that they were as good Englishmen as their blood brethren across the sea. It was an effective rhetorical touch in what was essentially a partisan war manifesto. The thought of applying it, say, to Negroes and Indians never so much as entered their heads. Within a generation after the Revolution, however, we find it thus literally applied to the Negroes by a few idealists. These in turn became the nucleus of the Abolitionist Party, whose leaders not only demanded the immediate emancipation of the slaves but also asserted that the Negro differed in no essential respect from the White man and should therefore be regarded as in every way the White man's natural equal. This strong belief in absolute human equality gave the Abolitionists their uncompromising, fanatical temper, which, in turn, inflamed the fear and anger of the slaveholding South. Two irreconcilable groups thus arose, mutually exciting one another to an ever-fiercer pitch, sweeping moderate men off their feet by emotional contagion, and plunging America into that Civil War of which they were the joint authors. And the trouble did not end there. After the War, the radical element in the victorious North, headed by fanatical theorists like Charles Sumner and Thaddeus Stevens, imposed Negro rule on the defeated South and even tried to enforce racial amalgamation. The upshot was a fearful embitterment of race relations and our present color problem, with all its tragic aspects and ominous possibilities.

Our modern immigration problem can likewise be traced to the idealistic novelties adopted at the beginning of our national life. At first it made little practical difference what men thought about immigration, because there were almost no immigrants. For nearly a generation after the Revolution, newcomers averaged only a few thousand a year, and not until over half a century had passed did the numbers swell to notable proportions. But when immigration did become not only a vast human tide but also a tide composed more and more of people strange in blood and equally strange in outlook and culture, America's acquired ideals prevented a clear-sighted understanding of immigration's full significance. For if all men were potentially equal and if such differences as did exist were due solely to environment, it followed logically that America, that wonderful young country with its boundless area, limitless natural resources, and peerless institutions, could easily and completely mold any number of immigrants into good Americans, whatever their origins or antecedents. That is unquestionably the way most of our forefathers felt about the matter. A good illustration of the popular temper in America's early days is the so-called "Liberty and Security" coins of the year 1795, which bore the oft-quoted phrase "A Refuge for the

Oppressed of all Nations." To be sure, our forebears were not wholly logical, because they limited their invitation to White men, our basic naturalization law admitting to citizenship only "free White persons." But with this single limitation, the gates of the young republic stood open to all—even to the pauper, the criminal, and the diseased. For a hundred years no attempt was made to exclude even obviously unfit individuals. As to undesirable or unassimilable groups and racial stocks, any warnings of that kind were reproved by the prevailing mood as "un-American." Not until our own days did the ugly facts of mass-alienage and aggressive "hyphenism" awaken the American people to the grim fact that our basic ideals, our culture, and our very nationhood itself were imperiled, and that even at best a long and crucial task of national reconstruction lay before us.

Such were the unpleasant consequences of the egalitarian and cosmopolitan doctrines of Rousseau and his fellows as applied to America. But, for our revolutionary forebears, the menace of color and the alien flood alike lay far below Time's horizon. The newborn nation was one in blood and consciousness, thrilling to the elixir of independence, and confident of a wondrous destiny. Let us now consider that great national forging that occurred between the Revolution and the Civil War and that is still like the foundation of the present and the inspiration of the future.

# CHAPTER III

# THE FIRST FORGING OF AMERICA

THE FIRST HALF OF THE nineteenth century was the springtime of American national life. It was an era of fine achievement and even finer promise. This truly happy epoch saw not merely a prodigious increase in material prosperity and population but also the welding of that population into a real "American people." Such a welding implies far more than political unity or common economic interests. It means, in addition, the achievement of a profound like-mindedness in basic ideals, which is the necessary foundation of a well-defined national character. From this, in turn, evolve those moral standards that determine a nation's institutions and traditions, together with the social *mores* that guide and control the conduct of its citizens. This foundation also forms the indispensable basis for a genuine culture, flowering in harmonious forms of literature and art. Furthermore, such a well-balanced, distinctive national life can arise only after a period of relative isolation and can fulfill itself only if measurably free from the impact of alien, antagonistic forces.

Now that was precisely the fortunate situation of America during the first half of the nineteenth century, especially in the period from 1815 to about 1850. Up to 1815, America was handicapped by the aftermath of the Revolution and was involved in foreign complications that culminated in the War of 1812. But the bonfires and joy-bells that welcomed the treaty of 1815 marked the dawn of a long era of peace and prosperity. Freed from foreign difficulties, America could devote all its youthful energies to national development and consolidation. The amazing material progress that ensued is so well known that it can be briefly summarized. The rapid settlement of the West, the growth of manufacturing industry in the East, and the binding together of the vast national domain by new methods of transportation like the steamboat and the railroad are reflected in the tremendous growth of population. We have already seen that at the end of the colonial period (1775) the total population was only about 2,500,000 (2,000,000 Whites and 500,000 Negro slaves). Despite the vital losses of the Revolution, the first national census of 1790 showed a population of 4,000,000. In 1820 this had more than doubled, standing at 9,500,000; in 1840 it had again almost doubled, to 17,000,000; in 1850 it was 23,000,000; and in 1860 it numbered nearly 31,500,000—over twelve times the population at the beginning of the Revolution! Of course, these figures include the Negroes, who increased from 500,000 in 1775 to 4,500,000 in 1860. Furthermore, the year 1847 saw the first great wave of immigration. Nevertheless, the Native White population rose from 2,000,000 in 1775 to nearly 25,000,000 in 1860 (a twelve-fold increase) and was thus in an overwhelming majority on the eve of the Civil War.

Such was the prosperous, virile population that was being forged into a nation. As already stated, the most favoring factor was America's isolation. Once the storm of the Revolution had passed, the Americans were left very much to themselves to work out their domestic problems. Already basically alike in blood, speech, and culture, the trend toward true nationhood was irresistible. State and sectional feeling was still strong but was overlaid with a growing sense of national loyalty and genuine patriotism. Even when the young nation was only a decade old, its welding had progressed so far that Washington could say in his Farewell Address, "Citizens by birth or choice, of a common country, that country has a right to concentrate your affection. . . . With slight shades of difference, you have the same religion, manners, habits, and political principles."

It was most fortunate for the stability of American nationhood that no large immigration occurred during this first formative period. Had great numbers of foreigners, even of kindred blood and culture, entered the country before its institutions and ideals had been established, assimilation would have been difficult even in the older settled areas; while if hosts of aliens had pushed westward and established themselves as the first settlers, they might have formed solid blocks impervious to Americanization. Luckily, during America's first formative period there was almost no immigration. The Revolution had interrupted the steady influx (chiefly from the British Isles) that had kept up throughout the colonial period, and a long time was to elapse before it revived. Previous to the year 1820, when national immigration statistics began to be tabulated, the number of immigrants was not accurately known but is supposed to have averaged only 5,000 or 6,000 per year. In 1820 the number of arrivals was 8,385, and by the year 1830 the newcomers averaged 20,000. During the 'thirties some 60,000 immigrants were annually admitted, while from 1840 to 1846 the average number was about 90,000. The year 1847 witnessed the first great wave of Irish fleeing from the terrible potato famine, while two years later political troubles in Germany sent a broad stream of Teutonic exiles to America. From 1847 to

1854, immigration ranged between 250,000 and 400,000 a year, dropping sharply thereafter until, at the outbreak of the Civil War, it sank temporarily to under 100,000 per annum.

These figures prove that previous to 1830, immigration amounted to virtually nothing and that from 1830 to 1846, it was a decidedly minor factor. Thus, for more than half a century after the nation's founding, the make-up of the population remained unchanged. Racially, the situation was absolutely unaltered. The few immigrants who did arrive were mostly English and Scotch, who fused rapidly with their native-born kinsmen. The vast pioneering tide that swept over the Appalachian mountain barrier and settled the empty West was therefore almost exclusively of the old Anglo-Saxon stock, and they stamped the virgin heart of the continent with the same ethnic and cultural imprint as the early English colonists had on the primeval wilderness of the Atlantic seaboard. It was the same story over again: the character of the first genuine settlers was of tremendous and lasting import, fixing the mold to which later arrivals were constrained to adjust themselves.

Now let us pause for a moment to consider how the young nation consciously averted what would have been a terrible (and probably fatal) disaster—the influx of a limitless horde of Negro slaves. We have already noted the opposition to slavery in colonial days, and we also saw how all efforts to check the evil had been vetoed by the British Crown. No sooner had they become their own masters than the Americans took steps to limit slavery and to stop the further importation of Negroes from Africa. In the North slavery had never really taken root, and slaves were few. Accordingly, all the Northern States extinguished the institution and became "free soil." Moreover, at the close of the Revolution, the trend of opinion in most of the Southern States was likewise unfavorable to slavery. Nearly all the great Southerners of the Revolutionary epoch were of that frame of mind. Washington and Jefferson, for example, though slaveowners, both deplored the institution and looked forward to its ultimate extinction. Only the far South (South Carolina and Georgia), where the culture of semi-tropical products like rice and indigo called for Negro labor, was bent on the continuance of slavery. Indeed, but for the resolute opposition of South Carolina and Georgia, it is possible that slavery would have been extinguished by some gradual process of law. As a matter of fact, slavery was legalized and perpetuated in the states south of the Mason-Dixon Line.[1] But two measures

---

1. This traditional line between North and South included Delaware as slave soil, although Delaware is not usually considered a "Southern" State.

of capital importance were nevertheless enacted, the effect of which was to restrict slavery to the South and to limit the future increase of the Negro element in America. These measures were the Northwest Ordinance and the constitutional prohibition of the slave trade after the year 1808. Both these measures were enacted in the same year (1787)—that momentous year when the Constitution was drawn up and the Federal Government established.

A moment's reflection on these measures is enough to reveal their tremendous ultimate significance. The Northwest Ordinance was passed to provide a civic basis for the vast region lying north of the Ohio River. In 1787 it was still an Indian-haunted wilderness, but the first ripples of the pioneer tide were already lapping its borders, and within a few decades the "Old Northwest" was to be transformed into prosperous, populous states of the Union. Now the Ordinance of 1787 specifically forbade slavery within the Northwest Territory, thus determining that the whole vast region should be "free soil." The momentous consequences of this are obvious. The Northwest Territory was settled by people from all parts of the country, including many men from the South. If these had been able to bring in their slaves, the Northwest would have had a large Negro element, their masters would have remained "Southerners" in feeling, and when the crisis over slavery later arose, the Northwest would have been sharply divided instead of being almost solid for the Union.

Even more momentous was the prohibition of the slave trade embodied in the Federal Constitution. We know from the reports of the Constitutional debates that not only the far South but also the new Western lands were calling for slave labor. Indeed, it was an anti-slavery Southern delegate to the Constitutional Convention (Mason of Virginia) who pointed out the potential peril, stating that the West would be filled with Negroes if the African trade was not stopped. In the end a sop was thrown to South Carolina and Georgia by extending the slave trade for another twenty years, but with the year 1808 it was to be absolutely and finally prohibited.

This decision was taken just in the nick of time. Only six years after the promulgating of the Constitution, Eli Whitney invented the cotton gin! The amount of labor involved in cleaning the fiber of seeds had hitherto rendered the raising of cotton unprofitable. Whitney's invention solved the difficulty. Cotton-growing expanded by leaps and bounds, and with it the demand for slave labor. Slavery was not only fastened firmly on the Old South but also spread to the new lands of the Southwest. This fresh demand began to be felt just about the time when the prohibition of the slave trade went into effect. The demand could, therefore, be supplied only from those Negroes already in America. That the domestic supply did not begin to meet the potential demand was shown by the rapid rise in slave prices that then took place. To be sure, the law was sometimes evaded, and a certain number of Negroes were smuggled in, as immigrants are "bootlegged" in today. However, the number of smuggled Negroes was not sufficient to produce any material effect.

Now consider what would have happened if the slave trade had not been prohibited. When we remember the vast hordes of Africans shipped during the first half of the nineteenth century to lesser New World markets like Brazil and Cuba, we may be sure that if the great American market had not been closed, the slave influx would have risen to many millions! The South would have probably become like the West Indies—a land inhabited by a solid Negro population overlaid by a small White aristocracy and a degraded "poor White" class. This vast Black nucleus would ultimately have given even the North a very large Negro element. Indeed, the Negroes might easily have come to form one-third or even one-half of America's whole population. When we think of what the Negro problem, even in its restricted form, has cost America, we may well shudder to imagine the frightful peril that the "Fathers of the Republic" averted. It is not too much to say that those twin enactments of the year 1787 mark a turning point in American race life unapproached in significance until the almost equally important Johnson Immigration Act of 1924, which may well go down in history as the second great turning point in America's racial destiny.

The ominous shadow from Africa thus happily averted, let us return to our story of the progress of White America. In our opening pages we saw how the primeval wilderness of the Atlantic seaboard rigidly selected the colonists and evolved a stock unsurpassed for vigor, tenacity, and courage. Well, the inland wilderness imposed the same stern conditions and produced the same splendid racial effects. The pioneers who, accompanied by their wives and children, shouldered their long rifles and followed the sun, left behind peace and security for lives of hardship and peril. The Indians were fierce and cunning, and the savage exacted a toll less costly than that paid to exposure and disease. The almost incredible hardships and dangers suffered by the early pioneers, together with the indomitable spirit that surmounted them, are immortalized in the stern figure of Daniel Boone, the hero of Kentucky. Yet Daniel Boone is merely an outstanding example of the pioneer breed. Consider that heroic band of 380 persons who trekked from North Carolina over the mountains to the site of Nashville, Tennessee. In those days Tennessee, like Kentucky, was "dark and bloody ground." Within a year, hardship and the Indians had reduced their numbers to 134 persons, while after another six months, only 70 remained alive. Their situation being apparently hopeless, a ballot was suggested to decide whether to take the desperate chance of staying on or to go back home. Not one voted to return! The settlement survived, and Nashville is today a flourishing city of over 120,000 souls.

That was the spirit of the pioneer breed: a spirit displayed generation after generation, as the frontiersmen pushed west, west, ever west—hewing their way through the trackless forests or floating down the rivers on their rafts and "broad-horns" to the Mississippi; crossing the great trans-Mississippi prairies and the vast desert plains to the foot of the Rockies; scaling the towering Rocky Mountain wall and descending the Pacific slope, until the waves of the Western Ocean set bounds to their epic progress and bore witness that Continental America had been wholly won.

Now this persistence of the frontier affected potently the character and composition of the American people. In the first place, it greatly increased the proportion of "pioneering" strains in the American population. For just as the colonists of the Atlantic seaboard, once acclimated, had multiplied exceedingly, so the hinterland, as fast as it was subdued and settled, provided fresh breeding grounds for the strongest and most forceful elements in the American stock; more land was for the taking and food was for the raising, and many children were a necessity as well as a blessing. Accordingly, the West became as amazingly prolific as the East was in colonial days. The new lands filled up like magic with a population almost wholly of picked stock. The frontier killed off wholesale, but the men and women who were left were an iron breed, fit to beget a progeny in whom there would be few weaklings.

And nationally as well as racially, the winning of the West had important results. All the older parts of the country contributed their quotas of pioneers. In that vast new Western land, they met and mingled. All of them were basically alike in blood and ideals; no real barriers hindered their rapid fusion. Accordingly, sectional differences were soon discarded. New Englanders and "York Staters," Northerners and Southerners, presently discovered that old grudges were fading before the larger fact that they were fellow Americans engaged in a common task—the upbuilding of a greater America. The further one went west, the more Eastern sectionalism dwindled and the stronger the "American" spirit became.

Yet, in the East also, sectional feeling was declining. The South alone, cursed by the blight of slavery, was beginning to stand apart. However, until the middle of the nineteenth century, the South felt itself an integral part of the Union. In those days few persons even dreamed of the terrible schism that was in store.

The first half of the nineteenth century saw, therefore, the emergence of a real American nation inhabited by a well-defined "American race." It was a splendid breed. Medical statistics show the high average physique in both the Northern and the Southern armies during the Civil War, while a recent scientific study of the old stock[2] shows that the "Native American" of unmixed descent has maintained his physical excellence unimpaired to the present day. This study shows, among other things, that the old stock is the tallest of any branch of the White race (averaging taller even than the proverbially tall Scotch) and also shows a striking homogeneity of type extending over all sections of the country, whatever may be the differences in climate, soil, and other environmental factors.

Thus, by the middle of the nineteenth century, a new and very superior breed had appeared, evolved from the mingling of closely kindred North European stocks, whose minor variations had been so fused that the "Native American" might (to borrow Kipling's fine characterization of the Englishman) be likened to "a built-up gun-barrel, all of one temper though welded of different materials."

This racial and national forging was accompanied by its natural corollary, the emergence of a distinct civilization and culture. All human history attests to the fact that when harmonious racial elements have been blended, and after sufficient time has elapsed to enable the various national factors to become unified and crystallized, we may expect, first, a budding and then a flowering of a new and distinctive cultural life. Now this was precisely what occurred in America during the period between the Revolution and the Civil War. And since the racial foundations were of excellent quality, the evolving culture was of a correspondingly high order. The number of great men that America produced during the Revolutionary epoch from a numerically insignificant population of two million reveals the racial treasures latent in the colonial stock, while from the Revolution to the Civil War the general level of ability continued high, and the output of talent remained extremely large. In proportion to our vastly more numerous present population, we can make no such showing today.

That old America of our forebears certainly provides an inspiring roster of truly great names in every phase of national life. Statesmen like

---

2. This scientific survey was conducted under the auspices of the Smithsonian Institution, by its leading anthropologist, Doctor Ales Hrdlicka.

Washington and Hamilton, jurists like Marshall and Shaw, orators like Clay and Webster, and epoch-making inventors like Whitney, Fulton, and McCormick—these are but the outstanding figures in a great array of talent displayed in the upbuilding of the nation. Even more surprising is the showing made in literary and intellectual fields. The arts and sciences inevitably take longer to develop in a new country, because much time is needed to evolve the standards, traditions, and culture groups that are the indispensable prerequisites of truly great production along these lines. That America developed so many literary lights in its first national epoch proves the amount of intellectual and artistic ability latent in the old stock. The early New York group headed by Washington Irving, Cooper, and Bryant; the remarkable efflorescence in New England, yielding a whole galaxy of names like Lowell, Emerson, Longfellow, Whittier, Holmes, Hawthorne, Prescott, Motley, and Parkman; and certain notable figures less identified with any group or section, such as Poe, Walt Whitman, and Bret Harte, all point conclusively to a wonderful cultural flowering that was clearly on the way.

For we must not forget that those early literary achievements, fine though they intrinsically were, should be regarded as merely the first budding of what normally would have been a sustained cultural flowering—if the unfolding blossoms had not been blasted by the fires of civil war and the blight of alien factors.

By the year 1850, then, America was nationally and racially forged and apparently stood on the threshold of a long, normal, and glorious evolution. Yet—already the first waves of the immigrant tide were beating on its shores, while a harsh note of domestic discord broke the national harmony—a discord significantly caused by the one really alien, unassimilable racial element (the Negro) that America then contained.

Down the long vista of the vanished years, we may look back with a sigh of regret to that bright dawning whose promised noontide never came. The Old America of our forefathers was fated to pass away in the storms of civil strife and in a deluge of alien forces. The work of centuries was in large part undone, and we Americans of today are faced by problems of national reconstruction that may well require generations of sustained and unremitting effort.

Yet Old America has bequeathed to us an infinitely precious heritage and inspiration. In our veins still flows abundantly the old blood, with its inborn energy, resourcefulness, and high idealism. In our hearts still dwells the memory of that bygone time when Americans lived, and thought, and felt as one: when beneath the minor diversities of the crude yet virile West, the cultured East, and the gracious South, there yet existed a profound like-mindedness in basic aims and ideals, enabling men to perfect a stable social order and to evolve a harmonious civilization. Those old days of national unity and spiritual concord have bequeathed us a high ideal toward which, through storm and stress, we may safely set our course toward the America of the future.

# CHAPTER IV

# THE SCHISM OF THE CIVIL WAR

THE CIVIL WAR IS THE supreme disaster of American history. This titanic struggle dealt the nation wounds from which it has never recovered. Indeed, the blow was, in a sense, mortal, because it shattered the original pattern of our national life beyond repair. Though the vanquished Confederacy suffered the heavier material loss, the idealistic and spiritual losses of the victorious North were even graver than those of the defeated South. When the war ended, the best part of that Old America whose forging we described in the preceding pages had passed away, and the America that emerged from the holocaust was an America maimed in soul as well as in body, an America whose spiritual uncertainty and idealistic impoverishment might be concealed but could not be remedied by the prodigious material expansion that was to ensue. In fact, this very material prosperity long blinded the country to the dangers that were arising to threaten the nation. Not until our own days was there to be an awakening of a new idealistic vision capable of grappling with national problems and infused with constructive zeal for the upbuilding of America's future.

A possibility of the disruption of the American Union had been latent from the very start. We have already noted how America's revolutionary origin provided both a logical precedent and a moral sanction for secession and rebellion. We have likewise noted that threats of disruption had been uttered in the North as well as in the South during the nation's early days. The first generation of Americans still gave their primary allegiance to their state or section rather than to the Federal Union, which many regarded as an experiment to be judged by results.

The results, however, were so splendidly successful and were so in line with the general unitary trend that a true national feeling quickly overlaid those older loyalties and rapidly generated an ardent patriotism. By the year 1820 the ideal of union was firmly established, except in one relatively small section of the country—the *Far* South. It is a grave error to think that secession had its roots in the whole region south of the Mason-Dixon Line. The heart of the *Old* South, Virginia, was one of the first strongholds of national feeling. Washington, Madison, Jefferson, Patrick Henry, and other great

Virginians furnished probably the largest and most eminent contingent to the "Fathers of the Republic." The presidency was long held by an almost unbroken "Virginia dynasty." Throughout America's early history, the "Old Dominion" was the proudest and most ardently patriotic part of America.

But what was true of Virginia and the rest of the tier of states lying just below the Mason-Dixon Line was not true of the Far South. At first the "Far South" meant only South Carolina and Georgia. Even before the Revolution, these two had stood somewhat apart from the other colonies. With their semi-tropical climate, "tidewater" South Carolina and Georgia (then the only settled parts of those colonies) had established slavery in its extreme commercial form. On the great rice and indigo plantations, slave gangs were worked like human machines for big profits, and Negroes were so numerous that they well-nigh outnumbered the White inhabitants. With its whole economic life based on commercialized slave labor, the attitude of the Far South toward slavery was very different from that of the Old South, where slavery was an easygoing, patriarchal system, not especially profitable. Indeed, we saw that in the Old South, public opinion tended to view slavery with disfavor and that most of its leading men, such as Washington and Jefferson, hoped to see it extinguished by some gradual process of law.

Now all this reacted disturbingly upon the Far South. Feeling themselves an imperiled minority, the planters of South Carolina and Georgia banded together to safeguard their interests at any cost. This accounts for the Far South's uncompromising policy at the framing of the Constitution. South Carolina flatly refused to join the Union unless slavery was guaranteed under the Constitution, and it was chiefly to placate her delegates that the Convention deferred prohibition of the slave trade for twenty years. The aggressive, threatening attitude of the South Carolina delegates in the Constitutional Convention of 1787 is a curiously significant forerunner of the attitude of the extreme pro-slavery leaders in the controversies preceding the Civil War.

Secession was, in fact, always latent in the Far South. South Carolina, especially, never unreservedly accepted the Union. Her citizens felt that their state had entered the Union on terms, and they tacitly reserved the right to use their own judgment if what they believed to be the terms of the contract should be transgressed. South Carolina showed plainly what was in the back of her mind by the "nullification" crisis of the year 1832. The crisis arose, not over slavery, but over a tariff law passed by Congress that South Carolina deemed injurious to her interests. A state convention was thereupon called, which passed an ordinance declaring the tariff "null and

## The Schism of the Civil War

void" and of no effect within the state's borders. South Carolina, however, soon learned that if such action had ever been theoretically possible, its time had passed. Outside the Far South, the new national patriotism everywhere rose to fever heat, and President Andrew Jackson (himself a Southerner) curtly warned South Carolina to back down or be broken by force of arms. Resistance being hopeless, South Carolina backed down and accepted the federal tariff law.

But South Carolina was not converted. On the contrary, her intellectual leaders, Hayne and Calhoun, confirmed her in her attitude. Calhoun especially, with his extraordinarily subtle mind, raised "nullification" to the dignity of a full-fledged constitutional doctrine whose logical cogency and persuasiveness appealed to the whole of the Far South. And the "Far South" was expanding. The invention of the cotton gin had made cotton-growing possible and was now spreading both cotton-raising and commercialized slavery over a broad belt of territory stretching from the original nucleus in South Carolina and Georgia westward through Alabama and Mississippi to Louisiana, Arkansas, and the borders of Texas. This "cotton belt" soon became the richest section of the South. And with economic prosperity came an increase of political power. In other words, political primacy was passing from the Old to the Far South—from the hands of moderate-minded Unionists to disciples of Calhoun.

Another point should be noted: despite its expansion and political prestige, the Far South remained uneasy. For if the South was growing, the North and West were growing even faster—and were growing more averse to slavery, especially in its commercialized form. It was the old story over again. Just as the South Carolina delegates had threatened and bargained in the Constitutional Convention of 1787, so the Far South (dragging with it the reluctant Old South) threatened and bargained in the councils of the nation. Compromise after compromise was extorted, but the North and West continued to outstrip the South in population and prosperity, and the South came to feel itself more and more an isolated minority with a mortgaged future.

Even so, anything like civil war seemed for a long time improbable. Most Southerners, like most Northerners, abhorred the very idea of disruption, and old-line Northern and Southern leaders such as Webster and Clay joined hands in upholding the Union they so loved. But two extreme factions were now in the field who were ready for almost anything. The aggressive tactics of the Far South were countered by the equally aggressive tactics of the "abolitionists" of the North, who demanded the immediate extinction of slavery, derided its constitutional status, denounced all Southerners as inhuman monsters, and lastly asserted the principle of absolute race equality. Such fanatical and indiscriminate attacks drove the Southern moderates into the arms of the extremists, who now saw safety only by abandoning compromise and demanding that the whole United States be made "slave soil." The denunciations of abolitionist fanatics were answered by taunting boasts like that of the famous Southern fire-eater who swore that he would soon call the roll of his slaves from Bunker Hill. So, matters went from bad to worse until Lincoln's election in 1860 gave the signal for secession and civil war.

Yet it was not the whole South that seceded. Once again let us note the important fact that secession was primarily the work of the Far South. The three arch-plotters of secession, for example, were all from that section,[1] and the first Confederate capital was Montgomery, Alabama—not Richmond, Virginia.[2] Virginia's subsequent adhesion to the Confederacy and the genius of her generals Lee and Jackson have somewhat obscured the beginnings of the secessionist movement. As a matter of fact, while Jefferson Davis and his colleagues were proclaiming at Montgomery their "Confederate States of America," Virginia was splitting in twain over loyalty to the Union. The mountainous northwestern part of the "Old Dominion" was solidly Unionist, and so strong was the national patriotism of these Virginians that when they failed in their efforts to keep their state in the Union, they broke away and founded a loyal government, which became the new State of West Virginia.

Furthermore, the whole tier of slaveholding states adjacent to the Mason-Dixon Line, from Delaware and Maryland through West Virginia and Kentucky to Missouri, refused to join the Confederacy and maintained their old allegiance. Lastly, the mountaineers of the great Appalachian chain running southward clear to northern Georgia and Alabama were prevailingly Unionist in feeling. In the mountains slavery had never penetrated, Negroes being rarely even seen. The individualistic, free-spirited mountaineers had, in fact, always been instinctively averse both to slavery and to the political domination of the slaveholding oligarchy. When, therefore, the planter aristocracy led the South to secession, the mountaineers hung back and, wherever possible, either stood aloof or actively aided the Union cause.

---

1. The three outstanding personalities of the early secessionist movement were: Jefferson Davis, of Mississippi, immediately elected President of the Confederate States; Alexander H. Stephens, of Georgia, Vice-President of the Confederacy; and Robert Toombs, also of Georgia.
2. Logically enough, the first shots of the Civil War were fired by South Carolina State troops against the Federal garrison of Fort Sumter in the harbor of Charleston, S. C.

## Chapter IV — The Schism of the Civil War

The presence of this great wedge of lukewarm or actually hostile mountain country thrusting down through the very heart of the South was one of the Confederacy's chief weaknesses and contributed powerfully to its undoing. The numbers and the patriotism of the Southern Unionists can be judged by the fact that they furnished more than 200,000 soldiers to the Federal armies.

Indeed, the more we reflect, the more astonishing does it seem that the planter aristocracy was able to mobilize the Southern White masses for secession and then to hold them steadfast to the Confederacy through four years of desperate and failing war. For the planter aristocracy was, numerically speaking, an insignificant minority. Out of a total Southern White population of about 8,000,000, the actual slave owners numbered only some 350,000. And it was this small minority alone that benefited from slavery. In fact, to the poorer Whites, slavery was an actual curse. In the South, as in ancient Rome, the free yeoman farmer and the free laborer could not stand against slave competition wherever slaves could be worked in gangs at a profit. This was the reason why the South lagged behind the North and West in the growth of the White population. In fact, hundreds of thousands of Southern Whites left their homeland and went West, where they ceased to be "Southerners" and afterward fought against the very slave power that had forced them to abandon their native soil.

That, in the face of all this, the slaveholding oligarchy was able to do what it did is striking proof of its extraordinary forcefulness and ability. No such masterful group has ever evolved in America, before or since. It is sad to think what those gifted strains might have accomplished for America if they had used their talents for national instead of sectional aims. As it was, they mostly perished in the Civil War, and their blood was thus for the most part irretrievably lost to the race.

Whatever their faults, those Southern gentlemen proved that they knew how to die! Disappointed in their hope of carrying with them the entire South and therefore faced with terrible odds, outclassed in wealth and natural resources, and cut off from the outer world by the strangling grip of the Federal sea blockade, the Confederacy fought a losing fight with unflinching determination. The Southern leaders had staked their all on a gambler's throw. They lost, but they lost like men.

Yet, if they lost, it was because the victors were their blood brothers, endowed with the same indomitable spirit as their own. For even with its superiority in wealth and population, the North confronted a herculean task. To conquer a vast region like the Confederacy, as large as several

European countries and desperately defended, meant a colossal expenditure of blood and treasure. At the beginning of the war, many qualified foreign observers roundly declared the task impossible, and Gladstone probably voiced the prevailing European opinion when he stated that Jefferson Davis had founded a new nation.

The Civil War was, in fact, a supreme death grapple between the two sections of Anglo-Saxon America. It was a veritable Moloch, devouring in its brazen maw the flower of the race. The war's stupendous material cost, running into many billions of dollars, was insignificant beside the racial losses. The expended billions could be (and were) replaced in a couple of generations. The splendid dead could never be restored.

How appalling the human costs were, a few figures will show. The census of 1860, taken on the eve of the war, gave the total White population of the United States as about 27,000,000. It was this relatively small people who were to engage in a fratricidal struggle of almost unparalleled fury. In the civil war that followed, North and South each lost about 300,000 fighting men—a total of 600,000 soldiers killed in battle or by disease. That, of course, does not include the vast number maimed for life or otherwise permanently incapacitated. It also does not include civilian deaths from privation, disease, or other causes due to the abnormal conditions of wartime. The director of the census of 1870 made a careful analysis of the human costs of the Civil War and concluded that it had caused a direct shortage of nearly 1,800,000 souls. He also estimated that the temporary reduction of the birthrate during the four war years was something like 750,000.

Yet these quantity estimates only partially indicate the loss in quality. As already remarked, the Civil War devoured the flower of the race. In its early stages it was fought on both sides almost exclusively by volunteers. No compulsion was at first needed to fill the armies with America's finest manhood, and in the four years of desperate fighting that followed, it was this picked soldiery that was mostly consumed. Conscription, of course, came later, to fill the terrible gaps in the ranks, and draft after draft was made upon the stock—especially in the South, where the merciless Confederate conscription seized practically every White male between sixteen and sixty who could possibly bear arms, thus (in the pungent words of a contemporary) "robbing both the cradle and the grave."

The racial impoverishment involved in all this is surely plain. The killing of hundreds of thousands of America's best young men was paralleled by the bereavement of hundreds of thousands of America's finest young women, who, deprived of their natural mates, either died childless spinsters or married inferior men who gave them inferior offspring. Thus, the racial level of the American stock was lowered, not only immediately after the war but also for subsequent generations.

The shattering effects of the Civil War upon the entire fabric of our national life will be analyzed in subsequent pages. We may here briefly summarize the matter by stating that every phase of the post-war period revealed an ominous lowering of tone. Old America before the war had displayed, even in its stormy politics and its rapid material expansion, a certain elevation of feeling and an instinctive sense of proportion, which sprang from a strong underlying idealism. But this idealistic quality seems to have been literally burned up in the fire of civil strife, and America after the war plunged into a veritable orgy of materialism. This new materialistic temper showed scant regard for principle and reckoned nothing of remote consequences. Politics became extravagant and corrupt to a degree that would have appalled the statesmen of former days. Business and finance developed methods and abuses hitherto almost unknown. The ruthless, selfish, short-sighted temper of the times was shown in national policies as diverse as Southern "Reconstruction," the wasteful exploitation of natural resources, and the encouragement of mass immigration for cheap and ignorant labor. The prevailing materialism also showed in a rapid decline of arts and letters, the decades following the Civil War being culturally almost barren.

Now, was not this melancholy epoch due primarily to the premature killing off of the best minds and the loftiest souls of that generation? When we scan the long "rolls of honor" inscribed on those countless Civil War monuments erected, North and South, to the memory of the Union or the Confederate dead; when we gaze at old daguerreotypes and faded photographs of soldier-boys with wonderful young faces, and then read below the curt announcement—"Killed at Antietam," or "at Gettysburg," or "in the Wilderness," or "at Cold Harbor"; when we ponder these things, I say, we must ask ourselves whether, if those glorious boys had been spared to take their rightful place as the leaders of their generation, they would not have furnished precisely that constructive vision which would have averted the errors and evils that were in store.

# CHAPTER V

# THE SHATTERING OF OLD AMERICA

When Grant and Lee held their memorable conversation at Appomattox Court House in April 1865, the omens betokened swiftly clearing skies. The early Southern spring seemed to be nature's promise that the long winter of civil war was indeed over. Never did a conqueror show more courteous magnanimity for a beaten yet heroic foe. Every effort was made to spare the feelings of the vanquished. The ragged, starving remnants of the "Army of Northern Virginia" were fed, cared for, and sent home on honorable parole. The Confederate soldiers were even allowed to take along the horses and mules "to help them in their plowing." That last homely touch of Grant's emphasizes his more famous phrase: "Let us have peace."

And behind Grant stood Abraham Lincoln, who, through the long war years had never once lost sight of his greater task: the reforging of the American people, as well as the rewelding of the Federal Union. And now his chance had come to bind up the nation's wounds. How Lincoln's heart must have leaped at the thought—that great heart, which then had only six more days to beat before it was to be forever stilled!

Lincoln's assassination by the half-crazed Booth was one of the most terrific blows that a malevolent fate ever dealt a nation. Yet at first the full magnitude of the disaster was not seen. The new president, Andrew Johnson, after a characteristic outburst of rage, set himself loyally to carry out Lincoln's policy of reconciliation. Lincoln's plan was to appeal to the goodwill and the good sense of all intelligent, moderate men and, through their united efforts, to damp down the fires of hatred, block the vengeful schemes of fanatical extremists, and genuinely weld the South once more to the Union in the shortest possible time.

That Lincoln's policy was as sound as it was exalted, there can be no reasonable doubt. A Southerner by birth and ancestry, though a Westerner by upbringing, Lincoln knew the South. He knew that secession was the creed, not of all Southerners, but of a relatively small ruling minority. Furthermore, Lincoln was profoundly American. Consequently, he realized that the war was a civil war between two sections of a people essentially one in blood and basic ideals. Lincoln thus judged (and judged rightly) that by stressing the many things that Americans had in common, the relatively few points on which they differed would no longer monopolize their attention, and the way would be paved for a genuine reconciliation in a relatively brief period. Lincoln's last official act was precisely along this line. On the afternoon of that truly "Black Friday," April 14, 1865, Lincoln held a Cabinet meeting devoted to the subject of Southern reconstruction. In it the president stated confidently that he expected to set up stable and loyal governments in the Southern States without too much opposition from embittered Northerners and without too much risk from unreconciled secessionists. As though stirred by some strange prophetic urge, Lincoln spoke with unusual emotion and spiritual exaltation. The final touch to this dramatic moment was given by the presence of General Grant, who evinced full concurrence with the President's ideas. It was from this last Cabinet meeting that Lincoln went forth to join a happy theater party—and to encounter death.

It is literally maddening to look back and think how the bullet of a crazy fanatic bedeviled the course of American history. Lincoln and Grant, the idols of the victorious North, had a wonderful opportunity to work something akin to a miracle. The nation was just emerging from a terrible war and was full of hatred, vengefulness, and all the other passions aroused by such a struggle. But there was also a sense of profound relief and solemn thankfulness at deliverance from the awful ordeal, together with an underlying emotional poise and much good common sense. America was thus for the moment in a critical state of balance and could be easily swayed for good or for ill. Lincoln's chief obstacle was the coming Congress, elected in the autumn of 1864 and composed mainly of fierce partisans chosen at the height of war fever. Yet even here fortune favored. The new Congress would not normally convene until December. Since peace had come in early April, Lincoln knew he had more than half a year before him to carry out his reconstruction policy and thereafter face Congress with an accomplished fact. To be sure, Lincoln would have had a big fight on his hands and would probably have been attacked and vilified by his political opponents worse than Washington was in his second administration. Nevertheless, supported as Lincoln would have been by Grant and by far-sighted moderates everywhere, he could have appealed to the country and would almost certainly have won through.

President Johnson faithfully continued Lincoln's policy, and by December the South seemed well on the upgrade. Material conditions were, of course, appalling. Bankrupt and impoverished, the South was economically

# CHAPTER V — THE SHATTERING OF OLD AMERICA

prostrate, while the presence of over 4,000,000 emancipated Negroes, totally untrained to look after themselves and largely wandering about in irresponsible vagabondage, presented a tremendous social problem. Yet the mood of the White South was, relatively speaking, hopeful. Bitter and sullen though it was over its defeat, the Southern heart had already responded to Lincoln's and Grant's magnanimity. Thus, President Johnson could count not only on the minority of Southern Unionists but also on the best and most clear-sighted leaders of the late Confederacy, such as the South's idol, General Lee—men who were ready to face facts and to work loyally for an honorable future inside the Union. Before December, therefore, President Johnson was able to establish Southern State governments that had met his terms by formally abolishing slavery and repudiating Confederate debts and that likewise enjoyed the confidence of a majority of the White population. Of course, many ex-Confederates held sullenly aloof or muttered wild threats, while a few even left the country in irreconcilable wrath. But the general attitude was to make the best of things and get down to the business of building anew.

Certainly, there was no likelihood of a second attempt at secession. As a recent writer admirably puts it, "The Southern people made up their minds after the war was over that the cause for which their soldiers had fought and died was a lost cause and was not something which could be revived. It was done with. After Appomattox, General Lee could not be described as anything but a Union man, and he carried the South with him. The velocity and completeness of the change were astounding and testified to the immense common sense and the political and moral wisdom of the people as a whole. I am frank to say I know nothing like it in history."[1]

Under these circumstances it really looked for the moment as though America was to give the world the almost miraculous spectacle of a great civil war followed by a speedy reconciliation. Such an event would not merely have re-established political solidarity; it would have also reknit the spiritual unity of the folk, so that substantially complete like-mindedness would have come within a generation and full co-operation would have been possible on all major national problems. This would have been highly extraordinary. Yet it was certainly possible, and it would have been an incalculable blessing for America's future.

But alas for the dawning vision of fraternal concord! December 1860 witnessed the convening of that Congress, which Lincoln had so justly dreaded, and in the twinkling of an eye the whole situation was compromised.

---
1. Mitchell, Langdon: *Atlantic Monthly*, August, 1926.

Instead of Lincoln's far-sighted plan, there ensued that most *unnecessary* tragedy of our entire history, ironically misnamed "Reconstruction." And even more than the war, it was "Reconstruction" that envenomed the war wounds, raised a barrier of bitter misunderstanding between the two chief sections of the American people, and turned the old slave problem into a new race problem in some respects worse than before.

In order to understand the tragic series of events that began with the opening of Congress in December 1865, let us cast a glance at political conditions in the North. The eve of the Civil War had witnessed a general breakup of old party lines. In the presidential campaign of 1860, several tickets had been in the field. The "Republican" party, which elected Lincoln, was itself a new organization, composed of elements varying from extreme abolitionists to moderate-minded patriots who saw in Lincoln and his platform the best safeguard for the threatened Union. The outbreak of the war had brought fresh accessions to the Republican party, which, during the war, was transformed into a general coalition of all strong Union men. The only other political organization that survived was the historic Democratic Party. Deprived of its best and most patriotic personnel, the party fell into the hands of narrow politicians who sought to make partisan capital by catering to the disaffected and even the disloyal elements in the North—these latter elements being dubbed "Copperheads." As the war went on, the Democratic attitude became steadily more deplorable. It condoned the terrible draft riots of 1863 and actually waged the presidential campaign of 1864 on the slogan, "The War for the Union is a Failure!" Justly enough, the mass of Northern voters punished the Democrats not only by overwhelmingly re-electing Lincoln but also by choosing a Congress manned by a tremendous majority of ultra-stalwart Union champions.

The covert disloyalty of the Democratic leaders had, however, done more than discredit their own cause; it had made the whole political atmosphere of the North unhealthy and abnormal. Convinced that they were fighting not only open rebellion in the South but hidden treason at home, the Union-Republicans grew more and more embittered and partisan in their attitude. The most drastic measures of repression were approved; legal and constitutional checks were flung to the winds; and the safety of the North was entrusted to a group of leaders masterful and arbitrary by nature, accustomed to political ruthlessness, and fiercely impatient of any opposition to their imperious will. The Congress elected in 1864 was thus composed of an overwhelming majority of fiercely partisan Union-Republicans and a small minority of equally partisan and covertly unpatriotic

# CHAPTER V — THE SHATTERING OF OLD AMERICA 47

Democrats. Lastly, the hatred and contempt felt by Union men for the cowardly Northern "Copperheads" inflamed still further their hatred of the Southern Confederates; though the latter, even if "rebels," were at least avowed rebels, staking their lives manfully upon the battlefield. Thus had the passions of civil war poisoned America's political life!

To have confronted such a Congress would have taxed even Lincoln's ability and popularity. His unfortunate successor was totally unable to handle the situation. To begin with, the new president was temperamentally unfit for the task. Opinionated and cursed with an ungovernable temper, Andrew Johnson made many enemies and few friends. Not only had he no popular prestige, but his political antecedents made him suspect to rigid partisans. A Southerner and a former Democrat, Johnson had been put on the ticket in 1864 as vice president in order to strengthen the loyalty of the Southern Unionist mountaineers, of whom Johnson was one. Because of his origin, Johnson could appreciate Lincoln's policy, but he could not win many Northern converts for it when Lincoln was gone and its execution fell into his hands. In fact, Congress came in spoiling for a fight. The Republican leaders in the preceding Congress had already shown what was in their minds by trying to enact a stiff reconstruction bill while the war was still on, and when Lincoln vetoed the measure, he had come in for much Congressional criticism, some of it decidedly bitter in tone.

Congress at once showed its mood by declining to recognize Johnson's new Southern State governments, by refusing to seat any congressmen or senators from the South, and by appointing a commission to investigate the president's whole policy. Johnson thereupon lost his temper and denounced the Congressional leaders by name as "traitors." The breach was henceforth irreparable. Furthermore, Johnson found himself virtually powerless, because the Congressional leaders, backed by huge majorities in both the House and the Senate, could pass any bill they liked over the President's veto.

By the summer of 1866 Congress showed plainly what it meant to do with the South. Its investigating committee had brought in its report, which declared that the Southern States had by their rebellion forfeited their constitutional rights; that Congress alone had the power to reconstruct these "rebel communities"; that the Johnson governments were illegal; and that the South was in anarchy, controlled by "unrepentant and unpardoned rebels, glorying in the crime that they had committed."

Though Congress had made up its mind, decisive action was deferred until after the autumn elections on which everything hinged, since unless the Congressional leaders could get a two-thirds majority in both houses, the President would block legislation by his veto. The political campaign of 1866 was the most vitriolic that America has ever known. Determined to win at any cost, the Congressional leaders recklessly inflamed war passions and partisan hatreds. As for the President, he unwittingly played into his opponents' hands by adopting the same violent tone. "Taking the stump," Johnson ranged the country like a wild man, roaring out coarse abuse and personal invective, thus disgusting those moderate elements who were his natural supporters. The upshot was that a Congress was returned with safe two-thirds majorities for the Republican party leaders.

When Congress reopened in December, it was in a truly ominous mood. The temper of its leaders was one of mingled triumph and apprehension: triumph for the present and apprehension for the future. They had gotten their requisite majorities, and therewith two more years of absolute power. But afterward? The elections had shown that the "Union League" of the war years was dissolved. "War Democrats" were drifting back to their old allegiance, the Democratic minority in the coming Congress being distinctly larger than it had been. Furthermore, many moderate Republicans, uneasy over Reconstruction, were beginning to murmur or openly to criticize. Veteran politicians that they were, the Congressional leaders realized that the popular tide was beginning to turn against them. If the White South were allowed to vote, it would vote Democratic, and in the presidential elections of 1868, a Democratic victory was far from impossible. An intolerable idea! To those stern party chiefs who had devoted themselves so passionately to the saving of the Union, the passing of political power into the hands of opponents whom they regarded as "Copperheads" and irreconcilable rebels seemed nothing short of treason. Let us be fair to the men of the Reconstruction period. Though they wrought evil, the basic fault was not in themselves but in the times. One golden opportunity had been vouchsafed America to avert the hateful aftermath of civil war. That divine hour had passed with Lincoln. Thenceforth, blind Fate took the helm, and events pursued their course with the relentless logic of a Greek tragedy.

The Congressional leaders who headed the "Republican" party in its narrower post-war sense now proceeded with ruthless and implacable determination. They even tried to remove the president by impeachment. Herein they failed, because seven Republican senators could not stomach such a partisan stroke at future constitutional stability, and impeachment was lost by one vote. The seven senators were politically ruined, yet their memory should be honored as that of staunch patriots who averted what would have amounted to a radical dislocation of our constitutional balance by subjecting the executive to the legislative branch of government. For the moment, of course, the outcome of the impeachment trial made no practical difference, since Congress could override President Johnson's veto as before.

Only one possible constitutional obstacle remained: the Supreme Court. The Republicans knew perfectly well that the constitutionality of some of the measures they had in mind was pretty dubious. Yet here again the Congressional leaders showed their ruthless disregard of legal scruples or ultimate consequences. The Supreme Court was given clearly to understand that if it blocked Congressional Reconstruction, it would be emasculated or perhaps done away with altogether. And the Supreme Court took the hint. For the first and (let us hope) the last time in our history, that august tribunal was plainly cowed. During the critical Reconstruction period, it carefully sidestepped embarrassing questions; albeit, later on, the Supreme Court handed down a series of decisions that undid much of the Reconstruction legislation and interpreted most of what remained in a manner quite different from that intended by its authors.

What, in a nutshell, was the Reconstruction aim of the Congressional leaders? It was to put, and keep, political control of the South in "loyal," Republican hands. But this meant, in practice, not merely disfranchising most of the Southern Whites but also enfranchising the whole mass of newly emancipated Negroes and the casting of these Black votes under the supervision of the small Southern White Republican minority—backed by the protection of Federal troops.

Now let us once more keep clearly in mind the logical sequence of events. The Republican leaders, as a whole, did not (as is so frequently asserted) set out with the deliberate intention of degrading the Southern Whites or of promoting racial amalgamation. Such ideas were confined to the "Radical" wing of the party, headed by such men as Charles Sumner and Thaddeus Stevens. These Radicals, however eloquent and influential, were a relatively small minority. Most Republicans undertook Reconstruction for a purely political objective: that of "saving the Union" from what they believed might be traitorous and rebel control.

However, this political reconstruction inevitably involved racial implications and as inevitably brought the Republican majority to accept more and more of the Radicals' racial policy as a necessary corollary of the political program. For, once embarked on "Reconstruction," there was no turning back. Thenceforth it was a fight to a finish with an infuriated and desperate White South, which, if the Republican grip should ever relax, would take an implacable political revenge. But the obvious way to perpetuate Republican control was to confirm and strengthen the Negro's new political status. Furthermore, as the Radicals did not fail to point out, full and lasting success for the Republican policy could be assured only by breaking down the color line and favoring miscegenation. If the White South were truly irreconcilable, the White South must disappear, and a more amenable Black or Mulatto South must take its place!

Such was the iron logic of the extreme Radicals. And *their* attitude was determined, not so much by political expediency as by moral conviction. The Radical Republicans were, of course, merely another name for the extreme Abolitionist group, which had done so much to bring on the Civil War by its unmeasured denunciations of the Southern Whites and by its fanatical preaching of race equality and amalgamation. Doctrinal heirs of the French Radicals of the eighteenth century, the Radical Republicans professed the same boundless faith in abstract principles and the same firm conviction in the power of environment to mold men almost at will, regardless of their origin or antecedents. Such was the Radical wing of the Republican party, led in Congress by Sumner and Stevens and represented outside Congress by orators and publicists like William Lloyd Garrison, Wendell Phillips, Theodore Tilton, and others, who conducted an eloquent and aggressive propaganda. Never really numerous, the strength of the Radicals lay in their fanatical sincerity and in the political trend of the times.

The Radical attitude toward the Negro was as naively simple as it was severely logical. Denying innate race distinctions, the Radicals looked upon the Negro as an unfortunate White man, deeply tanned by the tropic sun. Freedom, the ballot, education, and a few other favoring factors would so transform this unfortunate brother as to make him for all practical purposes indistinguishable from his White fellow citizens. To hasten and assure the process, full political and social equality must be obtained—and enforced. After that, amalgamation would normally ensue, and—the race problem would have been solved! There you have the doctrine expounded by the Radicals, not only to Northerners but also to the newly emancipated Negroes of the South.

The practical conclusions drawn by Radicals from their theories can be illustrated by a few examples. Toward the close of the Civil War, a Radical writer named Croley published a book advocating miscegenation as a general principle and warmly praising not only the amalgamation of Whites and Negroes but also of Whites and Chinese and all other races. Another Radical publicist advanced the decidedly original biological thesis that the blood of the White man was becoming dry and was thus in actual need of the extra sap to be found in the more primitive Negro blood. Wendell Phillips argued that the newly emancipated Negro was actually better fitted to vote than the Southern White man who had always had the ballot, for, declared Phillips, "The Negro inherits a brain which work has cultivated for four generations, and added to it the skill of a practical hand. The White man inherits a brain sodden by the idleness of four generations, and he has improved his birthright by a life of soddenness. Fairly considered, the only class ready for suffrage in the South is the Negro."

Under such auspices was Southern "Reconstruction" begun! At first everything went according to plan. The Whites were mostly disenfranchised, and the Negroes were given the vote. Many Negroes were likewise given political office, though the more responsible posts were entrusted to White Republicans, colloquially known as "carpetbaggers" or "scalawags." The carpetbaggers were Northerners—some of them honest men but mostly unprincipled adventurers who deserved their title from the fact that when they arrived in the South, all their worldly goods could go into an old satchel. The scalawags were Southerners—and they were the worst of the lot. The first breath of Reconstruction had driven all self-respecting Southern Unionists into a close alliance with the ex-Confederates to defend their threatened race life. Outside the mountain districts, therefore, no Southern White Republicans could be found except men who cared nothing for their own reputations or the opinion of their White fellow citizens. In addition to these unsavory local officials, Congress could count on the agents of the "Freedman's Bureau," a federal organization to aid the Negroes, which functioned throughout the South. Many of these agents were Radical propagandists who promised the Negroes all sorts of things, so that a legend became widely current among the freedmen that the Federal government intended to confiscate the property of their former masters and give every Negro family "forty acres and a mule." And of course, behind the Reconstruction regime stood the Federal army. Congress had divided the South into military districts heavily garrisoned by regular troops prepared to step in and quell resistance to Reconstruction by the application of martial law.

By the close of the year 1867, "Black-and-tan" state governments were duly installed throughout the South, and "Reconstruction" was in full swing. The local results are well described by the late Lord Bryce, surely a dispassionate and liberal-minded authority, whose verdict is, "Such a saturnalia of robbery and jobbery has seldom been seen in any civilized country, and certainly never before under the forms of free government."[2]

At first the Republican leaders were jubilant. Congress was filled with solid Republican delegations from the Southern States, while Southern electoral votes probably saved the party from defeat and elected Grant to the presidency in 1868. The North, to be sure, was registering disapproval of Reconstruction and many other acts of the Republican Party. But this made the Republican leaders all the more zealous for Reconstruction, which had become their political mainstay. For a while America seemed actually in danger of being ruled indefinitely by a fanatical oligarchy supported by Black votes and federal bayonets.

But the day of reckoning was at hand. Despite its apparently hopeless situation, the White South was girding its loins for decisive action. Maddened by the corrupt tyranny of ignorant Negroes and low-down Whites, the Anglo-Saxon South hardened into a veritable block of steel. The ruthless determination of the Congressional oligarchy encountered an adversary equally ruthless and even more determined. Legal action being impossible, the White South developed illegal measures that proved highly efficacious. Great secret societies like the "Knights of the White Camellia" and the "Invisible Empire" of the Ku Klux Klan systematically terrorized the superstitious Blacks by apparitions of weird night-riders in ghostly trappings. The most objectionable Negroes, carpetbaggers, and scalawags were frightened away or killed. The South became the battleground of political and racial warfare, obscure but terrible. Congress, of course, replied with "Civil Rights Acts," "Force Bills," and martial law, while the Reconstruction State governments raised Negro militia for their defense. All in vain! Nothing could long withstand that solid phalanx of the White South, wrought up to a cold, silent fury, and fighting for its very race-life. One by one the carpetbag governments fell, and state after state was regained for White rule. In 1877 a Republican president (Hayes) acknowledged the bankruptcy of "Reconstruction" by recalling the Federal troops from the South, leaving the Whites everywhere in full control.

Hayes' action undoubtedly reflected the weight of Northern public opinion. The North had never been solid for Reconstruction; still less had it approved the Radical attitude toward race equality and miscegenation. Reconstruction had, in fact, long been persisted in by the Congressional oligarchy against the plain evidence of Northern disapproval. But by Hayes' time the grip of that masterful group was practically broken. Some of the old leaders were dead, and more had retired to private life. Moderate men

---

[2]. Bryce, James: *The American Commonwealth*, vol. II, p. 498 (second ed. 1911).

# Chapter V: The Shattering of Old America

had taken office, war passions had cooled, and the North was interested in new issues. The poison gas of war hatred had mostly cleared away, and the political atmosphere was no longer abnormal.

The North was thus looking forward to a new day. But the South remained in the shadow. Those ten long years of horror had set upon the South a stamp that made it in many respects a land apart. The Congressional oligarchs had risked the great gamble of "Reconstruction" in order to create a Republican "Solid South." Their creation had given them a decade of political power, but it had now vanished, and in its stead appeared a Democratic South, more solid and more bitterly partisan than the framers of Reconstruction had ever dreamed.

Now a "Solid South," Republican or Democrat, was an ominous novelty in American political life. Before the war, party lines had bisected Southerners just like Northerners, and we have seen that not even in the Civil War did the South show a united front. But what secession failed to do, Reconstruction had done. The South was henceforth politically welded like a block of steel: consumed with hatred for the Republican party, obsessed with a terrible race problem, and so bitterly partisan that it stood ready to vote for the devil himself if he bore the Democratic label. And this frame of mind was to persist for almost two generations. Not until our own days has a "New South" arisen, with a truly national vision and a genuine urge to play its full part in American national life.

Meanwhile, the Southern people were for half a century to a large extent *denationalized*. Less than twenty years ago, one of the South's wisest and most far-sighted spokesmen thus depicted the prevailing Southern attitude: "Not rebelliously or bitterly, but wistfully, and with the real sadness of the patriot, an older friend once said to me, 'I think I love my country, and yet its general interests and its common life have been forced into the background and are far away. I sometimes feel that I have ceased to be a citizen of my country and have become, instead, but the citizen of a race.'"[3]

The tragedy of all this, not only for the South but perhaps even more for America as a whole, is surely clear. The old American stock was riven in twain, and its best men were prevented from common counsel and common action by a political cleavage that automatically ranged them in two opposing partisan camps. Indeed, the North, regardless of party, was almost wholly deprived of Southern aid and counsel in national affairs, because even when the Democratic party was in power, its Southern wing was too preoccupied with local problems to be able to give a tithe of the thought

---

3. Murphy, Edgar Gardner: *The Basis of Ascendancy*, p. 139 (1909).

and statesmanship to national problems that had been the pride of the Old South before the war.

Furthermore, the evil legacy of Reconstruction long tended to perpetuate the sectional breach within the nation and therewith to lower the political tone. War passions were burned out, but a few embers still smoldered beneath the ashes, and professional partisans on both sides industriously raked the ashes for sordid purposes. Republican hack politicians long tried to make a little cheap political capital by "waving the bloody shirt" and denouncing "Rebels"; while below Mason and Dixon's Line, Democratic party hacks similarly courted cheap applause by valiantly assaulting the stuffed scarecrow of the "dam' Yankee." It was a Southern wit who aptly characterized these "professional Southerners" by saying that they "lived by the sweat of their exclamation points."

Reconstruction was, of course, the crowning disaster of the Civil War period. Yet Reconstruction was itself merely the outstanding symptom of the ominous trend of the times. In every phase of national life, the war's shattering effects were disquietingly revealed; everywhere there was the same loss of constructive vision, the same degradation of sane idealism into blind partisanship, and the same replacement of patriotic devotion by a rampant and reckless egoism. Political life became increasingly characterized by extravagance and corruption. One political party was as bad as another: if the Republicans were disgraced by colossal scandals like the Crédit Mobilier and the Whiskey Ring, the Democrats were smirched by the brazen effrontery of Boss Tweed and the gigantic peculations of Tammany Hall. To this period, also, belong those sinister liaisons between politics and finance epitomized by the figures of Jim Fisk and Jay Gould, the wholesale spoliation of natural resources by predatory interests, and the "public be damned" attitude of the big corporations that then arose. America's growth in wealth and prosperity was, to be sure, amazing, but it was a growth accompanied by crass materialism and by that same reckless disregard of consequences that the politicians were showing in the handling of their affairs.

The post-war epoch was thus a critical transition period. The Old America of pre-war days lay shattered, and a new America was not yet forged. For a sound, constructive forging, the best possible situation would have been one of relative isolation like that after the storm of the Revolution. But America was to be vouchsafed no such boon. At the very time when the national fabric was perilously tattered, America was confronted with a new problem in the shape of an endless deluge of immigration; at the moment when its assimilative powers were thus at a low ebb, it was faced with the necessity of

# Chapter V: The Shattering of Old America

assimilating as never before. To America's domestic problems of sectionalism and color, there was superadded an alien problem of incredible magnitude.

# CHAPTER VI

# THE ALIEN FLOOD

MIGRATION TO AMERICA IS THE most stupendous human mass-movement in the world's history. Nothing even faintly approaching it, either in volume or variety, has ever been known. No other nation has had to deal with such a vast and continuous human flood. And no human flood of similar magnitude has ever arisen so unexpectedly or deluged a country within so short a space of time.

We have seen that during the early stages of our national existence there was little to betoken the human inundation which was in store. We have traced the stream of immigration from its first tiny trickles of 5,000 or 6,000 per year, and we have noted that immigration, though steadily growing, was a matter of minor importance down to almost the middle of the nineteenth century. From the birth of the nation to the year 1820 (a period of over forty years) the total number of immigrants is estimated at only 250,000; while from 1820 to 1846 immigration averaged less than 50,000 per annum. In other words, during the first seventy years of our national life the total number of immigrants was less than 1,500,000; whereas, in that same period, the American population grew from a scant 3,000,000 to a good 21,000,000.

Such was the situation in the year 1846. Then, suddenly, the human flood struck our shores! In the next ten years approximately 3,000,000 immigrants entered America—twice the total number which had previously arrived since national independence. During the Civil War epoch immigration slackened, but it again swelled to unprecedented proportions, until by the year 1890 the total number of immigrants admitted to the United States was over 15,500,000.

And even then, the human deluge had by no means reached full flood. It was in the period from 1890 to 1914 that immigration really inundated America. During those twenty-four years no less than 17,500,000 immigrants entered the United States! Furthermore, it was during just those years that immigration became most "alien" in character, since the bulk of these later millions were of South and East European or even of Asiatic origin; thereby bringing into America racial stocks, ideas, and attitudes toward life, which had previously been well-nigh unknown.

The outbreak of the Great War in 1914 caused a sharp drop in immigration. But it presently became evident that the end of the war would witness a new alien flood of even more colossal proportions. Experts on immigration estimated that the gathering deluge might run as high as 3,000,000 or 5,000,000 per year—that, in fact, the only definite limit would be the capacity of the ships which could be manned and built to ferry across the inconceivable human swarms struggling to get to America.

Then, at last, the American people awoke to their situation, and the gates of the Republic were closed to mass-migration—probably forever. Even as it was, over 5,000,000 more immigrants entered the country in the decade from 1915 to 1924—an average of over 500,000 per year. But the memorable Johnson Immigration Act of 1924 rendered any such influx thenceforth impossible. By that law immigration from the Old World was reduced to an annual maximum of 165,000 persons, while by the provisions of the same act this figure was to be later cut still further to 150,000 per year. With some minor exceptions, the gates had been closed against future immigration perils.

Yet, even though the gates were now barred, a century and a half of virtually unrestricted immigration had produced domestic problems of adjustment and assimilation bewildering in their complexity and scope. Under our "traditional" policy, some 37,000,000 immigrants had entered America—nearly 22,000,000 of them since the year 1890. To be sure, many millions of immigrants had been birds of passage, returning sooner or later to their homelands. Yet the majority had remained in America, so that, out of a total population approximating 110,000,000, almost 40,000,000 were either foreign-born or of foreign or mixed parentage. These foreign millions were of every race and nationality known to Europe and Western Asia, besides large contingents of people from various parts of the New World, and smaller contingents from Eastern Asia and even from Africa.[1] Such was the situation in the year 1924, when the closing of the gates to the alien flood gave Uncle Sam a chance to take stock and think things over.

Viewed from every conceivable angle, immigration is of tremendous importance. In the first place, entirely apart from questions of quality, let us consider the significance of such purely quantitative matters as *mass* and *time*. Contrast the difference between a relatively small foreign element,

---

[1]. Of course, this has no reference to importations of Negro slaves from Africa, which ceased legally in 1808. Since then Negro immigrants from Africa have been negligible. The chief source of modern immigration from Africa is the Cape Verde Islands, off the African coast, whence come the Black "Brava Portuguese."

arriving gradually and scattering among a large Native population, and a huge foreign mass, twenty or thirty times as numerous, coming in an endless series of waves literally piling on top of one another. And all in so short a time! Remember that the whole cycle of mass-immigration, which began in 1847 and ended in 1924, covered a period of less than eighty years. What is eighty years in the life of a nation? It is scarcely more than the span of life normally attained by robust individuals. Indeed, there are thousands of persons still living who were born before the alien flood began, at a time when immigration excited little popular interest. Think of the profound transformation of America which such persons have seen!

One thing is certain: immigration is, in the most literal sense of the word, a supremely "vital" problem. For immigration signifies not merely business or politics or dividends; in the last analysis immigration means men and women, and their children, and their children's children—in other words, *the nation's blood and soul.* For a "nation," in the true sense of the word (as distinguished from a mere government) must possess a national spirit; and that spirit is inevitably determined by the blood of its people. Before the first colonists came a certain area existed in the New World which was to furnish the geographical basis for the United States. But that vast wilderness was not "America;" neither were the Red Indians who roamed its forests "Americans." The same soil and climate which we now enjoy were there, together with an untouched store of natural resources; but the Indians made virtually no use of these splendid possibilities and affected the country scarcely more than the wild animals they hunted for a livelihood. It was the White colonists who endowed the virgin land with a true civilization, and who ultimately breathed into it a distinctive national soul.

Then, and then only, did *our America* come into being. And should that creative blood vanish or be radically altered by alien infusions, *our* America would pass into the limbo of dead nations and peoples, just like ancient Egypt, and Hellas, and Rome, and many a forgotten folk entombed in the dust of ages.

For every phase of national activity is as much the result of a nation's racial make-up as human activity is a consequence of the blood and temperament of a particular individual. Laws, institutions, ideals, the whole fabric of national life—these are but the outward manifestations of the creative racial spirit within. But if the nation's racial make-up changes, the national fabric can no longer fit people of different temperament and outlook; consequently, the laws, the institutions, the ideals, and all the rest of it are either radically transformed or are done away with altogether. Unlike an individual, a nation is potentially immortal. Yet there is one sure way of killing a nation—to destroy or fatally to dilute the blood of its creators. Whatever takes its place may, to be sure, assume the same name. But it is not the same thing.

Any factor which affects the blood of the nation is, therefore, of vital concern. And can we conceive of any factor which has more profoundly affected America than the mass-migration of the past eighty years? It is simply amazing to think that until recent years immigration was looked at mainly from the economic viewpoint, its "vital" aspect being almost wholly disregarded. Yet surely the admission of aliens should be regarded just as solemnly as the begetting of children, for the racial effect is essentially the same. Immigration is, from the racial standpoint, a form of procreation, and like individual procreation it may be either the greatest blessing or the greatest curse. Human history is largely the story of migrations, making now for good and now for ill. Migration, like other natural movements, is of itself a blind force. It is at once our privilege and our duty to direct this blind force in accordance with the known laws of life, for our betterment—lest it be our undoing. The way the immigrant was until recently regarded, not as a creator of race-values but as a mere vocal tool for the production of material wealth, was little short of madness.

Before proceeding with our survey of the immigration problem, let us pause to note one or two matters which, though not in the direct line of analysis, have a distinct bearing upon the subject.

In our entire discussion we have taken for granted the concept of a united, harmonious American *nation* as our ideal for the future, just as it was the ideal of Washington and Lincoln and unnumbered patriots throughout our history. Yet we may parenthetically remark that there exists among us a school of thought (small but disproportionately vocal) which rejects the national ideal in favor of a more or less pronounced internationalism. Now the internationalist philosophy causes its adherents to look at almost everything from a radically different angle. In nothing is this more striking than on the subject of immigration. Regarding this country not from an "American" but from a "world" viewpoint, internationalists tend to oppose restriction of immigration on principle. They assert that "America belongs to all the world;" wherefore all who wish to enjoy our special advantages have a sort of prescriptive right to come in and take their share, even if this brings all sorts of ill to Americans themselves, and even though it involves a troublous transformation of American life. Indeed, such a transformation is precisely what ardent internationalists desire. Their ideal is an "America" which would no longer be a nation, nor even a distinctive civilization, but which would have become a sort of microcosm of the whole world—a mosaic of races, cultures, and contrasting attitudes.

Now in so far as these internationalists are sincere, they have a right to their opinions. But to anyone except an internationalist such an ideal as that just described must seem the most dangerous of utopias, which should be vigorously combated wherever it appears to be making converts, muddling popular thought, or undermining patriotism. The ultimate consequences of "opening America to all mankind: would almost certainly be political and social chaos, frightful civil or racial war, and the destruction not only of American national unity but of everything worthwhile in American life. No worse fate could possibly be imagined for our country than an "internationalized" America.

In our discussion, therefore, we shall frankly consider the national ideal to be axiomatic, and we shall not turn aside to engage in any philosophical argument over the abstract merits of the national versus the international idea. In fact, we might not have mentioned the subject at all, were it not for the propagandist uses to which internationalism is being put by people who are not humanitarian idealists at all, but who have quite other aims in view. The genuine humanitarian internationalists are so few, and their doctrines are so visionary that, of themselves, they could never make much headway. Unfortunately, they lend respectability and furnish camouflage arguments to other elements by no means so innocuous in character.

The first of these is the aggregation of revolutionary radicals typified by the Communists—the believers in Russian Bolshevism. These radicals are, it is true, "internationalists," but their internationalism is something very different from that of the humanitarian idealists above described. Communist internationalism embraces not humanity but a definite class. Its objective in America is not a loosely federated mosaic of races, ideals, and cultures, but an iron "dictatorship of the proletariat," the banning of all ideals except the gospel of Marx, and the replacement of our existing culture by that "proletarian culture" which in Soviet Russia is yielding such dubious fruits.

Another aggregation which uses humanitarian internationalism for its own ends is the cluster of unassimilated alien elements. These elements may or may not be revolutionary radicals, but even those who are in no sense internationalists often use humanitarian phrases as a cloak to conceal their own aims. Many alien groups want to break down our immigration-restriction policy to get more of their kinsmen into this country and try to clothe their special interests by high-sounding humanitarian "principles."

These same alien groups employ similar arguments to conceal another aim of theirs. Disliking an America to which they are not adjusted, they long to break the traditional American pattern in order to remold it according to their own desires. Later on, we shall examine more closely these unassimilated aliens and their activities. The point to be here noted is the added strength which they derive from a pretense of high idealism.

Finally, humanitarian camouflage is often used by a third group wholly unconnected with those just mentioned. This group is made up of "hard-boiled" businessmen and big employers eager for cheap labor. The harm done by camouflage of this sort was especially great in the past, when the "sob stuff" ladled out wholesale by paid propagandists of big corporations, steamship agents, and other vested interests in unrestricted immigration did much to blind the public to the true situation. Today damage from this source is much less because public opinion is too aroused and too well informed, and also because many big employers have come to realize that the political and social perils of mass-immigration far outweigh the temporary profits from cheap, ignorant alien labor.

"America's good" should, therefore, be the criterion by which every phase of the immigration problem should be judged. The ideal of all genuine Americans can be simply and briefly defined. That ideal is: a united, harmonious American nation. Whatever furthers the attainment of that ideal should be warmly supported; whatever hinders it should be sternly opposed. The test governing the admission of all applicants, whether they be individuals, groups, or races, should be just this: does the weight of evidence show that these applicants will fit normally into the fabric of American life, accept our basic ideals, and come to form an organic part of a harmonious national whole? Unless our common-sense verdict on this question is "Yes," the applicant should be excluded. For remember: no foreigner has any "right" whatsoever to enter America. His admission is a *privilege*, extended to him solely because we think he can benefit America. The burden of proof is thus upon him to show why he should be admitted; not upon us to prove why he should be kept out.

Let us remember also that the national ideal is based not upon abstract theory but upon good common sense. No theoretical questions of "superiority" or "inferiority" need be raised.[2] It is perfectly true that our present immigration policy does (and should) favor North Europeans over people

---

2. The question of the relative standing of racial groups is one of great importance. The weight of scientific evidence shows that races not only differ widely from one another, but also that they can be qualitatively graded. However, we need not discuss the latter point, because it does not basically affect the matter which we are here considering.

from other parts of Europe, while it discriminates still more rigidly against the entry of non-White races. But the basic reason for this is not a theory of race superiority, but that most fundamental and most legitimate of all human instincts, self-preservation—rightly termed "the first law of nature."

We want above all things to preserve America. But America," as we have already seen, is not a mere geographical expression; it is a nation, whose foundations were laid over three hundred years ago by Anglo-Saxon Nordics, and whose nationhood is due almost exclusively to people of North European stock—not only the old colonists and their descendants but also many millions of North Europeans who have entered the country since colonial times and who have for the most part been thoroughly assimilated. Despite the recent influx of alien elements, therefore, the American people is still predominantly a blend of closely related North European strains, and the fabric of American life is fundamentally their creation.

Now this national and cultural fabric, whatever its shortcomings, has one outstanding merit: it fits the temperament and general outlook on life of its North European creators, who constitute the great majority of the population. Of course, most Americans draw from this the conclusion that our nation and our stock are the best in the world—all peoples, even Eskimos and Andaman Islanders, feel just the same way about themselves. But that is not the issue at all. The really important point is that even though America (abstractly considered) may not be nearly as good as we think it is, nevertheless, it is ours. We realize that it is not perfect; but we love it, we live it, and most of us would defend it to the last drop of our blood. Our national ideal is not static; we know that readjustments should be made. But we are resolved that whatever changes are made shall be evolutionary changes, in accordance with our basic ideals. Furthermore, we have recently become awakened to the fact that harmonious national evolution will be possible only if the blood of the nation remains predominantly of North European origin; because only thus will the existing fabric of American life continue to fit the temperament of the population. Thus, it all comes down to sheer self-preservation. And however, theorists may rail, self-preservation is the first law of nature.

The cardinal point in our immigration policy should, therefore, be to allow no further diminution of the North European element in America's racial make-up. This does not mean that immigrants from Northern Europe have any prescriptive right to admission. It does, however, mean that their origin is strong presumptive evidence that on closer scrutiny they will prove to be the sort of people who can best become real Americans. To get down to cases: a pure-blooded English criminal or moron should be barred as rigidly as any other criminal or moron, and a one-hundred-per-cent Nordic Scandinavian intellectual who turns out to be a "Red" agitator should be expelled as summarily as a bewhiskered Bolshevik from Moscow. Yet, while all applicants should, of course, be personally examined on their individual merits, it is nevertheless true that, generally speaking, North Europeans are to be frankly preferred, because they normally qualify much better as potential American citizens—which is the only valid reason why we should allow any immigrant to enter America. Can anyone who knows the facts honestly deny that Englishmen, Scotchmen, and Scandinavians come to us with an inborn temperament and a social upbringing which predispose them to true assimilation vastly more than is the case with, say, Russians, Sicilians, or Yugoslavs?

That is the meat of the matter, and when we discuss immigration, we had better stop theorizing about superiors and inferiors and get down to the bedrock of *difference*. America welcomes diversity—but diversity within limits. America should not encourage differences so great that assimilation is difficult or impossible. In other words: we want people who can understand us, accept our ways, and become whole-hearted partners in the great task of perfecting our America. But we most emphatically do not want people, *no matter how industrious or how intelligent*, who don't like us, don't fit into the national fabric, and instinctively want to change our America into something different, based upon different ideas and attitudes toward life. There is the whole thing in a nutshell. In later chapters we shall discuss its wider implications on various phases of national reconstruction. At present, let us keep it carefully in mind during the analysis of immigrant elements which we shall now essay.

The outstanding fact in the story of migration to America is that it falls into two great streams, profoundly unlike in character. These two human streams are usually termed the "Old" and the "New" Immigration. The terms are well chosen, for they accurately describe the difference between them. The Old Immigration is that from Northern Europe. The New Immigration is that from Southern and Eastern Europe and adjacent parts of Asia, which began about forty years ago. It is the Old Immigration which we will first consider.

The chief sources of the Old Immigration are: Great Britain and Ireland, Germany, the Scandinavian countries (Norway, Sweden, and Denmark), and a few minor sources like Holland, France, and Switzerland. Now the chief point to note about the Old Immigration is that it has in it nothing

## Chapter VI — The Alien Flood

really "new." All the countries of Northern Europe which we have just mentioned had furnished sizable quotas to the colonial population. When, therefore, the immigrant stream rose rapidly, toward the middle of the nineteenth century, it was essentially the same stream which had flowed since early colonial days. Of course, the stream was vastly larger, the quotas from the various countries had shifted their ratios, and the average quality of the immigrants differed considerably from that of colonial times. All these factors produced economic, social, and political effects on American life which were often disturbing and which frequently hindered assimilation. Nevertheless, these difficulties, however disturbing, were of an essentially temporary nature. The newcomers were basically of the same racial origins as the Native Americans, and they were thus temperamentally predisposed to assimilation in the long run. The Old Immigration, therefore, enormous though it has been, has involved no deep-going changes in the blood of the nation and has contained no basic threat to American ideals or institutions.

Until about the year 1880 the Old Immigration furnished practically all those who came to America. Only after 1880 did there appear the first trickles of that New Immigration which within fifteen years was to swell so prodigiously that it then came to outnumber the diminishing flow from the older sources.

Let us now analyze the Old Immigration, in order to discover the numbers and character of its various elements.

At the very start let us note one curious fact: in discussions of immigration one element is often barely mentioned or is even entirely overlooked. That element is the Anglo-Saxon. Yet this element, comprising as it does the English, the Scotch, the Scotch-Irish (Ulster Protestants), and the English-speaking Canadians, forms the most numerous and the most constant single stream of immigration which has ever entered America. It has flowed steadily from the very beginning to the present day. Its volume may be judged by the fact that the Anglo-Saxon "immigrant" stock[3] today constitutes between 11,000,000 and 12,000,000 of our population.

Why is there so little mention of the Anglo-Saxon element in immigration? For a very significant reason. The Anglo-Saxon immigrant usually fits into America so well and assimilates so rapidly that his great numbers pass almost unnoticed. To be sure, he often remains a British subject, and

---

3. The term "Anglo-Saxon 'immigrant' stock" refers only to such persons as entered America after the Revolution, and their descendants. All Anglo-Saxons here before 1783, and their descendants, are included under the colonial stock. The Anglo-Saxon colonial element today numbers about 43,000,000. Adding the "immigrant" element, the total Anglo-Saxon element in America today is about 55,000,000. This is well over one-half the total White population.

this slowness in adopting American citizenship has led some writers to declare that the Englishman is hard to "assimilate." That statement, however, ignores the real meaning of assimilation. "Assimilation" signifies genuine absorption, and as applied to immigrants it means their real incorporation into the idealistic and cultural fabric of American life—precisely as food is digested and becomes organically part of the human body. "Assimilation" should be clearly distinguished from "naturalization"—the legal act of being admitted to American citizenship. Assimilation is an instinctive process. Naturalization is a formal procedure. The new citizen may, or may not, be "assimilated." Indeed, great numbers of naturalized citizens prove conclusively that they have not been in the least assimilated, both by their conduct here and by their frequent return to their homelands, where they use their American citizenship for purely selfish purposes. Now the Anglo-Saxon immigrant is so like us in blood, language, customs, and ideals that he is, as it were, half "pre-digested" before he even sets foot on American soil. Therefore, whether he becomes technically "Americanized" or not, he is so similar to us that his political preferences usually do not much matter.

The other two main streams in the Old Immigration are the Celtic Irish[4] and the Germans. Both the Irish and the Germans have entered America in vast numbers, though neither element is quite so numerous as the Anglo-Saxon immigration. The Celtic Irish stock in America today numbers about 9,000,000; while the German immigrant stock[5] contributes between 10,000,000 and 11,000,000 to our present population.

Though the great Irish influx dates from the potato famine in Ireland of 1846-47, Irish immigrants had been entering America in considerable numbers during the preceding fifteen or twenty years. These early Irish immigrants were a fine, sturdy lot. For the most part lusty young fellows who promptly enrolled in the "pick-and-shovel brigade," they furnished much of the labor employed on the canals, turnpikes, railroads, and other public works which were then being undertaken. The great Irish influx which began in 1847, however, was of a very different character. The vast hordes of destitute, starving refugees from the potato blight, though still composed largely of sound individuals, contained many undesirable elements. The authorities in Ireland systematically aided the departure of

---

4. The term "Celtic" Irish is the term generally employed to distinguish the older Irish population (mainly Catholic) from the newer "Scotch-Irish" element settled in Ulster by the British Crown as a Protestant loyalist garrison. Having now made the distinction clear, I shall henceforth refer to the Catholic majority as "Irish," the prefix "Celtic" thus becoming unnecessary.

5. The term "German immigrant stock" does not, of course, include the German element of colonial times, which now numbers about 2,500,000. This makes the total German element in America today between 13,000,000 and 14,000,000.

useless members of society, and great numbers of paupers, ne'er-do-wells, and lunatics were dumped on America. The docks of New York, Boston, and other Atlantic ports witnessed harrowing scenes as the crowded immigrant ships discharged their human cargoes, which sometimes consisted chiefly of diseased or otherwise unfit persons. Even the majority of normal, able-bodied individuals constituted a serious problem, for they were so poor and destitute that they mostly stuck to the seaboard towns and cities, where they glutted the labor market and hived together in wretched slums. It was these unpleasant economic and social features of Irish immigration, rather than religious differences, that produced the friction between the Irish and the Native Americans which we shall later consider.

After the famine rush subsided, the stream of Irish immigration cleared, and thenceforth it was to contain, on the whole, the more enterprising and intelligent of the Irish peasantry. However, it has apparently never averaged so high in physical vigor as it did during the early period before the famine.

The great German influx begins with the year 1849, though here again a small immigrant stream had been flowing for the preceding two decades. Those early arrivals were mainly members of peculiar religious sects, who settled in agricultural colonies and, like the "Pennsylvania Dutch" of colonial times, kept pretty strictly to themselves. Some of these communities still survive as isolated islets of population, leading their own lives and out of touch with the world at large.

Very different in character was the great stream of German immigration which began in 1849, and which (except during the Civil War period) flowed mightily for over forty years. The failure of the German liberal movement of 1848 drove multitudes of political exiles to seek freedom in the New World. These "Forty-Eighters" were mostly of a high type. Nearly all of them were not only sincere idealists but also persons of education and culture. Their leaders made their mark in journalism, the learned professions, and many other fields of American life. After the Forty-Eighters, the stream of German immigration was for many years composed largely of yeoman farmers ("Bauern") who settled thickly on the new lands of the Middle West. Those Germans who settled in the towns and cities were mainly artisans and tradesmen. Down to 1890 German immigration contained very few undesirable elements. After that date the German stream rapidly dwindled. Germany had become prosperous, while most of our public land had been occupied. The result was that the Germans who came from 1890 to 1914 were fewer in numbers and were mainly townsmen of a less desirable type—though even so, they should be classed as mediocre rather than inferior. Since the late war German immigration has again become relatively large. Under our present immigration law Germany's annual quota is regularly filled. Germany's troubled post-war situation makes many of its best people desire to emigrate, so this latest German influx contains some excellent elements and averages well.

Another important stream of the Old Immigration is the Scandinavians—the people from Norway, Sweden, and Denmark, together with the Icelanders, who are of Norse blood. The Scandinavian stream did not begin to flow much before 1870, but thenceforth it ran strongly, so that today the Scandinavian element in our population numbers nearly 4,000,000. The Scandinavians are characteristically "outdoor" folk. They make fine farmers, and prefer the cold climates of our Northwestern States, where they are found in great numbers, from Minnesota to Washington and even in far-away Alaska. Others, heeding the call of their Viking forebears, follow the sea, and are fishermen or sailors. The town-dwellers among the Scandinavians are largely skilled artisans. The Scandinavians vary somewhat among themselves. The Norwegians and their Norse brothers the Icelanders are rugged individualists and are perhaps the finest of the lot. The Swedes are quicker, though somewhat less tenacious. The Danes are relatively gregarious and excel in pursuits like cooperative dairying. The general average of the Scandinavians is extremely good, with very few really undesirable elements. They are a most valuable addition to our population, especially since they assimilate better than any other element except the Anglo-Saxons. This is just what might be expected, because the Scandinavians are not only Nordic in blood but have political traditions, social ideals, and a general outlook on life very similar to those of the Anglo-Saxon stock.

The only other stream of real importance in the Old Immigration is the Dutch. A steady current of Dutch immigration, combined with a lesser inflow of their blood-kinsmen, the Flemings of Belgium, have together resulted in a "Netherlandish" immigrant element in our population which today numbers about 500,000.[6] Like their predecessors of colonial times, these Dutchmen are sturdy folk, somewhat slow to assimilate, but making good citizens in the long run.

So ends our survey of the "Old Immigration." Its tremendous importance is self-evident. Apart from any consideration of quality, its sheer mass is profoundly significant. For the five major elements[7] of the Old Immigra-

---

6. Adding the Dutch colonial element, the total "Netherlandish" element in America today is nearly 2,000,000.
7. There are a few minor sources of the Old Immigration, especially France and Switzerland; but immigrants from these minor sources are so few, relatively to the chief sources above discussed, that they need not be treated in a general survey like ours. Of course, immigrants from France should be clearly distinguished from immi-

tion which we have just analyzed furnish nearly 38,000,000 of our present population—in other words, well over one-third of all the White blood in present-day America!

Now the outstanding fact about the Old Immigration is that practically none of it is either racially or culturally "alien." A sizable sample of every one of its elements had been present as far back as colonial times, and they had all been successfully assimilated. It could, therefore, be safely assumed that none of the later instalments would prove refractory to assimilation or would present any permanent obstacle to the evolution of the "America" established by the colonial stock. That is probably the underlying reason why, despite the disturbance and friction undoubtedly caused by its first mass-influx, the Old Immigration aroused no general alarm in American public opinion. Instinctively, most Americans then felt that the economic advantages from this immigration outweighed the more or less temporary social and political problems which it raised. There was thus no growing sense of real peril culminating in a conviction that the gates must be closed, such as was later aroused by the "New Immigration" and which culminated in the decisive Johnson Act of 1924.

However, if we are to strike an accurate balance on the Old Immigration, we should not fail to note certain less obvious consequences. To begin with, the very fact that most of this immigration was sound and assimilable made people minimize its undesirable elements and delayed the passage of laws banning unfit individuals. It was not until 1882 that such legislation was really undertaken by Congress. Before that time such obviously bad elements as paupers, morons, criminals, and diseased persons could enter America practically at will. We have already noted how the governmental authorities and local charity boards in Ireland used the famine exodus as a fine opportunity to dump their undesirables wholesale on America. And this was merely the most striking example of a policy pursued deliberately by most European nations, until we stopped the practice by laws forbidding the entry of such persons. Meanwhile a lot of low-grade humanity had entered America even from those countries which normally form our best sources of immigration.

For we must not make the mistake of looking at even the most advanced nations as a unit. A moment's reflection shows us that just because a certain country is inhabited by a generally high-grade population is no reason for believing that population to be universally high-grade. Every human stock, no matter how good, has its dregs. Therefore, the good general average of a

---

grants from French Canada. The two elements are very different in character.

population is no guarantee that in its emigrants it is sending us a fair sample of itself. For instance: Scotland grows mostly a fine breed of men and has usually sent us a fine lot of emigrants. But if, suddenly, Scotch immigration should be made up largely of paupers and jailbirds, Scotland would cease to be a desirable source of immigration and would have to be regarded as a highly undesirable one. Here again, throughout the nineteenth century, American public opinion failed to grasp the essential fact that immigration is a very complex problem which needs careful watching lest new or unsuspected phases catch us unaware and work havoc before they are remedied.

Nothing more startlingly emphasizes this than the way new streams of immigration have suddenly swelled from a mere trickle to a veritable flood. Time after time this has happened. Furthermore, the cause has often been in no way connected with American conditions or needs. A potato blight in Ireland, a revolution in China, the crowning of a reactionary Czar in Russia—things like these, which the average American of the period had perhaps never even heard of, nevertheless caused immigrant floods as unexpected as though they had dropped from the skies. It took many, many years of bitter experience to teach the American people that the immigration problem was most emphatically loaded with dynamite, and that unless it was wisely and carefully handled it might wreck the whole fabric of American life.

Certainly, it was a great misfortune that throughout the nineteenth century American public opinion was lulled into short-sighted complacency by the doctrinaire humanitarian theories which had been grafted upon our thinking after the Revolution. It was also unfortunate that public opinion was confirmed in this "liberal" attitude by the fact that, up to about 1880, the racially and culturally assimilable Old Immigration was practically the only kind America knew. The American people was thus unprepared to grasp the significance of really "alien" immigration and vastly overestimated the assimilability of peoples racially and culturally remote. When, therefore, the New Immigration swelled portentously after 1880, the American people saw in it little more than a continuation of the Old.

If the American public of the eighties had been more observing, they might have profited by one startling warning which should have cautioned them on the subject of alien immigration. Perhaps they would have so profited if the warning had come *via* the usual Atlantic route, instead of as a distant episode on the shores of the Pacific. The warning was, of course, the Chinese influx into California.

Barely two years after the first great immigrant tide of 1847 had begun to fill our Atlantic ports, gold was discovered in California and caused an eager rush of pioneers. With everyone after gold, labor for ordinary tasks was scarcer than the precious metal. At that critical moment a few Chinamen turned up and exactly filled the bill. Here was labor, and satisfactory labor at that! Forthwith enterprising Yankee skippers sailed to China to get more of these marvelous workers. They had no trouble in loading full cargoes, for China itself was then in the throes of the great Tai-ping Rebellion and was filled with misery and unrest. This made multitudes of Chinese eager to emigrate, and surely nothing could be more attractive than the lure of golden California. More and more Chinamen landed on our Pacific shores and were promptly employed in all sorts of ways, from cooks in mining camps to construction gangs on railroads.

At first the Chinese were warmly welcomed. But as their numbers increased, the Californians began to consider, and they presently concluded that if the Chinamen continued to swarm in, they, the White Californians, would be literally pushed off the map. Soon only the big employers of labor continued to want Chinese immigration. From the employers' standpoint, the situation was perfect. The Chinese coolie is unquestionably the nearest living thing to the "Robots" of that justly celebrated satirical drama, *R. U. R.* The Chinese coolie can do more work on less food for less money than anyone else in the world. The employer can hire coolies in blocks from Chinese contractors, who handle all the details and guarantee satisfaction so long as the price is paid. It is perfection—for the employer.

But how about the rest of the community? Let us see. Unluckily, the coolie is *not quite* a machine. In fact, he is a man—with ideas, and desires, and aims of his own. He saves his wages—and stops being a coolie. He buys a little shop or a small farm—and still displays the same tremendous economic efficiency. As a coolie, he had cut the Native workman out of a job. Now, as trader or farmer, he proceeds to put those Native classes out of business. Having thereby made still more money, he climbs yet higher, and becomes a big merchant, a banker, or a great landowner. And all this time he has been sending home for his kinsfolk, men and women. These women produce children—many children. The Chinese element expands by leaps and bounds. Chinese villages, Chinese city quarters, grow like mushrooms. Ultimately the land is transformed into something like a New China. And the Native is, for the most part—no more!

Such was the nightmare possibility which flashed before the Californians' startled eyes—a nightmare which they promptly swore should never become a reality. As a matter of fact, it did not happen. But it *would* have happened if the Californians had not stopped the Chinese influx. They stopped it by drastic means. But this was because Congress for a long time refused to give them legal protection in the shape of an exclusion law. So the Californians, fighting for their very race-life, used violent, extra-legal methods. Chinese were mobbed, beaten, and killed, and Congress was frankly warned that if something were not done there might be a general massacre. Congress still hesitated, because American public opinion was, on the whole, indifferent or disapproving of the California attitude. Humanitarian liberals spoke eloquently of "America's duty" to "give the Chinaman a chance." But the situation in California was so tense that Congress reluctantly passed the Chinese Exclusion Act—and our Pacific Coast was preserved as a White man's land. The Chinese were kept from doing to California what they threatened to do at that same period to other White lands like Australia,[8] and what they are today actually doing to Asiatic lands like Malaysia, where the Native inhabitants are being literally crowded off the earth by Chinese "peaceful penetration."

We know today that the Californians were right, and we have extended Chinese exclusion to Hindus, Japanese, and all those other vast Asiatic reservoirs of potential immigration, aggregating fully 900,000,000 people, who would swamp the whole of America if they were given the chance. That the poor Chinese in California were brutally and unjustly treated is unquestionably true. But who was really to blame? In the immediate sense, it was Congress; in the last analysis, it was Nature. Deprived of the legal protection they sought, the Californians were roused to desperation by the most imperious of all passions—self-preservation. After Congress had passed the Exclusion Act and the Chinese no longer flocked in, there was no more trouble.

The Chinese episode teaches several very useful lessons. In the first place, it shows us that, when confronted by a new situation, we should look at the facts of that situation and should not be blinded by cherished theories. Secondly, when public opinion becomes aroused and alarmed over what it believes to be a pressing and vital issue, legal relief should be promptly given, lest public feeling grow desperate and turn to desperate means of self-defense.

And there is yet another point which the Chinese episode drives home. It is, as already stated, that any sound immigration policy must be based

---

8. In Australia, as in California, a rapidly growing influx of Chinese excited an alarmed popular agitation which was quieted by an exclusion law. No non-White immigrants of any kind are permitted to enter Australia. The cornerstone of Australia's immigration policy is that Australia shall be kept a "White man's country."

on the bedrock of *difference*. The Chinese, for example, are in many ways a wonderful people. They are hard-working, temperate, likable, intelligent, and much more besides. But—the Chinese are *different!* They are so different from us in blood, culture, ideals, and general outlook on life that they cannot be assimilated, and we know that if they came to us in vast numbers, they would either destroy us or hopelessly mongrelize us. Therefore, no matter how intelligent, or industrious, or anything else they may be, we do not want them and we will not have them. And this applies to any race or nationality that is so different from us that its presence among us would threaten the harmonious evolution of our national life. We are unalterably resolved that *our* America shall survive. And any theoretical arguments against that resolution, however high-sounding or eloquent, are so much waste of breath. They are worse than useless.

Thank Heaven, that is today the attitude of the great majority of Americans; and their conviction is embodied in our present wise and sound immigration laws, which are our best guarantee for a happy national future. But alas! Those immigration laws were passed only after forty years of the "New Immigration," which has resulted in the presence of some 14,000,000 people of diverse South and East European or West Asiatic origins, who are for the most part massed in our Northeastern States. Many of these new elements present grave problems of adjustment to American life, while a few of them may never be really assimilated. The effect of the New Immigration on America will be discussed in subsequent chapters. For the moment let us analyze the various elements of the New Immigration, in order to understand the human factors involved.

A glance at the European homeland is enough to explain why the New Immigration differs so profoundly from the Old. The basic reason is, of course, the vast difference between Northern Europe, on the one hand, and Eastern and Southern Europe, on the other. As compared with the other portions of the continent, Northern Europe displays marked simplicity and stability. Racially, culturally, and politically, this is equally the case. Northern Europe is the home of the blond Nordic race, and practically everywhere in Northern Europe Nordic types constitute either a majority or at least a notable minority of the population. The only other racial elements[9] in Northern Europe are the brunette "Mediterranean" stock found chiefly in the British Isles, and the round-headed "Alpine" stock of many parts of Germany and Switzerland. Both these stocks are, in Northern Europe, pretty well mixed

---

9. There are of course, one or two very minor racial groups, like The Mongoloid Lapps of northern Norway. Also, a few vestigial traces of very ancient races like the Cro-Magnons of central France and the "Old Black Breed" types of western Ireland and the Hebrides occasionally crop out in the present population. But these elements are, of course, too negligible to affect the essential truth of the statement made in the text.

with Nordic blood, which thus forms at once a connecting link between them and a sort of ethnic cement for the racial whole. Furthermore, racial mixtures in Northern Europe are relatively stable, because mass-migrations in that part of Europe ended long ago. When we turn from race to culture, we find similar conditions of stability and basic unity. Northern Europe has possessed the same general culture since the early Middle Ages. Therefore, despite a rich variety of cultural forms, they are on the whole harmonious, because the basic ideals and intellectual standards are on the same general plane. Turning to the political aspect, we find that the national groupings of Northern Europe are mostly old and well-established.

How different is Eastern Europe! It is the direct opposite of what we have just discussed. Conditions in Eastern Europe can be described in two words: complexity and instability. Eastern Europe is next door to Asia, and time after time Asiatic hordes have swept over it, upsetting its political and cultural life and altering its blood. The "Slavic" peoples who occupy most of Eastern Europe belong technically to the Alpine race, yet they are very different from the Nordicized Alpines of Germany and Switzerland, because they are all more or less impregnated with Asiatic Mongol or Turki blood. "Scratch a Russian and you'll find a Tartar" is a saying which applies not only to the Russians but also in varying measure to the other Slavic peoples, from Poland to the Balkans. Again, these mixtures of widely unlike racial stocks are relatively recent, and hence unstable. Furthermore, class distinctions are largely along racial lines, so that often the aristocracy, the middle classes, and the peasantry of a particular East European country differ strikingly in ethnic make-up. Lastly, large blocks of people have remained for centuries quite distinct from the surrounding population, from which they are sundered by deep religious and cultural gulfs as well as by differences in blood. This is notably the case with the East European Jews, who, by the way, are not Semitic "Hebrews," but are descended either from West Asiatic stocks akin to the Armenians, or from a Central Asiatic (Mongoloid) folk—the Khazars. Eastern Europe thus presents a bewildering complexity of races, creeds, and cultures, which reaches its climax in the Balkans—that unhappy abode of jarring, half-barbarian peoples. Eastern Europe, therefore, does not possess anything approaching Northern Europe's basic unity in ideals and cultural standards, and nothing like its relative simplicity of blood. On the contrary, in Eastern Europe there is neither unity nor simplicity of any kind.

In Southern Europe conditions lie midway between the extremes of the North and East. Italy, Spain, and Portugal, which are the chief South European nations, possess old, well-established, kindred cultures, and thus have basic ideals and standards, quite as stable as those of Northern Europe. Politically, however, Southern Europe is less stable than the North, while racially it is much more complex. The Italian and Iberian Peninsulas, open as they are to penetration both by land and sea, have undergone pronounced racial changes in the course of their history. The original stock is "Mediterranean," but the modern Mediterranean stocks of Italy and Spain are very different from those of the British Isles. This is because the British Mediterraneans have been isolated for ages, mixing only with Nordics, whereas the stock of Southern Europe has been repeatedly and profoundly modified by Alpines and Nordics coming from the North, and by West Asiatic, North African, and even Negro blood coming by sea. Modern Italy, despite its political and cultural unity, is nevertheless inhabited by two distinct stocks which divide the peninsula between them. The North Italians are chiefly of Alpine blood, with strong Mediterranean and Nordic infusions. The South Italians are a complex mixture of Mediterraneans with Asiatic and North African strains (chiefly Arab and Berber), together with a slight dash of Negro blood. The racial make-up of Spain is somewhat similar to that of Italy. In Portugal, the lower classes have so much Negro blood that they are practically light Mulattoes.

Such, in brief, are the racial, political, and cultural conditions prevailing in Eastern and Southern Europe, which, together with certain West Asiatic regions like Turkey, Armenia, and Syria, form the sources of the New Immigration. From small beginnings, about 1880, the New Immigration swelled with portentous rapidity until by the opening of the present century it swamped the Old Immigration and from then until 1914 constituted from three-fourths to four-fifths of all the immigrants admitted to America. In the years immediately preceding the Great War the average number of immigrants from Southern and Eastern Europe and Western Asia averaged well over 1,000,000 per annum. This heterogeneous mass had only one thing in common—it was thoroughly "alien" to America in blood, culture, and outlook on life. In the deepest sense, therefore, it was undesirable; because, whatever economic services it rendered by its muscular power and mechanical skill, and however eminent some of its more talented members were to become, these advantages were more than counterbalanced by the acute problems of adjustment and assimilation provoked by the mass-alienage saddled upon the nation—perhaps for generations.

Think of the circumstances under which the nation was forced to shoulder this new burden—say, in the late eighties, when the New Immigration began to attain notable size. It was only about twenty years since the Civil War, whose shattering effects we have previously described. Now ever since the Civil War, America, owing to its weakened condition, had had its hands full assimilating the millions upon millions of North European immigrants who had been pouring in at a tremendous rate. True, the human material was promising, and the job was being done successfully; but it was slow work at best and the job was far from completed. Suddenly, almost without warning, the American people was faced with a new tax on its assimilative powers beside which the unfinished job looked like child's-play. What wonder that, beneath a hectic surface of material prosperity, the national life soon became politically fevered and socially diseased? Talk about assimilation! Uncle Sam was suffering from acute indigestion, if not from ptomaine poisoning! What wonder that Uncle Sam's whole digestive system came to be painfully upset?

The New Immigration is so complex that instead of describing it by national origins we shall divide it into a few main groupings according to the general character of the immigrants we receive. For our present purposes this is a much more useful method; because, in Eastern Europe especially, nationalities are bewilderingly cross-cut by ethnic, cultural, and religious lines. What we are here concerned with is not the national homelands but the sort of immigrants we get from them. And we shall discover that, while the ruling classes and their cultures may vary widely from one another, the uneducated peasants, who in many cases form the bulk of immigration from those countries, differ comparatively little in habits and general outlook on life. In analyzing the New Immigration, we must always remember that the upper social levels in the homelands do not necessarily indicate the sort of immigrants we get from those countries. In Eastern Europe especially, a particular nation may possess an able, cultured, and progressive ruling class; whereas in that same nation the peasantry (perhaps of a different racial stock) will be still in the Dark Ages, and the lower-class townsfolk will be almost equally ignorant and backward. Therefore, it is quite beside the point to argue, as is so often done: "Just look at the men such-and-such a country has produced! Just look at what it has done in the past, and what it is doing today! I guess the immigrants from there must be pretty good stuff!" Such arguments, in themselves, mean nothing; because all the good things said about a particular country may be absolutely true—and yet it may be one of our worst sources of immigration for the simple reason that it may send us mainly its worst human material. Offhand, you simply can't tell.

Bearing these points in mind, let us now survey at close range the New Immigration, which falls logically into four main groups: (1) the East

European peasants; (2) the East European Jews; (3) the Southern Europeans (mostly peasants) ; and (4) the Western Asiatics (chiefly Syrians and Armenians).

The great mass of East European immigrants (the Jews of course excepted) are peasants, whatever their national origins. But, though fresh from the soil, most of them come to America seeking jobs rather than land. Unskilled and uneducated as they usually are, they gravitate naturally to our mines, steel mills, and other industrial plants requiring hard labor. Considered as a whole, the East European immigrants are backward, primitive folk who herd together in foreign "colonies" which remain distinctly "alien" in tone. The ultimate effect of these people on America depends primarily on the extent to which they bring over their families and settle down as permanent residents. Certain nationalities are chiefly "birds of passage." Some of the Balkan elements, especially, consist almost entirely of men, who plan to save their wages and return home. Obviously, such elements, whatever their temporary economic effect, will exert no lasting influence on America. Other elements, however, like the Poles, not only are very numerous but tend to bring over their women and remain in America. The Poles especially present a serious problem for assimilation. Whether they get jobs or go on the land, they always strive to form compact urban or rural colonies, which become real "Little Polands." Since they have enormous families, these Polish colonies grow rapidly but never lose their alien character and remain undigested foreign blocks set down in American cities or on American soil. Other immigrants, however, are more promising. Perhaps the most desirable of the East European elements are the Bohemians or "Czechs." The Czechs are better educated and are more intelligent and progressive than most East European immigrants. To be sure, they are clannish and self-centered, but they do come to understand us and fit gradually into the American national fabric.

Another promising element is the Hungarians or "Magyars."[10] For a thousand years the Magyars have been a ruling race, and even the poorest peasants feel a keen pride and self-respect which makes them ambitious to do well and win the respect of their American neighbors. The Magyars are, however, relatively a small element in the great immigrant stream. Much more numerous are the Letto-Lithuanians, who rank above the East

---

10. The "Magyars" must, of course, be clearly distinguished from the much more numerous Slavs, Rumanians, and other racial elements which were included in the Kingdom of Hungary before the Great War, and which made up most of the immigration from that country. Although they are listed in immigration statistics as from Hungary, they are not "Magyars." Most of the rough labor colloquially known as "Hunkies" are, therefore, not Magyars but Slavs.

European immigrant average in intelligence and mechanical skill. The Letto-Lithuanians, however, are so self-centered and clannish that they are generally refractory to assimilation.

Reviewing the East European immigrant group as a whole, we find that it consists mainly of backward peasants decidedly alien to American ideals and American ways. Their average intelligence seems to be considerably below that of North European immigrants. Thus, save for the exceptions above noted, the East European immigrants do not appear to be very promising material for harmonious incorporation into American national life. The East European elements in America today total somewhere between 5,000,000 and 6,000,000, massed almost wholly in our Northeastern States.

Let us now consider the second main group of the New Immigration: the East European Jews. Right here we should note one point which underlies the whole matter—*The Jews are not a race*. Considered as a whole, the Jews are a religious and cultural group, divided into at least two absolutely distinct racial branches. These are: (1) the "Sephardim" or Mediterranean Jews; (2) the "Ashkenazim" or Eastern Jews. Racially and temperamentally, they have about as much in common as Christians of Western Europe have with Christians of Syria and Armenia. Now the East European Jews (who have come to America only since 1882) are Ashkenazim, and it is they who alone constitute that "Jewish problem" which today undoubtedly exists in America.

Jews of a different sort have been in America since early colonial times. We noted quite a group of Sephardim way back in old Dutch New Amsterdam, long before the town became "New York." But these Sephardic Jews were no "problem." On the contrary, they were well esteemed and proved a valuable addition to the population. Some of those old Sephardic colonial families are deservedly prominent in New York today.

A second Jewish element to enter America were the German Jews. In blood they were partly Sephardim and part Ashkenazim; but they likewise constituted no "problem." The German Jews formed part of the great German stream of immigration which began in 1849. In culture and ideals, they were practically Germans, and they soon adjusted themselves to American ways. Mostly small tradesmen, they scattered broadcast over the country and seldom raised any real friction between themselves and the rest of the population. In 1880 there were about 200,000 Jews in America—all either of old Sephardic or German extraction.

The year 1882, however, saw the beginning of the vast flood of Eastern Jewish immigration. In Eastern Europe a great mass of Ashkenazic Jews

# CHAPTER VI — THE ALIEN FLOOD

have lived for ages. They are descended mainly from a remote branch of Israel which entered Southern Russia from the Caucasus and Armenia, over a thousand years ago. By the time they reached Russia, these Jews were no longer racially "Hebrews" but were mostly of blood akin to the Armenians. In Southern Russia they converted to Judaism a Central Asiatic tribe, the Khazars, and thereby further mingled their blood. It was this mixed population which drifted westward to Poland and the Ukraine, where they have remained for the last eight hundred years. Here they received reinforcements in the shape of a stream of German Jews fleeing from persecution. These Western Jews were so superior in culture that they imposed their Germanic dialect, which became "Yiddish." The former theory that all the Polish Jews came from Germany has thus been disproved. We now know that the Western stream, however culturally important, was numerically only a small addition to the mainstream from the East. Therefore, the modern Polish and Russian Jews are chiefly of West Asiatic Armenoid stock, together with a strong infusion of Central Asiatic Khazar blood.

Such is the racial make-up of the Eastern Jewish flood which reached America after 1882. The first arrivals averaged best, including as they did many religious leaders of deep learning. The masses which followed, however, were for the most part composed of the very poorest elements, which had existed for centuries in appalling poverty and squalor. These people were about as thoroughly "alien" to America as it is possible to conceive. For instance: we set great store by our ideal of national life. But to the mass of Eastern Jews the very phrase "national life" was not only meaningless but was positively distasteful. They had never been a nation; nor had they ever formed part of a nation. From time immemorial they had led a closed life as a persecuted tribal sect. The only "national life" they knew was that of their hostile Polish or Russian neighbors. The only government they knew was that of the despotic Russian Czars. Hence, the Eastern Jews instinctively hated both nationality and government. This explains why international and radical revolutionary theories have gained such a hold upon the Eastern Jewish element in America.

The Eastern Jewish immigration was a genuine "exodus." They came in families, and they came to stay. They are very prolific, and they now number well over 3,500,000. Counting the old Sephardic and German Jewish elements as 300,000, America today contains nearly 4,000,000 Jews, rapidly increasing. In passing, we may remark that the Sephardic and German Jewish groups have no liking for their Eastern co-religionists, so there has been little intermarriage, and the stocks remain distinct.

The third main group of the New Immigration is the South Europeans. Its most numerous and important element is, of course, the Italians. But the Italians themselves divide into two sharply contrasted branches. We have already noted that Italy is inhabited by two virtually distinct stocks. This home division is faithfully repeated by the immigrants on American soil. The immigrants from Northern Italy are vastly different from those we get from the Italian South. The North Italians are a decidedly desirable folk. They are mostly skilled artisans or expert agriculturists, together with many merchants and professional men. The Northern Italians usually keep carefully aloof from their Southern compatriots, whom they dislike. In fact, the Northern Italians generally try to Americanize as quickly as possible, and they usually succeed.

Very different are the Southern Italians, who are many times as numerous in America as their Northern compatriots, and who thus form the bulk of Italian immigration. Mostly backward peasants, the Southern Italians tend to become manual laborers, especially in construction gangs or in the building trades. The Southern Italians are thoroughly alien to America and instinctively crowd together in "Little Italys," where they can lead their own gregarious, colorful life. Even so, neither the climate of our Northern States nor the American scene seems really congenial to these typically Mediterranean folk, who look back fondly to "Sunny Italy" as home. More than perhaps any other element, the Southern Italians have been "birds of passage," coming here to make quick money and then returning whence they came. For this reason, the present size of the Italian element in America is not nearly so large as might be supposed from statistics of immigrant arrivals and from the proverbial fecundity of their women. Although by the census of 1920 nearly 4,000,000 Italians have entered America, so many had left again that this census showed only 1,600,000 foreign-born Italians then in the country. An analysis of the net increase from the beginning shows that the Italian element, Northern and Southern, in America today numbers about 3,000,000.

Of the immigrant Spaniards little need be said. They average better than the Southern Italians, but they are relatively few in numbers, keep very much to themselves, and usually intend to return home after they have "made their pile." As for the immigrant Portuguese, they are an undesirable element. Most of them come, not from Portugal itself, but from the Azores Islands. It is a curious fact that the Azoreans are Whiter than the lower classes of the Portuguese mainland. Still, our Portuguese immigrants are mediocre folk with a low average of intelligence. The so-called "Brava" Portuguese from the Cape Verde Islands off the coast of Africa are really Negroes, with only a dash of White blood.

# The Alien Flood

The fourth and last group of the New Immigration are the Western Asiatics, most of whom are Syrians and Armenians. While both these immigrant elements contain individuals of commercial and intellectual ability, the Syrians and Armenians are, as a whole, too remote racially and culturally to be really assimilated. Compared to the preceding groups, the Western Asiatics are numerically insignificant. Even including minor elements like Turks and Arabs, their total number in America is not over 250,000. However, we have every reason to believe that those small trickles of immigration were but the forerunners of what would have been another great human flood if our restriction laws had not intervened. The lure of the New World was stirring Western Asia, and on the eve of the Great War several steamship companies were planning to expand their Mediterranean and Black Sea services to accommodate hosts of Syrians, Armenians, Caucasians, Tartars, Persians, and other Asiatics who were planning to come to America.

The "New Immigration" was, in fact, a boundless flood, and although by 1914 it was coming into America at the rate of over 1.000,000 a year, it was really only just getting under way! Had it been allowed to flow unchecked; it would have literally drowned *our* America. Not merely the old stock but all the later North European arrivals would have been ultimately crowded to extinction by these swarming, prolific aliens, drawn from ever lower and lower economic levels, undermining our living standards, and making life on the high American plane impossible. In President Roosevelt's vigorous words, America would have become "polyglot boarding-House"—the crowded abode of a jostling throng of alien peoples.

# CHAPTER VII

# ON THE ROAD TO RUIN

"For what shall it profit a man, if he shall gain the whole world, and lose his own soul?" And what shall it profit a nation if it shall recklessly exploit its natural and human resources, gaining thereby a whole world of hectic prosperity which shall soon turn into the Dead Sea fruit of a harassed present and a mortgaged future? That, in short, is the melancholy story of the fifty years between the Civil War and the Great War. That entire period of over half a century is characterized by an ever-increasing materialism, a deflection of constructive vision into short-sighted egoism, and a blunting of instinctive poise and sense of proportion by a ruthless lust of immediate gain coupled with a reckless disregard of ultimate consequences. With the fabric of its national life badly tattered and with its idealism burned away by the cataclysm of the Civil War, America plunged into a materialistic orgy which so careful an authority as Carver roundly terms an economic and social "nightmare."[1]

Now a nightmare lasting more than fifty years and getting worse all the time is apt to leave deeply disturbing traces, even after the victim has waked up. And that is precisely where we are today. We realize what we have been through, and we are resolved it shall not happen again. But it is going to take a long time before the havoc wrought is repaired and our national life becomes truly sound once more.

To comprehend fully the evil days on which America entered after 1865, let us cast a glance at the economic and social condition of Old America as it was before the Civil War. We have already sketched the marvelous growth of the West, and we saw that this was a thoroughly healthy movement—the natural expansion of a vigorous people, which resulted not only in the development of hitherto untouched natural resources but also in a marked increase of the fine "pioneer" stock. Thus, the material and the human wealth of the nation were alike fruitfully multiplied.

While this Western agricultural expansion was going on, a parallel process of industrial development was taking place in the settled Eastern

---
1. Carver, T. N.: *The Present Economic Revolution in the United States*, p. 262 (1925).

States. Almost from the hour of independence, New England had begun to harness its waterpower for mills of various kinds, while the advent of steam-power tapped the vast coal and iron deposits of Pennsylvania and adjacent regions. By the middle of the nineteenth century, New England, especially, was dotted with manufacturing towns inhabited by a relatively large working-class population.

This industrial development, however, was as normal and healthy as was the agricultural development of the West. Those early New England "mill-towns" showed none of the squalor which was later to debase them. The mill-operatives were frugal, self-respecting Yankees, who lived decent, orderly lives, and who insisted upon fair treatment and just wages. And these things they nearly always obtained; not only because there was then no inpouring tide of low-standard labor for employers to turn to, but also because the employers were then for the most part old-school New Englanders—men of principle, who respected their fellow-Yankee working men and working women and were ready to give them a "square deal." Of course, we do not mean to imply that conditions were perfect—as a matter of fact, hours were long, and wages, while sufficient for a decent livelihood, needed Yankee thrift to make them stretch much beyond plain needs. Nevertheless, industrial conditions in America were then probably better than they were anywhere else in the world. Foreign travelers of those days have left abundant testimony of their surprise and delight at the refreshing aspect of the clean, wholesome mill-towns of Old America.

To give our mind's eye a clearer vision of those vanished days, let us scan a few excerpts from the recollections of a mill-girl of that period. "The young women who worked at Lowell," she writes, "had the advantage of living in a community where character alone commanded respect. . . . Work, study, and worship were interblended in our life. The church was really the home-center to many, perhaps to most of us. . . . The two magazines published by the mill-girls, the *Lowell Offering* and the *Operatives' Magazine*, originated with literary meetings in the vestry of two religious societies; the first in the Universalist Church, the second in the First Congregational; to which ray sister and I belonged. ... In recalling those years of my girlhood at Lowell, I often think that I knew then what real society is better perhaps than ever since. For in that large gathering together of young womanhood there were many choice natures—some of the choicest in all our excellent New England. . . . We were allowed to have books in the cloth-room. Our superintendent, who was a man of culture and a Christian gentleman of the Puritan school, dignified and reserved, used often to stop at my desk in his daily round to see what I was reading. It was a satisfaction to have a superintendent like him, whose granite principles, emphasized by his stately figure and bearing, made him a tower of strength in the church and in the community. He kept a silent, kindly, rigid watch over the corporation-life of which he was the head; and only those of us who were incidentally admitted to his confidence knew how carefully we were guarded."[2]

Another resident of the same city, a minister whose long pastorate enabled him to see both the "good old days" and the darker days which were to follow, thus contrasts the changes wrought by the years: "There are still those in Lowell who remember the 'former days' and pine for their return—the happy days when life was homogeneous, and all were one in their loyalty to the new mill-town on the Merrimack; when the Yankee girls worked leisurely thirteen hours a day in the mills and wrote poetry at night. . . . It is a far cry indeed from the city of more than 100,000, made up of fifty or more nationalities, with 50 per cent foreign born and 80 per cent foreign parentage, to the days of 'auld lang syne,' when all knew each other, thought the same thoughts, spoke the same language, and worshipped in the same way."[3]

Now the conditions just portrayed in Lowell, Massachusetts, apply in the broad sense to industrial conditions throughout Old America. In the early days even the lower-paid ranks of manual labor were not squalid or degraded. Poverty of course there was, and many individual cases of destitution—usually the result of too much hard liquor. Again, the waterfronts of the port towns harbored tough and criminal elements—mainly of foreign origin. But even the largest cities of Old America had no real "slums" before 1840; just as the medium-sized cities of the Far West, inhabited as they are almost exclusively by descendants of pioneers and the best of the Old Immigration, have no real slums even today. We must always remember that if slums make slum people, slum people also make slums. In the absence of low-grade, pauper, or degenerate elements, slums simply do not arise.

These happy social conditions were first disturbed by the great immigrant influx which began in the late forties. We have seen that the Old Immigration, while sound in the main, contained undesirable elements which congested the cities and towns of the Atlantic seaboard. The market for manual labor was temporarily glutted, the relatively high standards of the Native American laborers were upset, and in time this immigrant labor worked its way into the mills, disturbing the economic and social status

---
2. Larcom, Lucy: *A New England Girlhood* (1889).
3. Kenngott, G. F.: *The Record of a City* (1912).

of the Native factory operatives in New England and adjacent regions. The Old Immigration thus produced a milder phase of the unfortunate consequences which the New Immigration was later to produce in vastly aggravated form—the upsetting of living standards; the appearance of slum conditions in the cities and factory towns; the undermining of old ideals; and the disruption of the traditional like-mindedness, by the introduction of foreign cleavages in ideas, languages, and creeds.

Another consequence of even more profound and lasting significance was the downright *replacement* of a large portion of the Native American population by the immigrant newcomers and their children. Driven from many lines of labor, the displaced American workmen either went West or, even if promoted to better jobs at home, limited the size of their families, refusing to raise children unless these could be so educated that they could enter the more desirable occupations and could thus avoid competition with low-standard foreigners under working conditions which, in American eyes, had become degrading. This "social sterilization" of the Native stock revealed itself by a rapid decline in their previously high birth-rate, this decline in fecundity being everywhere exactly in proportion to the intensity and character of the immigrant influx. Indeed, nearly all students of the problem now agree that even the Old Immigration, especially where it stayed in the East mid competed directly with the established Native stock, was essentially a *replacement* of a certain portion of the Native American element; that every such immigrant prevented a Native American baby from being born; and that if there had been no immigration at all, we should today have just about as large a population, but entirely of Native American blood.

However, we need not stress unduly this replacive aspect of the Old Immigration, because, considered as a whole, it did not involve any marked alteration of the nation's racial make-up or any basic threat to American ideals. The Eastern Seaboard States did unquestionably suffer a certain lowering of human quality, because it was there that almost all the undesirable elements in the Old Immigration stuck. Yet these undesirable elements after all formed but a small portion of a sound and assimilable total. Especially was this true of the vast hosts of North Europeans who came seeking, not Eastern jobs, but Western land. These people did not stay East but usually went directly West to settle the areas as yet but thinly occupied by the Native American pioneers. And those immigrants, whether British, Irish, German, Scandinavian, Dutch, or other nationality, were nearly all of good quality, and exerted no injurious influence on existing living-standards.

They therefore did not "socially sterilize" the Native stock and were thus a genuine addition to the population instead of a mere replacement.

Surveying the Old Immigration as it reached its peak in the early eighties, we find that in the West both its temporary and its permanent results were favorable. In the East it had caused temporary economic and social disturbances, and it had introduced some undesirable elements which were to be a permanent burden, yet even in the East the bulk of the Old Immigration was of sound, assimilable stock. If the New Immigration had never come, America would, by now, present about the same racial and social aspect as Australia. Like America, Australia was settled mainly by people from the British Isles; but, unlike America, Australia had the wise foresight to welcome only immigrants from North European sources. This immigration did, to be sure, contain some undesirable elements, just as we got undesirable elements, mixed up with the good, in our Old Immigration. In its early days, especially, Australia was afflicted by the convict stream which the British Government had previously sent to its American colonies. Although that muddy human stream ceased long ago, Australia is still paying the price, because the descendants of the worst elements today infest the slum quarters of Sydney and Melbourne. However, this slum element is practically confined to Australia's two chief cities. The rest of the Australian population is a high-grade, homogeneous people.

Now that would have been about the situation in America today if we had adopted Australia's immigration policy. New York, Boston, and a few other big cities would have had bad slums with a vicious, criminal element. But these would have been exceptions to the general rule. The rest of the country would have been inhabited almost entirely by a high-grade North European population which would have been pretty thoroughly Americanized in a couple of generations.

That, indeed, was what seemed most likely to happen in the early eighties. By that time the worst economic and social disturbances produced by the Old Immigration had abated. The tremendous industrial development which set in after the Civil War had taken up the slack in the formerly congested Eastern labor market, and with higher wages and better living conditions, the North European working men were being rapidly Americanized. The mill-towns of New England recovered from the first slump and improved in tone; while the coal regions of Pennsylvania, purged of criminal foreign elements like the "Molly Maguires," showed decent villages, inhabited for the most part by self-respecting Cornish, Welsh, and Irish miners, often owning their own homes and usually rearing their children under proper surroundings.

But already the first trickles of the New Immigration were seeping into the Eastern States, and within a decade the whole industrial trend was going from bad to worse. These strange newcomers were not only alien in blood but equally alien in living standards and social ideals. Accustomed to existence on an economic plane much lower than that prevailing in Northern Europe and infinitely lower than that of America, the first Slav and South Italian peasants who landed found America almost as much an economic paradise as had the Chinese coolies in California. Poor and hungry, these South and East Europeans were only too glad to work for wages and under living conditions which North Europeans as well as Native Americans indignantly rejected as impossible and degrading. Snapped up eagerly by America's expanding industry, the New Immigrants saved good money where the Old Immigrants and Native Americans would have literally starved, and the glowing tales sent home stirred fresh multitudes in far-off lands to quit their cramped, pinched existence for the wonderful El Dorado across the sea.

By the early nineties the New Immigration was fairly under way, and any one with half an eye could see that, unless checked by restriction laws, it would rapidly attain vast proportions. Already the New Immigration was producing economic and social disturbances far graver than those which the first influx of the Old Immigration had caused half a century before. As early as the year 1892, a trained observer of social conditions, investigating the sinister transformation of Pennsylvania's decent raining towns into filthy slums, which was then taking place, thus reported his findings: "When a stranger visits the anthracite regions he is filled with sympathy for the poor Italian and the Slav. He considers the American resident heartless in the extreme. He is amazed at the way the foreigners are regarded. But a single year spent in that land will show him the truth, no matter how tender-hearted he is. He will then know that disgust should take the place of surprise. He sees a thousand idle Americans and a like number of foreigners slaving for eighty or ninety cents a day. He sees the Americans sending their children to school, supporting churches, living in decent houses, trying to be cleanly and wear presentable clothing. He also sees the scum of Europe taking the place of the former, content to swarm in shanties like hogs, to contract scurvy by a steady diet of the cheapest salt pork, to suffer sore eyes and bodies rather than to buy a towel and washtub, to endure typhoid fever rather than undergo the expense of the most primitive sanitary apparatus."[4]

At about that same date, General Francis A. Walker, then superintendent

---

4. Rood, H.: "The Mine Laborers in Pennsylvania," *The Forum, September* 1892.

of the Federal Census Bureau, and America's leading authority on population problems, uttered the following poignant note of warning regarding the broader aspects of the New Immigration: "The entrance into our political, social, and industrial life of such vast masses of peasantry, degraded below our utmost conceptions, is a matter which no intelligent patriot can look upon without the gravest apprehension and alarm. These people have no history behind them which is of a nature to give encouragement. They have none of the inherited instincts and tendencies which made it comparatively easy to deal with the immigration of the olden time. They are beaten men from beaten races, representing the worst failures in the struggle for existence. Centuries are against them, as centuries were on the side of those who formerly came to us."[5]

Thus, from the very start, clear-sighted observers were warning the American public of the perils which the New Immigration involved. But those warnings were mere voices crying in the wilderness. For the most part, American public opinion in the nineties was indifferent or even complacent to what was taking place. The sinister aspects of the New Immigration did not awaken a fraction of the alarmed protest which the much less serious economic and social disturbances of the Old Immigration had aroused in the generation before the Civil War. To us, who have analyzed the shattering effects of the Civil War on American national life, this apparent enigma is perfectly explained. Sunk in materialism and lusting after quick profits, the America of the nineties was in no mood to forego present prosperity to avert future consequences. Indeed, what little idealism did remain was of the old doctrinaire "liberal" variety which still proclaimed America to be the "refuge" for all the world and was supremely confident that we could easily "Americanize" the most unpromising human material by the simple virtue of ideas and institutions. Thus, idealism joined hands with materialism in blinding the American people to the grim realities of the situation; and in consequence, public opinion gave the "captains of industry" free rein to drive the industrial machine as fast and as far as they desired.

The leaders who directed American industry after the Civil War indeed typified the spirit of their times. How different they were from their predecessors of former days! The founders of American industry in the early nineteenth century, exemplified by such outstanding figures as Lowell and the Lawrences, were men who combined daring and determination with high intelligence and vision. Possessing an instinctive poise and sense of proportion, they looked at industry, not as a thing in itself, but as part of

---

5. Walker, General Francis A.: *Discussions in Economics and Statistics,* vol. II, p. 446.

a larger whole: to wit, America. And they did this, not only because they were good patriots, but also because they were good businessmen. Regarding their enterprises, not as a gamble for quick profits but as a sound investment for continuous returns, they took the long rather than the short view and built-up plants intended to operate successfully for generations.

Now these industrial pioneers of the early nineteenth century realized that the best guarantee of industrial progress and stability is intelligent, contented labor. And they also realized that the only way to get and keep such labor is to pay fair wages and give just treatment. Accordingly, they looked after the physical and moral welfare of their employees and tried to enlist their loyalty as sharers in a common enterprise. And those old industrial pioneers not only succeeded in getting intelligent, loyal workers, *but made good money as well.* Understand: they never dreamed of being philanthropists. They were there for *business*. But they showed themselves actually better businessmen than most of their successors, because they knew how to make good money without recourse to the ruthless methods which were afterward employed. Thus, they not only had clearer vision but also better business brains. To put the thing in a nutshell: they were hard-headed, but not "hard-boiled."

The "captains of industry" who came after the Civil War were, on the contrary, mostly of the "hard-boiled" type. Now a hard-boiled man is nearly always a short-sighted, narrow-minded man. Wherefore, the captains of industry of the last half of the nineteenth century were usually as lacking in true insight and broad understanding as the industrial leaders of the first half of the century had been conspicuously possessed of those qualities.

Therefore, the captains of industry displayed the same ruthless concentration on immediate aims in reckless disregard of ultimate consequences that we saw the politicians of that period displaying in the handling of their affairs. Yet, what we remarked about the makers of "Reconstruction" applies substantially to the captains of industry; though they wrought great evil, the basic fault lay, not in themselves, but in the times. Those industrial leaders were as much selected for their temperament and outlook by their business constituents as the political leaders were by the majority of the voters. If they had run counter to the prevailing national temper, they would have been quickly curbed or retired to private life—precisely as was to happen later on, when the popular mood had changed.

What, then, was the policy of the industrial leaders of the later nineteenth century? It was precisely that of their colleagues, the "lumber kings," who were then stripping our noble forests from Maine to Michigan and from Michigan to Oregon, leaving behind a scrubby "second-growth," to be perhaps devastated by forest fires which would reduce the whole area to worthless "barrens." Why did the lumber kings do this? Because they were after quick profits, regardless of consequences. Well, just so did the captains of industry strip our mines and factories of high-grade Native American or North European labor, replacing it with a scrubby "second-growth" of cheap, alien labor, regardless of the possibility that those mines and factories might ultimately be destroyed by the fires of class hatred or social revolution. Little did the industrial leaders of that period bother their heads about such remote possibilities. They were there for "business" in its narrowest and most immediate sense. The future could look after itself.

The upshot was that American industry entered upon a veritable "Rake's Progress," which needed the caustic pencil of a Hogarth to portray its sordid and dreadful realities. For a quarter of a century (1890 to 1914) the New Immigration was in full swing, degrading living standards and replacing Native Americans and North Europeans by ever-cheapening alien labor drawn from ever-lower economic levels. The industrial leaders had made the (to them) delightful discovery that immigrants, freshly arrived from home surroundings of chronic poverty and semi-starvation, would eagerly accept pitifully low wages and would live under the most sordid conditions—especially since many of them were mere "birds of passage," intent on saving every cent and then returning home to live "rich" for the rest of their lives. These "greenies," as the new immigrants were called, could be herded like cattle in filthy "bunkhouses," sordid boarding-shacks, or old railroad cars—a mobile labor army, ready to go anywhere and do anything. Of course, these ignorant, backward peasants, straight out of the Dark Ages, were, man for man, not nearly as efficient as the Native American or North European workman. Nevertheless, under skilled direction, these low-paid, low-living aliens left the employer a big margin of profit. And that settled the matter! The Native American or North European workman was curtly given the choice of holding his job by degrading his living standards or of going "down the road."

The American and North European workman did not go without a fight. Throughout the nineties and the opening years of the present century, America's industrial life was frequently convulsed by great strikes. But in most cases the strikes failed and merely hastened the "alienizing" process. Fresh hordes of "greenies" were always on hand to take the jobs and send yet more Americans "down the road." Where did they go? Some stayed in their home localities and got better jobs calling for intelligence and skill above what the alien could supply. Others went West, where the alien had not yet penetrated and where "American" standards still prevailed. A great host of unfortunates, however, continued to go "down the road." This was the chief source of that veritable plague of "hobos" which afflicted America during the nineties and continued into the opening years of the present century. Those "hoboes" were usually of a type quite different from our vagrants of today. The present-day vagrants are nearly always either restless "rolling stones" who can't or won't keep even a good job, or they are bums and petty criminals who will not work at all. Of course, such vagrants existed a generation ago. Nevertheless, the typical "hobo" of the nineties was usually a decent American workman who had been squeezed out of his job by alien competition, had lost his grip, and was going "down-and-out." These unfortunate victims of circumstances must have numbered hundreds of thousands—perhaps millions, if we survey the entire period. When we think of all the American homes broken up or never founded, and all the American children who were never born, we begin to get some conception of the "sterilizing" effects of the vast alien tide, sweeping into America, million after million, and year after year, undermining standards and drowning out older populations as relentlessly as the incoming waves of the sea.

And mark you: the tide of ocean ebbs after it flows; but to that alien tide sweeping into America there was neither ebb nor end. Source after source yielded its swirling human floods. In Eastern and Southern Europe, potential immigrants could be numbered by the tens of millions; while beyond Europe's eastern marches lay teeming Asia, ready to pour forth its incalculable supply. The one sure thing about the "New Immigration" was that the longer it lasted, the more "alien" became its character and the lower it sank in the economic scale. We have just seen how it was ruining American and Old Immigrant workmen, and how it was killing American children by preventing them from being born as effectually as though the alien immigrants had been embattled barbarians cutting American throats. But the "sterilizing" process did not end there. As the New Immigration increased, it literally dried up the Old. For ambitious, self-respecting North Europeans, America ceased to be a land of promise. The slum and the bunkhouse? No, thank you! So, hundreds of thousands of North Europeans, who would have made excellent immigrants, either stayed at home under better conditions than America could offer them, or migrated to lands like Canada, or Australasia, where immigration laws were framed with some regard for the nation's blood and future.

Lastly, as the human tide lowered in quality, it kept out the better elements of even the New Immigration, who likewise discovered that America's degenerating living standards had lost some of their whilom charm. Thus "Gresham's Law" of labor, like all natural laws, ground inexorably on, driving high-standard men before low-standard men as surely as bad money drives out good. And what was the logical end of it all, if no restriction law should intervene? Clear-sighted old General Walker had answered the question very concisely when he had warned, far back in the nineties: "Hard times here may momentarily check the flow; but it will not be permanently stopped so long as *any difference of economic level* exists between our population and that of the most degraded communities abroad."[6]

At this point perhaps some readers (particularly those who belong to a generation later than that of the period we are describing) may ask: "Granting the materialistic temper of that time, why did not at least a considerable minority see the danger and rouse the national spirit by their protests?" To which we may answer that, strange though it may seem, the average American of those days had practically no idea of what was going on! If this answer appears unsatisfactory, consider the facts. In the first place, the alien influx, though vast, was strictly localized. America is a big country, and nearly all the New Immigration flowed into the Northeastern States, especially the States of the Atlantic seaboard. Furthermore, even in those States, the alien influx huddled into the city slums or packed closely into the industrial centers. There they stayed and were seldom seen by the average American except as stray individuals or construction gangs. The average American farmer did not even get the city man's occasional glimpse of the incoming hordes and had not the faintest inkling of what was afoot.

Another reason why the average American of those days did not suspect that anything was seriously wrong and was thus prevented from investigating the real situation, was because the alien influx *temporarily benefited* all classes except the American or Americanized workingmen of the Northeastern States. Later on, of course, the whole nation would have to pay dearly for this abnormal prosperity; yet, for the moment, there was real prosperity—albeit of an increasingly hectic kind. So the average American of the nineties and of the dawn of the present century looked complacently upon the alien, and if his instinct of self-preservation ever did stir, it was usually put to sleep again by the soothing assurances of "liberals"— who were sometimes paid propagandists of the "big interests," cannily aware of the appeal of the time-worn shibboleth: "America, the refuge for all the world—so let 'em all come!"

---
6. Walker, *op. cit.*, p. 441.

The fact is that the American people of the generation between 1890 and the Great War was suffering from a blindness which seemed strange in retrospect, yet which is perfectly comprehensible if we put ourselves back in that period. History shows that the thing has happened many times—has happened, indeed, whenever a country has mortgaged its future by mass-importations of "cheap labor." In the seventeenth and eighteenth centuries the tiny "Sugar Islands" of the West Indies bought Negroes wholesale and enjoyed a prosperity which was the wonder of the world. And old Rome must have had marvelous "boom times" when millions of slaves were driving the Roman artisans and yeomen to the wall but were earning their masters' big dividends. Old Rome was dying, but the average upper- or middle-class Roman never noticed it in the "prosperity" which then prevailed. That was why occasional objectors like the Gracchi were called the impolite Latin equivalent of "calamity howlers" and were summarily disposed of.

To be sure, things never got to that pass in America. Heaven be praised, the American people waked up in time, and are today well aware of the fate which would have been in store for them if they had not soon awakened. Nevertheless, the grim fact remains that for more than a quarter of a century, America, with the smiling blindness of a sleepwalker, was following old Rome, and the Sugar Islands, and her own hoboes "down the road" —*the road to ruin.*

How utter the eventful ruin would have been if the alien flood had not been stayed, a few further reflections on the New Immigration will clearly show.

Up to this point we have treated the alien influx as though it were a natural flow. It was that in the beginning; but it soon became more and more an artificial process stimulated by a variety of special "interests." In its later stages, the New Immigration was the exact opposite of the Old. We have seen that the Old Immigration was fundamentally like that of colonial days, consisting, as it did, chiefly of enterprising persons who had to undergo some hardship and expense to reach America at all, and who came here mostly with the intention of living an independent life on the land. The New Immigration, on the contrary, was from the first made up chiefly of jobseekers, and as the kinds of available jobs deteriorated, so did the quality of the applicants.

However, the great vacuum of American industry, now basing itself more and more on "greenie" labor, sucked up almost anything that could work, and about this central nucleus a whole group of "interests" developed, to satisfy industry's insatiable demands. The most prominent of these interests were the great steamship companies, which made enormous profits from the immigrant traffic, and which, being virtually all foreign-owned, had absolutely no interest in what the immigrants they transported might do to America. The "steamship lobby" was one of the many selfish interests which long blocked effective immigration-restriction laws.

These steamship companies had thousands of agents, and the agents had many more thousands of "runners," who systematically combed the remotest parts of Europe and even Western Asia drumming up "business" by every artifice they knew. Since these agents and "runners" were after mere "immigration fodder," quality was not considered. A ne'er-do-well, a moron, or a criminal had to have a ticket and yielded the same commission as the sturdiest peasant lad or the most skilled artisan.

Thus, the festering purlieus of Old-World cities and the filthy villages of backward countrysides were industriously raked for human material—any old stuff that could possibly "get by" our then almost wide-open immigration regulations. Consequently, vast hordes of poor, mongrelized creatures were gathered for shipment to America, to furnish the cheap, ignorant, docile labor which American industry had learned how to use. These masses of low-grade humanity were "way-billed," like so much freight, right through from their Native towns or villages to some "boarding-boss" or saloonkeeper in distant America, who kept them until a "labor-broker" finally delivered them to a contractor, a mine, a packing-plant, or a mill of some kind. The transportation charges on this kind of freight were very moderate, even though the amount handled assured the steamship companies good profits. During the period between 1890 and 1914, immigrant transatlantic rates averaged between $20 and $35, and they occasionally sank to absurdly low figures. During the "rate-cutting war" of 1904, certain steamship companies carried immigrants from Liverpool to New York for $8.75, while the rate to Philadelphia went as low as $7.50!

In other words, almost anybody, anywhere, could have his vacillating mind made up for him by a solicitous steamship "runner," and could thereupon be carried passively, easily, and cheaply,[7] many thousands of miles, to an American destination. This process has been well termed "Pipe-Line Immigration." Thus, had migration to America utterly lost its original character. In the early days it had been a natural selection of the best. By the year 1900 it had become mainly an artificial selection of the worst.

---

7. Immigrants often had their fare paid by various agencies anxious to get them to America, the immigrant reimbursing them later from the proceeds of his labor. When Congress imposed a head-tax and required a minimum sum of money to be shown, etc., such moneys were likewise often provided the immigrant by the same agencies on the same terms.

One of the most ominous aspects of the prevailing trend was a revival of that "assisted immigration" of paupers and criminals which we have previously noted in earlier periods. The steamship agents and their "runners" were too shrewd to overlook such profitable sources, and many foreign officials did not even need to be bribed to assist the departure of their countries' most undesirable citizens. As our present Secretary of Labor, an authority on immigration problems, well remarks: "America, known to all the world as a land of refuge for the oppressed and persecuted peoples of other countries, seems to have become an asylum for bandits, Black-handers, and land pirates."[8] He reveals one source of our foreign criminal elements by quoting a statement made by an American police official,[9] who says: "The United States has become a refuge for all the delinquents and bandits of Italy, Sicily, Sardinia, and Calabria. About a year ago the authorities of Tunis[10] decided to cleanse the Italian quarter of that city where there were a great number of crimes. The French Government proceeded to make a rigorous inquest which resulted in the expulsion of ten thousand Italians from that country. Where did that flower of manhood go? They were welcomed with open arms by Uncle Sam!"[11]

Perhaps at this point some reader may arise to remind us that after 1882 Congress passed a series of laws prohibiting the entry of criminals, paupers, etc. To all of which we will answer that, given the unholy alliance of "vested interests" in "liberal" immigration which then existed, ranging as it did from big corporations and steamship companies down to innumerable shady "labor brokers," boarding-bosses, saloonkeepers, and "White-slave" agents, there was tremendous pressure to get undesirables in—and nothing but a small body of overworked immigration inspectors to keep them out. Wherefore the immigration laws were mostly a joke, and the alien tide flowed in practically at will.

We have just mentioned "White-slavers," those infamous panderers to sexual vice. But to be candid about the matter, was not the whole system of "Pipe-Line Immigration" something very like a modern revival of the old slave-trade? The wretched creatures who were shipped in batches to "consignees," usually foreigners themselves, only recently domiciled in America, sometimes fared as ill as the Negroes shipped from Africa a hundred years before. Those delivered to big corporations were frequently the lucky ones. Others were turned over to small employers of foreign origin,

---

8. Davis, Hon. Janies J.: *Selective Immigration*, p. 81 (1925).
9. The well-known expert on crime, Lieutenant Petrosino.
10. A French protectorate in North Africa.
11. Quoted by Davis, *op. cit.*, pp. 80-81.

who exploited them mercilessly. The "padrone" and "sweat-shop" systems (both run exclusively by foreigners) were nothing but slavery, from which the green immigrants, ignorant of their legal rights, did not know how to escape. Many corporations were almost as bad and held their immigrant workers in a thinly disguised form of servitude known as "peonage." Here, again, we see how the New Immigration was breaking down wage-scales and living-standards, and how impossible it was for American labor to compete with the semi-servile hordes which were pouring into the country. Thus, in the Northeastern States, as formerly in the South, slave methods were working their immediate effects—and were preparing their ultimate consequences.

On both these points the sociologist Ross warningly wrote: "Our captains of industry give a crowbar to the immigrant with a number nine face on a number six head, make a dividend out of him, and imagine that is the end of the matter. They overlook that this man will beget children in his image—two or three times as many as the American—and that these children will in turn beget children. They chuckle at having opened an inexhaustible store of cheap tools, and lo! the American people is being altered for all time by these tools. Once before, captains of industry took a hand in making this people. Colonial planters imported Africans to hoe in the sun, to 'develop' the tobacco, indigo, and rice plantations. Then, as now, business-minded men met with contempt the protests of a few idealists against their way of 'building up the country.' Those promoters of prosperity are dust, but they bequeathed a situation which in four years wiped out more wealth than two hundred years of slavery had built up, and which presents today the one unsolvable problem in this country."[12]

How ominous was the trend of American industry between 1890 and 1914 can be seen when we compare conditions then with conditions today. A few years of restricted immigration have sufficed to produce firm wage-scales, favorable living-standards, practically no unemployment, and widely diffused prosperity. In the period before 1914, American industry was getting to be based on "greenie" labor. That was a system in some respects more odious than out-and-out slavery, because employers did not own the bodies of their workmen and so had no continuing interest in them. A "greenie" was employed until he "got wise" and demanded better pay and better laboring conditions; whereupon he was "fired," another "greenie" was hired, and the process was repeated. This put America's labor system on more and more of a "casual" basis. Employers no longer sought

---

12. Ross, E. A.: *The Old World in the New*, pp. 286-287 (1914).

to keep permanent labor forces composed of family men with local ties; instead, they went on a "hire and fire" basis, "scrapping" workers without compunction, because they were largely homeless "greenies" to whom one job or one town was about as good as another. The labor "turnover" in that period was enormous; in many lines it averaged over 100 per cent a year. All this explains the chronic unemployment problem of those days. In the "hard times" of 1896-97, an average of 6,000,000 persons were unemployed. Of course, this meant enormous social losses, but the losses fell, not so much upon industry as upon the community, which had to care for unemployed and pauperized workers by public and private charity. Cheap labor also held back industrial progress by retarding the introduction of labor-saving machinery and efficiency methods. These are making great strides today, when labor is a high-priced commodity which cannot be ineffectively used.

One of the most refreshing results of our present immigration restriction policy is the way it is reviving the traditional dignity of American labor. Before the New Immigration began, some grades of manual labor were badly paid; nevertheless, there was no general stigma attached to labor as such. Nothing better reveals the essentially "servile" character of the New Immigration than the way it degraded every line of work it touched. It was not merely a matter of wages; it was also a question of dignity and self-respect. The Native American and Americanized workers simply would not stand for the bad conditions, rough "driving" and "cursing out" which went with "greenies," even where good wages were paid. Such lines were abandoned to "wop" or "hunkie" labor, and were as much taboo to American workmen as lines given over to "nigger labor" are taboo to White workmen at the present time. How refreshing it is to note that today the tendency is all the other way! Now that the supply of "greenies" has been cut off, "greenie" standards are fading as well. Of course, in those industrial centers where aliens are thickest, it is going to take a long time to get back to anything like the traditional American attitude, but we are moving that way just the same.

This time element must be frankly faced in all our problems, and we need not be discouraged if improvement is slow. We must remember that effects are inevitably proportioned to their causes. Thus, even at best, our social system will long bear the scars of the terrible blows dealt it during the melancholy period between 1890 and 1914. The alien blight on our Eastern cities and factory towns, for example, is too sadly familiar to us present-day Americans to need detailed description. Those urban slums and sordid mill-towns, with their lack of civic spirit, their political corruption, and their generally blatant, vulgar tone, accurately reflect the low-grade, polyglot masses who inhabit them, and who, despite all efforts at Americanization, have acquired only a partial grasp of American ideals and a thin veneer of American culture. We shall discuss those aspects later on, when we come directly to consider present-day problems. Here let us note that those problems which now so vex us were imported for the most part as recently as a generation ago. We are meeting the first instalment of the price which we must inevitably pay for the lack of foresight which the past generation displayed.

For let us make no mistake: there are other instalments which will fall due and which must be paid, not only by us but by our children, and very likely by our children's children as well. By this we mean particularly the harm done to the blood of the nation by permitting the entry of undesirable and more or less unassimilable racial elements. Economic blunders can usually be soon remedied. Already our industry and business are no longer a hectic series of "booms" and "depressions"—an improvement due, in our opinion, even more to the stoppage of mass-immigration than to the Federal Reserve banking system, to which our economic stabilization is usually ascribed.

Economic damage is thus relatively easy to repair. Not so, damage to the blood of the nation. Tamper with the well-springs of racial life, and you tamper with the heritage of generations yet unborn! Verily, the sin of our fathers in permitting the mass-influx of the "New Immigration" will be visited upon the children, probably far beyond the third and the fourth generation. Let us not mince words on this matter! Considered as a whole, the New Immigration is for America a disaster comparable only to the disaster of the Civil War. Indeed, for aught we know, the future may show that the New Immigration, rather than the Civil War, is the supreme disaster in American history.

Understand: we pass no sweepingly undiscriminating judgment. In the previous chapter we reviewed the New Immigration in detail, and we found that it contained some elements of excellent average quality, while we also found that many individuals, even from the most unpromising immigrant sources, had proved themselves highly desirable American citizens or Americans in the making. We recognize with joy and thankfulness that a large fraction of the New Immigration "deserves well of the Republic." But we should likewise honestly face the unpleasant fact that those desirable elements, while unquestionably a considerable minority, are nevertheless a *minority*; and that the majority of the millions who have come to us from the "New Immigrant sources are frankly undesirable. Below the better elements, who are being genuinely and harmoniously incorporated into the fabric of American life, there lies a polyglot mass of undigested and indigestible material, refractory to assimilation, which already causes us much trouble, and which will continue to be a burden, a weakness, and a potential menace, probably for generations to come.

Understand again: this is no mere personal opinion or "prejudice;" it is a deliberate statement of fact, proved beyond all reasonable doubt by the careful investigations of competent authorities, who have approached the problem from many angles and have conducted their studies with scientific accuracy. The best general source of information for the inquiring reader is the immense collection of data to be found in the hearings before the Congressional Committee on Immigration which framed the Johnson Act of 1924. Those hearings have been published as official documents, and if the reader will study the thousands of pages packed with information, he will find that the overwhelming weight of expert testimony shows unequivocally that the vast alien mass which congests our Northeastern States is, on the whole, of an undesirable character.

To cite merely one out of many authoritative statements: Dr. H. H. Laughlin, recognized as being one of America's leading specialists in his field, made a careful study of the mental capacity of immigrants, as a result of which he testified before the Congressional Committee that between the years 1900 and 1923 we had admitted over 6,000,000 immigrants who ranked so far below the average intelligence of our White population that they must be graded as either "inferior" or "very inferior."

Think of it! Over 6,000,000 individuals let into America, who must be considered not only as "undesirable" from the special American viewpoint of assimilability, but also as "inferior" or "very inferior" from the general scientific standard of mental soundness and capacity! Under decent immigration regulations, properly enforced, not one of all those 6,000,000 and more gross undesirables should have ever been allowed to pass our gates.

Over 6,000,000 "inferiors" and "very inferiors!" That is about two-fifths of *all* the immigrants, from all sources, who entered America between 1900 and 1923. And since the evidence shows conclusively that the proportion of inferiors is much greater among "New" than among "Old" immigrants, it follows that fully one-half of all the New Immigration admitted during those years was of an inferior character. Now add to the original inferior immigrants the millions of children that they have already produced—often at a rate several times that of the birth-rates of Native Americans or North European immigrants in the districts where these low-grade aliens settled.

Now add still other elements of the New Immigration which, while not "inferior," must be considered as being below the general average of our population; and add to those original immigrants their very numerous progeny. Finally, add still other immigrant elements which, while mentally at or even above the general mental average, are yet so different in blood and ideas that they do not fit into the national fabric and instinctively dislike American ideals and institutions. Now add all these elements and their rapidly multiplying progeny together. Can any unprejudiced reader honestly assert that we exaggerate when we state that the bulk of the New Immigration has been thoroughly "undesirable," and that those inferior, alien elements above enumerated will long constitute a hindrance, a weakness, and a latent peril to American national life?

Without stressing further the harm which we saw the alien influx doing to living standards and social conditions in our Northeastern States, let us here consider the far more profound and lasting damage which those aliens have already *indirectly* done to the blood of the nation by "socially sterilizing" the older stocks. There can be no question that every low-grade alien who landed prevented a Native American baby or a North European immigrant baby from ever being born. Furthermore, there can equally be no question that the New Immigration prevented hundreds of thousands of better-grade potential North European immigrants from ever coming to America. And, of course, this indirect damage is only the prelude to the *direct* damage to the blood of the nation which low-grade aliens will do by injecting inferior or discordant strains into the nation's ethnic make-up.

The replacive and lowering effects of the alien masses are already plainly visible in many parts of our Northeastern States, especially in New York, New England, and the industrial districts of Pennsylvania. A recent book, significantly entitled *The Conquest of New England by the Immigrant*,[13] exposes with terrible clarity the inexorable thoroughness and the appalling rapidity with which the alien deluge, entering a geographically small and industrially urbanized area, has in the space of a single generation racially "conquered" New England, in the sense that alien elements now form an actual majority of its total population. This book also tells in ominous detail how the alien influx has so "sterilized" the old Yankee stock that it is a dwindling minority, failing even to reproduce itself; and the book further shows that "Old" immigrant elements, like the Irish, have also been so "sterilized" that they are barely holding their own. Lastly, the book shows that the alien elements are multiplying with great rapidity. Now, of course,

---
13. By Daniel Chauncy Brewer (1926).

unless novel factors arise to reverse the present trend, there can be but one end to all this: another fifty years will see New England racially transformed beyond all recognition, with the Yankee and the Irishman alike standing forth as mere remnants in a heterogeneous mass composed for the most part of Slavs, Southern Italians, French-Canadians, and Ashkenazic Jews.

And we must likewise remember that about the same thing is going on in New York, New Jersey, considerable portions of Pennsylvania, many parts of Ohio, Indiana, and Illinois, and some other sections of our Northern States. On the other hand, we should note that throughout the South and West—wherever, indeed, the alien has not penetrated in large numbers—the Native American and North European immigrant stocks are flourishing, with good normal birth-rates and with no signs of social decline. A final proof (if further proof be needed) of the blight cast by low-grade men, against which high standards, high ideals, high intelligence, physical vigor, and other superior qualities are a weakness rather than a defense! "Gresham's Law" of labor is indeed inexorable; for just as debased money drives sound money out of circulation, so low-standard men tend to drive high-standard men economically to the wall.

From this survey one hopeful fact emerges: the low-grade alien elements are pretty much localized in the Northeastern States. Furthermore, it appears that they will on the whole remain thus localized. To be sure, they are very numerous. The "New Immigrants" and their children today number something like 15,000,000.[14] But America is a big country, and its total White population is at present over 100,000,000—practically all of which, except the 15,000,000 East and South Europeans just mentioned, is of old colonial or "Old" immigrant stock. America is thus still overwhelmingly inhabited by persons of North European blood, and the American people is becoming so decidedly aware of the situation that it is incredible to think they would ever allow another alien invasion which would spell their ultimate ruin. Yet, think of the problems which confront our Northeastern States. And think of what would have happened to the whole of America if the alien flood had been allowed to pour in for another ten or twenty years!

Let us face the situation squarely. Short of some unforeseen disaster, America is going to win through. But that hopeful outcome must not blind us to the very serious fact that America has a big, tough job on its hands which will probably keep us busy for the next fifty years. As already remarked, a considerable minority of the "New" stocks now dwelling among us are excellent people who will, after a longer or shorter period,

---
14. Including the French-Canadians.

be genuinely assimilated into as good Americans as anyone else. But below them lies the "alien" mass, which offers scant promise for the future. This low-grade mass is made up mostly of backward, primitive folk who are more or less thinly veneered barbarians. *The New Barbarians* is, indeed, the title of a recent book on the problems they present,[15] while many years ago that clear-sighted prophet, Prescott F. Hall,[16] warned us that "the 'barbarians' of the present time do not come from the plateau of Central Asia or from the jungles of Africa; they are the defective and delinquent classes of Europe— the individuals who have not been able to keep the pace at home and have fallen into the lower strata of its civilization."[17]

Consider this vivid description of the incoming "barbarians," written in the days just before the Great War, when the alien tide was at full flood: "It is fair to say that the blood now being injected into the veins of our people is 'sub-common.' To one accustomed to the aspect of the normal American population, the Caliban type shows up with a frequency that is startling. Observe immigrants, not as they come travel-wan up the gangplank, nor as they issue toil-begrimed from pit-mouth or mill-gate, but in their gatherings, washed, combed, and in their Sunday best. You are struck by the fact that from 10 to 20 per cent are hirsute, low-browed, big-faced persons of obviously low mentality. Not that they suggest evil. They simply look out of place in Black clothes and stiff collar, since clearly, they belong in skins, in wattled huts at the close of the Great Ice Age. These ox-like men are descendants of those *who always stayed behind*. . . .

"To the practiced eye, the physiognomy of certain groups unmistakably proclaims inferiority of type. I have seen gatherings of the foreign-born in which narrow and sloping foreheads were the rule. The shortness and

15. By Wilbur C. Abbott (1925).
16. Every true American should know about this great patriot, who, though he lived and died practically unknown to the general public, was, more than any other man, the preparer of that "great awakening" which, beginning in 1914, culminated in the Johnson Act of 1924, which closed our gates to mass-immigration and thus saved America from impending ruin. Prescott F. Hall was unquestionably the first to grasp the full peril of the "New Immigration." He came to this conclusion as far back as the late eighties, when he was barely grown to man's estate. Once his keen vision had pierced to the heart of the matter, he devoted his whole life to this supremely vital cause. At first, he stood quite alone. Gradually he gathered about him a small group, mostly young men of Boston and vicinity, like himself, who founded the Immigration Restriction League in the year 1894. From then on, this little band fought a discouraging fight, apparently making scant headway against the prevailing temper of the times, but in reality, sowing seeds which were to produce a rich harvest of success. Of course, it was always the leader, Prescott Hall, who bore the brunt of the battle. Renouncing a brilliant legal career (he is the author of standard legal textbooks and was considered one of the ablest minds of the Massachusetts bar), Prescott Hall devoted his modest means and delicate health to the patriotic cause with an intensity which unquestionably shortened his days. His untimely death, early in the year 1921, prevented him from witnessing the triumph of the Johnson Act of 1924. Yet he died in the serene conviction that the tide had definitely turned and that victory was nigh. It was the author's deep privilege to have personally known this great spirit, though only in his last days. Perhaps when future generations come to realize the debt they owe him, Prescott F. Hall will be remembered as he surely was: one of the saviors of our country.
17. Hall, Prescott F.: "The Future of American Ideals," *North American Review,* January 1912.

smallness of the crania were very noticeable. There was much facial asymmetry. Among the women, beauty, aside from the fleeting, epidermal bloom of girlhood, was quite lacking. In every face there was something wrong—lips thick, mouth coarse, upper lip too long, cheekbones too high, chin poorly formed, the bridge of the nose hollowed, the base of the nose tilted, or else the whole face prognathous. There were so many sugar-loaf heads, moon-faces, slit mouths, lantern jaws, and goose-bill noses that one might imagine a malicious jinn had amused himself by casting human beings in a set of skew-molds discarded by the Creator."[18]

Such was the nondescript, mongrel tide which, for more than thirty years, poured in ever-increasing volume into America. Yet, despite everything, the American people delayed decisive action. The captains of industry were still obsessed with cash surpluses and big dividends, while the well-to-do classes generally were as yet content with hectic "prosperity." So materialistic and short-sighted was the temper of the times that a reputable economist could actually write: "The cost of rearing children in the United States is rapidly rising. In many, perhaps in most, cases it is simpler, speedier, and cheaper to import labor than to breed it" (!); while another "economically minded" writer could complacently say: "a healthy immigrant lad of eighteen is a clear $1,000 added to the national wealth of the United States." And, of course, all this time the "liberals" were chanting their parrot-like refrain: "America, the refuge for all nations!"

So, the American people, blinded alike by false prosperity and false ideals, quickened its pace down the road to ruin. Well might an observer of those days, who, though an "economist," was likewise a clear-sighted patriot, thus despairingly forecast America's future: "Already America has ceased to allure, as of yore, the British, the Germans, and the Scandinavians; but it strongly attracts the Italians, Greeks, and Slavs. By 1930, perhaps, the opportunities left will have ceased to interest them, but no doubt the Khivans, the Bokhariots, the Persians and the Afghans will regard this as the promised land. By 1950, even they will scorn the chances here, but then, perhaps, the coolies from overpopulated India will be glad to take an American wage. But by the last quarter of this century there will remain possibly no people in the world that will care for the chances left in America, when the blood of the old pioneering breed has faded out of the motley, polyglot, polychrome, caste-riven population that will crowd this continent to a Chinese density."[19]

This despairing patriot did not exaggerate. That was just where America

---

18. Ross, E. A.: *op. cit.*, 285-286.
19. *American Economic Review*, Supplement, vol. II, no. 1, March 1912.

was headed when he penned those lines in the year 1912. It was, indeed, the darkest hour. But—it proved to be the darkest hour before the dawn! Yet a little farther "down the road," and the roar of Armageddon was to shock the American people wide-awake, not only to possible perils abroad but to certain perils at home. The story of that "Great Awakening" will be the subject of our next chapter.

# CHAPTER VIII

# THE GREAT AWAKENING

August 1914. Who that then had eyes to see can forget the awe, the strangling terror, which gripped us as we watched the Old World suddenly burst into a flaming hell of war? So incredible was the cataclysm that in those first days, with one accord, we termed it *Armageddon*. And as time passed, even the least reflective came somehow to realize that an historic epoch was in its death-throes and that a new age full of unknown possibilities was at hand.

Since those momentous August days more than a decade has passed. No part of the globe has escaped Armageddon's transforming touch; and we, who live in the post-war world, are daily made aware of deep-going changes of every kind. Armageddon indeed shook the foundations not only of the old material order but also of traditional viewpoints and attitudes toward life in a manner best epitomized by Nietszche's trenchant phrase: "a revaluation of all values."

Now this applies to America just as to the rest of the world. The cataclysmic summer of 1914 marks for America the beginning of mental and spiritual changes so rapid and so fundamental that our pre-war attitude seems in some respects as distant and unreal as the naively simple attitude of childhood appears in retrospect to the man or woman grown to the complex realities of adult life. Like the stress of adolescence in the individual, so the storm of Armageddon was for America a national "coming of age." For the American people, the "Great War" produced the "Great Awakening" to national, cultural, and racial realities.

Down to 1914 the traditional American attitude had been a naive optimism. And that such should have been the prevailing popular attitude was quite natural. In our survey of America's foundations, we saw that even in colonial days there was a half-conscious faith in a high destiny, and we likewise saw how the attainment of independent national life acted like a splendid elixir, quickening men's minds and souls. Of course, the long cycle of marvelous growth and prosperity between the Revolution and the Civil War confirmed America's robust optimism and deepened it into a faith which was almost unshakable.

Not even the disaster of the Civil War shook America's traditional optimism. In fact, the Civil War really exaggerated it in a manner highly dangerous for the future. Instead of sobering America's optimism, the Civil War intoxicated it! The Civil War's destructive spiritual influence and the slaughter of the loftiest souls of the rising generation, shattered the idealism and sense of proportion which had hitherto kept the exuberant popular optimism within bounds. The rampant materialism which followed the Civil War showed how unbalanced the popular temper had become. American optimism, indeed, grew more naive and irrational than it had been in the nation's early days. The boundless complacency and self-glorification felt by the average American of the later nineteenth century is well summed up in a phrase current in those times. "America is God's Own Country." The average American then actually believed that there was some mystic virtue in our air, our soil, and our institutions which made America a land apart, and which somehow exempted us from the pains and penalties suffered by less fortunate peoples. It was this belief, instinctive rather than pondered, which blinded the American people to the blunders it was making, and which made it so susceptible to the sentimental "liberal" sophistries which we have already analyzed.

The traditional optimism of the American people thus accounts both for its complacence toward mass-immigration and for its equal complacence toward the alien elements which became domiciled in the country. The rapidly growing alien "colonies," not only in our cities but also over many parts of our countryside, sometimes stirred us to annoyance but were usually viewed with amused tolerance as picturesque bits of "local color" which would soon pass away. Our promising (but as yet by no means complete) assimilation of the "Old Immigration" led us to imagine that the "New Immigration," however alien from us in blood, culture, and ideals, would be just about as easy to digest into the body politic; or, at least, if not the original immigrants themselves, then surely their children. The American public school, the Fourth of July oration, and, above all, the overwhelming sense of being citizens of "God's Own Country," would do the trick; and the next generation would be full-fledged Americans, indistinguishable (for all practical purposes) from all other "good Americans." So ran the chain of popular reasoning before the war.

Wherefore, although the "Little Italies," the "Little Polands," and the "Little Ghettos" swelled into Big Italies, Big Polands, and Big Ghettos; and although the "next generation" which grew up in these foreign "colonies" neither looked nor acted like other Americans—still the American people, generally speaking, refused to read the signs of the times.

Then came the Great War! And thereupon something happened—*America woke up!* As a lightning-flash illumines a dark landscape, so the flare of an exploding Old World revealed the perils obscurely present in the New World overseas.

Whatever loss it was to inflict upon us, the Great War certainly did America one inestimable service—it aroused us *in time*. Even before the war. America was showing signs of awakening. The warning voices of its seers and the painful symptoms of social ill-health had begun to rouse a growing minority to alarmed protest. In the course of time America would have awakened anyway. But—time was precisely the essence of the situation. With mass-alienage pouring in at the rate of nearly 1,500,000 per year, a relatively brief delay would have rendered conditions so bad that a disastrous convulsion m our national life would have become practically inevitable. The Great War telescoped what would perhaps have been a long process of education into a brief course of intensive enlightenment as to national and racial realities, from which the American people emerged, not only with open eyes, but also with eyes open to a situation which had not yet got out of hand. In other words, America had waked up just in the nick of time.

So fully have the realities, which we then learned, become part of our general outlook that we often find it difficult to realize what a shattering of old illusions took place in our minds and hearts during those hectic war-days. The "Great Awakening" has never been more vividly portrayed than in the following pungent lines: "We have chattered about the 'asylum of the oppressed' and wake up to find we live in Bedlam. We have prattled about the "melting-pot' and have wakened to find the stomach of the body politic filled to bursting with peoples swallowed whole, whom our digestive juices do not digest. Wise doctors have compounded a prescription called 'Americanism' which we are assiduously pouring down our throat, in the hope that it will disintegrate these knots that give us such pain and allow us to absorb the meal we have gorged ourselves with. We hold numerous consultations to determine what 'Americanism' is doing to these alien bodies. But what are the aliens doing to America?"[1]

*"What are the aliens doing to America?"* That was a question which the average American never asked himself before the war. His thought had reached no further than speculation upon the rate at which the various immigrant groups would be "assimilated." That the immigrants might dream of changing *his* America never so much as entered the average American's

---
1. Strother, French: "The Immigration Peril," *World's Work,* October, 1923.

head. That the American-born sons of immigrants might actually try to alter *his* America was simply beyond the bounds of his imagination. The average citizen visualized America either as it had been before 1860, or as it had been before 1880. To the Westerner or the Southerner, who knew of mass-immigration only by hear-say, America still appeared the homogeneous nation of 1860. To the Easterner, who experienced mass-immigration at first-hand, America seemed about as it had been in 1880—a nation with such solid American" foundations that the immigrants, however numerous, were bound to be ultimately absorbed.

Then, athwart this inveterate complacence, there suddenly shot the lightning-flash of Armageddon, and in its searching glare Americans, North, South, East, and West, were alike faced with hard realities. Instead of the united nation of their fancy, they saw an America in which even the North European elements of the "Old Immigration" were in many cases imperfectly assimilated, while the bulk of the "New Immigration" was either passively or actively "alien." Indeed, the "America" of 1914 bore a certain ominous resemblance to President Roosevelt's warning description of a "polyglot boarding-house."

The war thus dramatically showed up what really *was*, in place of that with which Americans had been fondly deluding themselves. To his horrified amazement, the average American learned that the real "America" was merely a large nucleus, shading off through more or less Americanized elements until it encountered solid "alien" groups refractory to Americanization or even downright hostile to everything distinctively "American." The Great War was, in fact, an acid test, revealing latent alienism and "hyphenism" which had drifted along for decades or even for generations, unnoticed by the American public and only half-consciously felt by the aliens themselves. During the war, it was the unassimilated portions of the Germanic element which displayed the most overt signs of "hyphenism." But the period of the peace-settlement showed the American public what clear-sighted observers had already realized—that every immigrant element had its "hyphenates," whose primary loyalty was to the "old country," and who put its interests before those of America. The way America was swept by rival foreign propagandas, and the way "hyphenate" elements of every kind responded to such foreign appeals, completed our education about hyphenism and "mass-alienage," and showed us how they paralyzed our capacity to think and act as a united nation.

The shattering of old popular illusions was shown not only by the way the average citizen came to grasp the vital significance of national

# The Great Awakening

unity; it was also amusingly revealed by the sudden conversion of many erstwhile champions of unrestricted immigration and the beauties of the "melting-pot." How grimly humorous it was to see quondam champions of the alien turn a mental somersault and publicly lament alike the menace of "hyphenism" and the ominous shortcomings of "assimilation!" Scan, for instance, the following lines from the pen of one who before the war had been a leading advocate of "liberal" immigration: "We now know that we are not in a position to participate disinterestedly and courageously in the international adjustments that will take place at the close of the war. . . . We see a conglomeration of colonies and ghettos and immigrant sections in our large cities, and the country dotted with settlements quite as un-American as anything to be found abroad. We face the fact that America is not first in the hearts of every resident, that not every man works for America, and that not every man trusts her present or believes in her future. This is still the land of promise for the 'bird of passage' who exploits us, and whom we pluck in return. Thanks to the war, we have been freed from the delusion that we are a united nation, marching steadily along an American highway of peace, prosperity, common ideals, beliefs, languages, and purpose. Security and prosperity have blinded us to the fact that we do not all speak the same language nor follow the same flag."[2]

Just so. And—what a complete confirmation of that which a few seers and prophets had been telling the American people for many, many years, in face of popular apathy and the bitter opposition of those who, panic-struck, now admitted the realities of the situation!

The education of the American people on national realities was not to end with the war. It was in the post-war period that the larger menace of mass-alienism was disclosed. The "hyphen"—the man who puts the "old country" before America in his affection—was bad enough. But how about the man animated not so much by love of any country as by hatred of America and things American? The war's psychological effect had been twofold: it had awakened the American people to the alien peril; but it had also aroused the alien to the full sense of his alienism! In the easy-going "liberal" days before the war, when the immigrant could be as "alien" as he liked, and when he was swarming in so fast that he obscurely sensed he might ultimately possess the land, he had been quite satisfied with the trend of the times. But the awakening of the American people and their determination to safeguard their threatened national life spelled a converse threat to alienism and therefore roused the refractory elements to conscious hostility

---

2. Kellor, Frances: *Straight America,* pp. 3-5 (1917).

toward Americanism. The rebellious, aggressive alienism which has arisen since the war, and which confronts us today is the inevitable by-product of the reforging of our nationhood. The alien "colony" fights for its continued existence as naturally as the American people strives for the attainment of national unity. In both cases it is the primal instinct of self-preservation. The larger aspects of this problem will be treated in subsequent pages. Let us here stress only that phase of aggressive alienism which most impressed American public opinion during the war and post-war periods—the alarming symptoms of revolutionary radicalism, almost wholly of alien origin.

Revolutionary radicalism in its extreme sense—a fierce hatred of the entire existing order and a wild desire to smash the whole framework of our national life—has never gained any real foothold either among old-stock Americans or among Americans of "Old Immigrant" origin. A few more or less "queer" American "intellectuals," and a small group of American workingmen embittered chiefly by destructive immigrant competition, comprise the slender results of "Red" propaganda among real Americans. On the other hand, "Red" radicalism appeals strongly to many elements of the "New Immigration," and it is these alien followers who constitute the strength of the "Red" movement in America.

How thoroughly "alien" that movement is in character can be judged by the record of the Socialist party during the Great War. When America entered the conflict, the Socialist party maintained its "international" viewpoint and displayed a flagrantly unpatriotic attitude. This, however, so angered and disgusted its genuine American members that, when they found themselves hopelessly outvoted by the immense majority of East and South European "Comrades," they left the party in disgust. As one of these "American" Socialists, Allan Benson, who had been the Socialist candidate for President in 1916, remarked: "I resign as a protest against the foreign-born leadership that blindly believes a non-American policy can be made to appeal to many Americans."

How "non-American" the policy of those foreign-born Socialist leaders was, may be judged by the campaign slogan of perhaps the most widely known of them—Morris Hillquit, a Russian Jew. Hillquit's slogan, in wartime, was: "Patriotism, the great sham!" Many alien radicals were jailed during the war for seditious activities, and after the war many more were imprisoned for similar acts of various kinds. Do we not still recall the radical unrest of the post-war period, punctuated by conspiracies, bomb outrages, and an epidemic of "outlaw" strikes? The radical alien attitude of hatred toward our whole national life was never more vividly expressed than it was by a banner borne on the streets of Boston during a strike of garment-workers—mostly Russian and Polish Jews. That banner bore the charming legend, "To Hell with the United States!"

The post-war period completed the process of popular education and enlightenment which the war itself had begun. The American people at last had their eyes open to the perils of "hyphenism," mass-alienage, revolutionary radicalism, and other ills which threatened the very life of the nation. And the American people saw clearly the root of all those evils: mass-immigration. Yet at that precise moment of awakening, America was menaced by a mass-immigration vaster in quantity and worse in quality than anything which had ever been known before. The Great War had shattered the Old World, and now the Old World was getting ready to dump its human wreckage wholesale on the New!

This prospect was made doubly alarming by the fact that during the war immigration had fallen to virtually negligible proportions. The dramatic suddenness of the change was striking indeed. The year 1913 had witnessed the high-water mark of the immigrant tide, no less than 1,427,000 persons having entered America. The year 1914 at first promised to break even that record, and notwithstanding the wars disturbing influence after August, the number of arrivals for the year totaled 1,403,000. But in 1915 emigration dropped to about 400,000, while by 1918 it had sunk to a trifle over 200,000. Furthermore, the departure of multitudes of foreign reservists, called home to the colors, produced such an out-flow that it almost equaled the inbound tide. In 1915 the net increase by immigration was only 50,000, while in 1918 the excess of arrivals over departures was a mere 18,000. For the first time within living memory, America was virtually "deprived" of immigration.

Now what happened? Remember that one of the stock arguments of those who favored a "liberal" immigration policy was that America's prosperity depended upon copious immigration. Here surely was a test of that thesis. Even during the war's early years, when we were still neutral, our industry was enormously stimulated, while, after we entered the war, we not only still further raised our industrial output but also mobilized millions of able-bodied young men for soldiers. Well: did American industry languish for lack of labor? It did not. It merely put itself on a more efficient basis, installed more labor-saving machinery, stimulated Native labor by higher wages—and carried on nicely, thank you. In other words, the war proved what clear-sighted thinkers had long asserted—that no real labor-shortage existed, but only a shortage of :cheap" labor; that American labor could be had in plenty at fair wages and under proper working conditions; and that the way to put American industry on a sound, healthy basis was to replace mass-immigration by higher efficiency, more machinery, and a reduction of labor "turnover."

Thus, even from a purely "business" standpoint, mass-immigration was shown to be unnecessary. And of course, on social and patriotic grounds, the stoppage of the alien flood proved an unqualified blessing. Every charity board and settlement-worker was astonished at the improvement of slum conditions, the subsidence of unemployment, and the generally better social tone which even the brief immigration-stoppage of the war years sufficed to produce.

Such was the situation at the end of the war. And then, at the very moment when America was engaged in deflating its war-industries and finding jobs for millions of demobilized soldiers, it was faced with an alien deluge of limitless proportions! Immigration, which had almost ceased during the war, swelled portentously once more. In 1920, over 600,000 immigrants arrived. In 1921, almost 1,000,000 persons entered the country. And all signs showed that this was merely the beginning of a human flood of inconceivable proportions. Every report of our consular and diplomatic agents, every survey of special investigators abroad, emphasized the crisis with which America was faced. As the Immigration Commissioner for the Port of New York then put it: "All records are going to be shattered from January on. Whole races of Europe are preparing to remove to the United States. Never since the early days of barbarian Europe has there been such a wholesale migration of people as that which is now in contemplation, with the United States as the destination." Competent students of the problem estimated that, unless promptly checked, the mass-migration might easily reach 3,000,000 or even 5,000,000 per year; that, in fact, the only practical limit was the capacity of the ships which could be manned and built to ferry across the human swarms eager to quit war-wrecked Europe and Western Asia for the New World. Such a situation had never before confronted us. This was not "normal" immigration, not even "pipeline" immigration It was a frenzy, a panic, a stampede, a mob without calculation, without sound judgment—a seething mass of humanity with but one idea—*America!*

And this threatened deluge was as bad in quality as it was huge in quantity. The immigration which threatened us was literally a *poisoned* immigration of the offscourings of the Old World. The harassed, debt-ridden governments of post-war Europe saw in mass-migration a golden opportunity to lighten their burdens by dumping their worst elements on America.

A high official of one of the East European nations frankly stated that his country's sole concern with American immigration was the hope to get rid of the "old men and rubbish." The report drawn up by the Immigration Committee of the House of Representatives, based on confidential consular and diplomatic reports and submitted to Congress at the close of 1920, was of a truly alarming tone, stating as it did that a majority of these prospective immigrants were "physically deficient," "mentally deficient," of low standards of living, and "economically and socially undesirable."

The huge horde of low-grade humanity which was then on the march for America is vividly described by an expert American investigator who had studied post-war conditions in Eastern Europe and thus reported his findings: "These emigrants are, as far as the great majority of them are concerned, the weakest and poorest man-material of Europe. They are the defeated, incompetent, and unsuccessful—the very lowest layer of European society. They are paupers by circumstance, and parasites by training and inclination. They are expedited out of their countries by governments who do not want them. They are assisted to America by the largest and best organized society that ever assisted and unconsciously stimulated immigration to America or to any other country, and they invariably travel on money they have begged or demanded from America. Nor do these people consider that they are going to the 'uncertainty of a new life in a new land.' They are going from countries where business is rotten, taxes are high, food is scarce, money is hard to get, military service is apt to seize the menfolk, and armies are likely at any time to start marching and simultaneously begin seizing all the cattle and poultry and other edibles in sight. They are going to America, the world's greatest sure thing; America, where all the money in the world comes from; America, who has so much money that she sends her sons all over the world to give it away to people who often don t need it; America, where conditions at their worst are better than conditions in other countries at their best. These are the universal opinions of the emigrants. Suggest to them that they are going to the 'uncertainty of a new life in a new land,' and they will wonder privately whether you are weak-minded. The land to which they are going is no uncertainty; it's a lead-pipe cinch. The only Europeans who are taking a long chance today are the ones that stay at home."[3]

But only the advance-guard of that sinister horde was destined to reach our shores. The American people was at last thoroughly aroused to the peril which threatened the very foundations of national life. So, the voice of an aroused America called a stern "Halt!" to the oncoming alien hosts. And the

---
3. Roberts, Kenneth L.: *Why Europe Leaves Home*, pp. 52-53 (1922).

gates of the Republic closed to mass-migration—probably forever.

# CHAPTER IX

# THE CLOSING OF THE GATES

THE IMMIGRATION ACT OF 1924 is unquestionably the second great turning point in American national life. No such momentous and far-reaching decision had been made since the prohibition of the slave trade, embodied in the Federal Constitution by the Convention of 1787. That first decision, taken by the "Fathers of the Republic," averted a fatal mass influx of unassimilable Negroes and thereby kept America a "White man's country." The second great decision, taken a century and a half later, averted an almost equally disastrous mass influx of low-grade aliens who would have undermined the national foundations and would have thus either disintegrated or shattered the nation. The two chief personages in this great decision were well aware of its epoch-making importance. Representative Albert Johnson, chairman of the Immigration Committee of the House of Representatives and the primary framer of the act, termed it "a second Declaration of Independence," while President Coolidge, whose signature made it law, stated with characteristic terseness, "America must be kept American."

*"America must be kept American!"* Those few words sum up the whole situation. The Johnson Act of 1924 embodies the awakening of the American people to national and racial realities. It is the natural culmination of a long process of education and enlightenment, which had exposed the fallacy of traditional illusions by the stern logic of facts. Practical experience, confirmed by scientific discoveries, had for years been opening the eyes of intelligent, patriotic Americans to the grim fact that our institutions, ideals, and culture could be maintained only if the blood of the nation continued to be predominantly the blood of the stocks that had created those institutions and that had evolved our ideals and culture as instinctive expressions of their racial temperament and attitude toward life. Since the preservation of *that* America is extremely precious to all true Americans, it needed only the awakening of the American people to the dangers that beset them to assure prompt and decisive action. The Johnson Immigration Act therefore reflects not a passing popular mood but a firm national conviction—which will endure.

The year 1924 is thus one of the decisive dates of American history, marking, as it does, the beginning of a new epoch of national reconstruction and racial stabilization that should normally culminate in a *reforged America*. We of today live too close to the event to grasp its exalted significance. But future generations, looking back athwart the years, will see the Great Decision of 1924 rising like a lofty mountain peak across the plain of Time. Those future Americans will also better appreciate its dramatic aspect. For what could be more truly dramatic than this decision, taken only at the eleventh hour and barely averting national ruin? For nearly half a century, alien mass immigration had been steadily undermining America's foundations. Then, in its weakened condition, the nation was faced with an even vaster alien mass migration. A few years of that alien deluge would have wrought irreparable disaster. The American people were thus offered a last chance of national salvation. The opportunity was grasped, and America was saved!

How it recalls the old Roman legend of the Sibylline Books! Much had been lost, and many difficulties had been needlessly created by past blunders, yet enough was preserved to insure America's future if what remained should be wisely and constructively used.

Why the American people awakened so tardily to the peril that confronted them is explained by our survey in that preceding pages. The evolution of America's immigration policy is well summarized by the present Secretary of Labor, who describes it as having passed through three sharply contrasted phases: (1) the ideal of "asylum"; (2) the economic attitude; (3) the biological ideal.[1]

In our second chapter we explained how the idea of America as a refuge for all peoples (at least, within the limits of the White race) was grafted upon American thinking by the popularity of the humanitarian internationalism of Rousseau and his followers, relying as they did upon abstract principles and political institutions to mold men almost at will.

However, we should note that this popular attitude characterized the generation after the Revolution much more than it did the actual founders of the nation. The "Fathers of the Republic" had pondered deeply on the problems of national construction, and they had a much better grip on basic realities than did their successors. It is a highly interesting fact that the most eminent of the "Fathers" foresaw dangerous possibilities in immigration. That is a remarkable proof of their vision, because at that time immigration was negligible, and no likelihood of mass migration of any sort had appeared.

---

1. Davis, Honorable James J.: *Selective Immigration*, pp. 27-29

Nevertheless, the pronouncements of Washington, Jefferson, Madison, Franklin, and others have a startlingly "up-to-date" ring, forecasting, as they do, all the main problems that mass migration was to raise generations afterward. Thus Washington, writing to John Adams in 1794, stated: "My opinion with respect to immigration is that except for useful mechanics and some particular descriptions of men and professions, there is no need of encouragement, while the policy or advantage of its taking place in a body (I mean the settling of them in a body) may be much questioned; for by so doing they retain the language, habits, and principles, good or bad, which they bring with them."

Even more striking was Jefferson's attitude. Although in many ways deeply influenced by "French principles," Jefferson was under no illusion as to the dangers inherent in mass alienage and had scant faith in rapid assimilation. As early as 1781 we find him questioning whether the desire of some of his contemporaries "to produce rapid population by as great importations of foreigners as possible" was really good policy. And his answer was that "in proportion to their numbers, they will share with us the legislation. They will infuse into it their spirit, warp and bias its direction, and render it a heterogeneous, incoherent, distracted mass. Is it not safer to wait with patience for the attainment of any degree of population? May not our government become more homogeneous, more peaceable, and more durable?" Surely, there was foresight! For, we may ask, could even a modern witness of wholesale immigration and mass alienage pen a better summary of their disintegrating and disruptive effects?

To cite one more instance of the "Fathers'" prevailing attitude, we may note Madison's disapproval of a bill before Congress providing for the quick naturalization of foreigners to hasten the settlement of vacant lands. Madison, who was then president (1809-1817), called the attention of Congress to "considerations of a higher nature than those connected with filling up the country by an accession of mere brute numbers."

These characteristic quotations of the "Fathers" prove, in the first place, the arrant falsity of an argument advanced by advocates of "liberal" immigration. Such persons often claim that the United States was deliberately founded as a "refuge for all peoples." The voices of America's creators, above quoted, effectually puncture that argument. The actual founders of this country had had too hard a job building a nation to entertain any such utopian idea. It was not the "Fathers," but the children and the children's children, lulled by prosperity and beguiled by specious theories, who lost touch with basic realities.

Another point worth noting is that those words of the "Fathers" aptly illustrate a matter that we have so often stressed: the sane idealism, poise, and instinctive sense of proportion displayed by America's early leaders, which sufficed to temper popular enthusiasm and self-assurance down to the Civil War.

That a leaven of patriotic insight into immigration's unfavorable aspects continued to persist despite the growing popularity of sentimental and economic arguments for immigration is shown by the opposition aroused when immigration began to reach sizable proportions in the thirties and forties. This opposition was at first a healthy protest against the landing of numerous paupers, criminals, and other undesirable elements, which was then taking place. Unfortunately, the whole situation was so novel that the popular protest mistook the real problem and, instead of demanding sound immigration selection and restriction, got involved in religious controversies, was used by designing politicians, and culminated in the violent "Know-Nothing" movement, whose aftermath of bitterness long handicapped intelligent discussion of immigration problems.

Nevertheless, had it not been for the rapid absorption, after 1850, of America's best minds in the controversies over slavery, which culminated in the Civil War, it is probable that the widespread opposition to wholesale immigration, which undoubtedly then existed, would have shed its vagaries and would have resulted in immigration laws of a sensible character. That would have been an inestimable blessing, because if America had followed the example of Australia and New Zealand and had from the beginning adopted a sound immigration policy, most of the ills of later times would have been averted. But the opportunity was let slip, and the Civil War rendered it impossible, not only by enthroning materialism but also by entirely diverting the nation's best minds from immigration to other issues.

Concerning European immigration, from the Civil War through the opening years of the present century, little need be said here. Our previous survey showed that public opinion then generally regarded immigration as a purely economic matter. Thus, such laws as were passed after 1880 were designed chiefly to prevent the entry of obviously unfit individuals, like paupers, criminals, and lunatics. No attempt was made to limit numbers or to check the inflow of relatively unassimilable European elements. The only exception was that of Asiatic immigration. We have already discussed the crisis in California that led to the passage of the Chinese Exclusion Laws, and we have noted their wider significance as marking the first breach in the "traditional" American attitude. Thenceforth, though restriction of

# CHAPTER IX — The Closing of the Gates

European immigration was long delayed, restriction of Asiatic immigration became a settled policy. When, after 1900, a Japanese influx alarmed the Pacific coast, the Federal government gave partial relief by negotiating a "Gentleman's Agreement" with Japan, by which the Japanese government agreed to limit the entry of its subjects into the United States. The principle of Asiatic exclusion was further confirmed by the Act of 1917, which put practically all of Asia except Japan into the so-called "Barred Zone," from which immigration was prohibited. The principle reached its logical conclusion with the abrogation of the "Gentleman's Agreement" and the inclusion of Japan within the "Barred Zone" by the Johnson Act of 1924.

This provision of the Johnson Act has been widely criticized as being a needless affront to Japan. Yet a moment's reflection will show that it was good foreign policy as well as sound immigration legislation. The "Gentleman's Agreement" had placed Japan in a special, favored position, not only as regards other Asiatics but also as regards the whole world. To Japan we gave a privilege extended to no other government on earth—the right to denote the individuals who should come to us and whom we were bound to accept on the Japanese Government's "O.K." To have continued to grant Japan this favored position after passing a drastic law like the Johnson Act, which aroused bitter disappointment in many parts of the world, would have given many peoples a just sense of grievance against us and would have weakened our moral position in maintaining our principle that immigration is a purely domestic matter, of which we must be the sole judge. Therefore, whatever resentment it has aroused, or may arouse, in Japan would have been more than outweighed by the resentments and other difficulties that we should ultimately have experienced from other quarters if the "Gentleman's Agreement" had been retained.

Returning to our main theme (European immigration), let us now trace the rise of the modern restriction movement. For we should remember that, while the war greatly hastened the conversion of public opinion, the public was being steadily converted to the need for restrictive legislation during many years before 1914. The beginnings of a restrictionist movement can be clearly traced back to the early eighties, when the appearance of the "New Immigration" instantly alarmed a few far-seeing minds. At first this attitude was confined to a mere handful, but that handful was composed of tireless patriots like Prescott Hall, and their combined zeal and moderation enabled them to conduct propaganda that appealed effectively to intelligent, forward-looking men. Thus, by the close of the nineteenth century, the foundations of a sane, well-considered immigration policy had been firmly laid. The general public was, to be sure, as yet but little interested. Nevertheless, the existence of an ably led and well-considered restriction movement was of capital importance, because when public opinion should be stirred on the immigration question, it would find a literature and leaders able to direct popular feeling along proper channels, instead of letting it fly off the track, as it had in the "Know-Nothing" movement of half a century before.

Besides the movement just described, there existed another restrictionist force—organized labor. The "New Immigration's" destructive effects on wage scales and living standards had thoroughly aroused both Native American and North European working men to the peril of mass immigration, and the organized strength of American labor lined up almost solidly for restriction legislation.

The combined strength of these two restrictionist elements was increasingly shown as time went on. President Roosevelt greatly aided the movement by appointing a government commission authorized to make a complete survey of the problem. In 1910 the Commission turned in a 41-volume report packed with material, which threw a great light on every phase of the question. This report had an enormous effect. It proved to unbiased, patriotic citizens the urgent necessity of decisive action. The Commission's verdict, that immigration restriction was "demanded by economic, moral, and social considerations," received the hearty endorsement of most thinking Americans. That verdict, indeed, marks the end of the purely "economic" attitude toward immigration. The social, political, and moral aspects of the problem were now clearly recognized, and the whole question was raised to a higher plane! Furthermore, the swelling tide of mass-migration was opening the eyes of the general public as nothing else could have done. The year 1907 had witnessed the arrival of almost 1,300,000 immigrants—mainly from Southern and Eastern Europe and Western Asia. Even the most unthinking citizen began to sense dimly that America was being literally submerged by such alien floods.

The Roosevelt Commission suggested a remedy—a restriction law on a percentage basis, thus foreshadowing the policy that the nation has now adopted. Yet—why did so many years elapse before the decisive step was taken? The melancholy answer is because of the selfish power of "vested interests" in wholesale immigration. In our previous survey we described that group of interests, ranging as it did from big corporations and steamship companies down to labor brokers, touts, and "red-light cadets." To these commercial interests should be added the frantic efforts of various foreign-language groups to hold open the doors for fresh masses of their kinsfolk eager to get to America. Now all these interests had "lobbies" in Washington, which knew how to put pressure on Congress. And of course, propagandist backfires were started all over the country, spreading "liberal" appeals and "sob stuff" wholesale to blind public opinion to the true situation. So skillful were these tactics that they staved off the inevitable until the close of the war.

But the post-war crisis put lobbies and propaganda to rout. Before the commanding voice of an aroused American people, the "interests" went down in defeat. In 1921, Congress passed a stopgap restriction measure that checked the alien flood and gave time for the working out of a permanent, constructive immigration policy that was embodied in the Johnson Act of 1924.

This epoch-making law combines the idea of restriction with the ideal of national conservation. In the first place, it recognizes that mass immigration of any kind is undesirable, and so assigns a temporary maximum limit of about 160,000 to the number of European[2] immigrants to be admitted in any one year, that number to be ultimately reduced to 150,000 per annum.

Even more important is the act's second feature—the embodiment of what Secretary Davis so aptly terms "the biological attitude" toward immigration. The Johnson Act rests upon the undeniable truth that *the blood of the nation* is the basic fact of American life and that our institutions, ideals, and everything else should be regarded as mere manifestations of the vital spirit that has created them. Now the evidence of all recorded history and the evidence of modern science combine to prove conclusively that if the blood of the nation changes, the national temperament will likewise so change that existing institutions and ideals will no longer fit the population and will therefore be either radically altered or done away with altogether. But the overwhelming majority of the American people, being of the racial stocks that evolved our present institutions and ideals, are unalterably determined that these normal expressions of their temperament and outlook shall be preserved. So the Johnson Bill enacts into law the will of the American people by preserving our present ethnic make-up against change through immigration. It does this by its most striking feature—the "National Origins" clause.

---

2. Including, of course, also immigrants from a few West Asiatic sources like Turkey, Armenia, and Syria. The Johnson Act does not, however, disturb the "Barred Zone" principle of the Law of 1917, but, rather, logically completes it by putting Japan under that category. The theory is that, since no members of the non-White Asiatic races can become American citizens (as has been definitely decided by the Supreme Court), such Asiatics should not be admitted as immigrants—though provision is made for the entry of travelers, students, and merchants engaged in bona fide international trade. Lastly, the Johnson Act omits countries in the western hemisphere from the quota provisions.

That clause, due to the patriotic vision of Senator David A. Reed, of Pennsylvania, is truly a masterstroke of constructive legislation. Although at the moment of its passage in 1924 the act assigned an allotment of immigration quotas from European countries that corresponded roughly to the various ethnic elements now in America, it provided for a thorough investigation of the nation's present racial make-up, the object being to apportion the future annual immigration of 150,000 according to the national origins of the entire White population. Now, strange though it may seem, all previous restriction plans had been based upon the foreign-born elements, thereby totally ignoring the rights and claims of the native-born Americans! Could anything be more unjust? On the other hand, could anything be more just and fair than to give each element in the population its proportionate share of those new arrivals who are destined to form part of the nation's blood and thus to influence its future? Here, indeed, is "proportional representation."

The National Origins clause is, in the last analysis, a declaration that what we are now racially, we propose to remain. As former Immigration Commissioner Curran well put it, "Each year's immigration is to be an exact miniature of what we are as to stock." If ever there was a sound, fair bedrock immigration policy, the National Origins clause is one. That justice to all was the motive of its framers is shown by the statements of Representative Vaile, of Colorado, one of the leading members of the Immigration Committee, in a recent speech before the House. "To those who are in the least familiar with the recent development of the immigration policy of the United States," said Mr. Vaile, "there is one fact that stands out as clearly as any fact can possibly stand out, and that is that, far from discriminating against or in favor of any racial group, Congress has endeavored to treat them all with the most even-handed justice. . . . Let me make a preliminary observation in order to emphasize the generosity of the American Congress. We have an undoubted right to discriminate if we wish to do so. There are some countries whose immigrants, notwithstanding notable individual exceptions, have not on the whole done well here. We might, in the proper exercise of sovereignty, have said, 'We will give those countries a smaller proportion of the total.' We said nothing of the kind. . . . I have yet to see any plan suggested that meets more general approval than that of basing the proportion of immigration from different countries upon the proportion of our total present blood that those countries have contributed. It is a plan of which no country can justly complain. It is a declaration to all countries: 'We don't want the blood of the United States to be further changed, but we are willing to accept people from all of you at their face value on the basis of your aggregate past contribution to our present blood.' Let those who are dissatisfied with this plan propose a fairer one—always bearing in mind that if they advocate a scheme that will favor themselves, some other group will be working for something that will put the advantage in their own laps. . . . Are we to understand that we should embark upon a policy of considering the merits of different races in fixing immigration quotas? There is much to be said in favor of it, if matters of opinion could readily be reduced to matters of fact in an applicable form. But, as already stated, we rejected that plan in favor of an absolutely non-discriminatory law. . . . Let those who have a fairer plan propose it. But remember: Any plan that involves leaving out elements that founded this country, won its independence, and established its government—elements that were here since the very beginning—will be out of court before its case is submitted. . . . The National Origins plan is fair to all; it completely avoids all racial discrimination, and it will preserve the blood of the United States in its present proportions."[3]

This analysis of the National Origins clause by one of its makers is a convincing refutation of the cries of "Discrimination!" and "Race Prejudice!" that we hear from certain quarters. For, in Heaven's name, is it "discrimination" to include the whole population, even unnaturalized aliens, in apportioning immigration quotas? And is it "race prejudice" to allow even those elements that have proved least assimilable and least desirable their proportionate share in contributing to the blood of the nation? Surely, every fair-minded person must acknowledge that such accusations are inspired either by blind passion or by designing propaganda. America's immigration policy is based not upon theories of race superiority or inferiority but upon the bedrock fact of *difference*. As President Harding well said in 1920, "There is abundant evidence of the dangers which lurk in racial differences. I do not say racial inequalities—I say racial differences."

To sum up the matter: the American people have come to realize the fundamental fact that no country can be a true "nation" without a spirit of unity, and that no such spirit can exist without a basic like-mindedness among its citizens—which, in turn, can arise only through basic similarity in blood. The American people look back longingly to the unity and like-mindedness that existed down to the middle of the nineteenth century, and they are determined that the nation shall be welded anew. They know

---

3. Extension of remarks of Honorable William N. Vaile, of Colorado, in the House of Representatives, December 16, 1925, as published in the *Congressional Record*.

that the only way to accomplish this is through race stabilization. The Johnson Act is thus the first step in the re-forging of America.

Many other steps, of course, remain to be taken. But the great thing is that we are now on the right track and that a promising beginning has been made. When we remember that the Johnson Act has been in operation only three years, the results achieved are truly astonishing. Even under the provisional quota schedule,[4] the new law instantly accomplished its main purpose—the apportionment of immigration according to the ethnic make-up of our present population. Of the quota immigrants now admitted, fully 75 per cent come from Northern and Western Europe, while only 12 percent come from Southern and Eastern Europe. In other words, the "Old Immigration" has been raised to its fitting preeminence, while the "New Immigration" is restricted to precisely its just ratio, since the "New" immigrant stocks now in America form approximately 12 percent of the whole population. Again, since the total number of quota immigrants is today only a trifle over 160,000 and will be ultimately reduced to 150,000, all danger of mass migration from Europe has been averted. Contrast the present situation with conditions before the war, when, out of a mass immigration averaging close to 1,500,000 per year, fully 80 percent came from Southern and Eastern Europe or Western Asia, and only about 20 percent came from North European sources!

Furthermore, not only has immigration been restricted in quantity and justly apportioned in racial make-up, but it has also been improved in quality from all quota sources. This is due largely to another excellent feature of the Johnson Act—the preliminary inspection "at the source." All prospective immigrants must obtain visas for their passports from our consular officers abroad, and visas are granted only if the consular officers are satisfied that applicants are legally admissible to the United States. Thus, many undesirables are rejected at the start, and final inspection at our ports of entry is much simplified.

And, just as the immigrant stream is being purified of its worst elements,

---

4. This provisional schedule is based upon the numbers of foreign-born of the various European nationalities in America at the time of the census of 1890. That date was chosen because the census records showed that the numbers of foreign-born then corresponded better than later censuses to the racial make-up of our present population. This schedule was, of course, designed as a temporary measure, to hold the scales of immigration even until official investigation should ascertain the racial make-up of our population. Three years were allowed for this investigation—which, as a matter of fact, is now successfully completed. The law provides that the permanent schedule, based upon the "national origins" of our population, shall go into effect on July 1, 1927. It is this clause which immigrant elements tried hard to abrogate in the last session of Congress. They did succeed in having its application postponed for a year and are meanwhile striving to discredit the National Origins plan so that it should never go into effect. That, of course, would be a great misfortune, because the clause is the Johnson Act's most statesmanlike feature.

# The Closing of the Gates

so the improvement that immigration restriction has wrought in our economic and social conditions is attracting a better grade of immigrants from all quarters. We have already seen how the lowering of working conditions and living standards by mass immigration before the war was discouraging self-respecting, ambitious persons from coming to America and thus not only was drying up the Old Immigration but was worsening the quality of the New Immigration as well. Now that the trend is reversed, and wage scales and living standards are on a healthy basis, America attracts the right sort of people once more. Our immigration officers (who are certainly the best judges) are loud in their praise of the remarkable betterment that the law effected from the very moment of its operation. Here is what Commissioner Curran, chief immigration officer of the Port of New York, had to say only a year after the enactment of the Johnson Law: "As an affirmative performance, the Immigration Act of 1924 has already done great good to our country, and it gives promise of doing more. The immigrants who come to us now are fewer and better. They are cleaner nowadays. They possess better health, better intelligence, and a better promise of industry that produces than did their predecessors. In the main they are outdoor folk, pink-cheeked, long of limb, and muscular. They will labor rather than barter, and work in the open rather than buy and sell in the alleys. They are self-contained and confident. And they are young. It is the youth of Europe that is coming through Ellis Island these days." The latest annual report of the Commissioner General of Immigration is couched in a thoroughly optimistic tone. "For the first time in the history of the United States," comments the Commissioner General, "we have a well-grounded and well-considered set of laws relating to immigration which, while not shutting us off from a reasonable contribution of Old-World peoples, are at the same time responsive to the demands of the American people for an effective immigration control."

The Johnson Act has thus proved its excellence beyond all argument. However, we must never forget that the most perfect law is only as good as its enforcement. And unfortunately, we are faced with one very serious weakness in the present situation—the menace of the "bootlegged alien." How great that menace is, a moment's reflection will show. Remember the huge mass immigration that threatened us a few years ago? That deluge was *legally* prohibited by our immigration law. But the law did nothing whatsoever to lessen the *desire* of would-be immigrants to come to America. In fact, the law has actually increased that desire because the more American wages and living standards rise, the more America becomes a "land of promise." To get down to hard realities: we have set up a legal barrier against the greatest mass migration of all recorded history. But, unless that legal barrier is backed by official force strong enough to make it stand, the human pressure from abroad will crumple it up like what (if unsupported) it really is—a bit of printed paper. And the alien pressure to get into America is so tremendous that only eternal vigilance and strong enforcement will protect us against an illegal alien infiltration of a most insidious and destructive character. Competent observers have estimated that at least 20,000,000 people in Southern and Eastern Europe and Western Asia alone today *long* to come to America! With such a huge reservoir of unsatisfied desire, it is easy to see how multitudes will take the most desperate chances and pay any price to get in.

That is the reason why a great "bootlegging" business in immigrants has developed, closely knit with the smuggling of liquor and drugs, richly financed, ably directed, and so well organized that the system's tentacles reach from America's "underworld" to the remotest parts of Europe and Asia. Every mile of our long land frontiers to the north and south and every league of our Atlantic and Pacific coasts are possible "leaks" in our legal dike, by which the alien flood can trickle through. The revelations that have been made in regard to this bootleg immigrant traffic are literally astounding. In the first period after the Johnson Act was passed, before the government had really grasped the situation, it has been authoritatively estimated that immigrants were being smuggled into America at the rate of 1,000 a day—an illegal immigration with a volume aggregating nearly 400,000 per year! Since then protective measures have been so improved that illegal immigration has been markedly reduced. Still, even today, it is presumed to number between 50,000 and 100,000 per year. Now remember that a majority of these smuggled aliens are of the most undesirable types of Eastern and Southern Europeans and Asiatics, including many dangerous criminals and persons afflicted with loathsome and contagious diseases, and you will realize still more vividly what "bootleg" immigration is doing to us.

What can we do about it? Well, practically every government official in touch with the problem, from the Secretary of Labor and the Commissioner General of Immigration down to local inspectors and border patrolmen, asserts that there is only one effective way to stop the illegal influx and to cleanse America of the human dregs that have been foisted upon us. That way is an alien-registration law, coupled with wholesale deportation. At present there is no adequate method of tracing smuggled aliens once they get in, nor is there any satisfactory way of checking up on those actually among us. We know that the number of aliens illegally in America today must run into the hundreds of thousands. A registration system would detect these people, while the establishment of suitable deportation machinery supplied with sufficient funds[5] would make possible a general house-cleaning of gross undesirables who are now making all sorts of trouble, including dangerous crimes and revolutionary propaganda.

The outcry today being raised against an alien-registration law in some quarters as being "un-American" is mere sentimental twaddle. As Secretary Davis well says, alien registration "is based upon a principle always recognized in our American scheme of things. Every American citizen must register to qualify himself to vote. Practically every state in the Union provides for compulsory education of children, both native-born and alien. ... This system would enable us to weed out the alien who has entered the country in violation of the law or who is here to preach the downfall of our institutions, and the overthrow of all law and order. It would provide help for the alien who seeks to become a real American and would check the activity of the alien who is here for no good purpose.... These proposals are put forward in the interests of the immigrant who comes to us from abroad, the alien who is within our gates, and all-American citizens, today and in the future."[6]

Another step that must soon be taken is the putting of the Western Hemisphere on a quota basis. When the Johnson Act was framed, New World countries were not limited as to numbers of immigrants. This was done to facilitate neighborly relations. At that time, it was not believed that New World immigration would be likely to become troublesome. Our chief source of New World immigration had, up to that time, been Canada, a land with less than 10,000,000 inhabitants, which had sent us immigrants of good average quality and with many very fine elements.

Since then, only three years have passed. And yet, within that brief period, our experience with our southern neighbor, Mexico, has driven home in our minds one stem fact: the fact that, with our high living standards and abounding prosperity, any low-standard country that is exempted from our restriction laws will sooner or later (and usually sooner) become a source of mass immigration. Mexico has a population of nearly 15,000,000, mostly low-grade Indians and mixed breeds. That Mexico possesses an intelligent, cultivated upper class is entirely beside the point, because the immigrants

---

5. At present, deportation methods are so cumbrous and expensive that our officials cannot proceed against more than a fraction of the aliens whom they know to be deportable. This is a scandalous situation, which should be remedied at once.
6. Davis, Hon. James J., *op. cit.,* pp. 213-214.

that Mexico sends us are the poorest, lowest elements of the population.

Down to the stoppage of low-grade European labor, Mexico was not an important source of immigration. Considerable numbers of Mexicans did cross the frontier to do the rough labor in our Southwestern border states, but they did not constitute a "problem," because they were mostly seasonal male laborers who went home after their work was done. However, as soon as cheap labor from Europe was stopped, many lines of American industry that had been run on a cheap-labor basis turned to the Mexican supply. For here, right at our doors, was a great reservoir of the cheapest and most docile labor. The Mexican "peon" (Indian or mixed-breed) is a poverty-stricken, ignorant, primitive creature, with strong muscles and with just enough brains to obey orders and produce profits under competent direction.

It was the same old story! Big employers were delighted, labor agents drummed up recruits, and Mexican immigration swelled to mass proportions. No one knows how many Mexicans there are now in the United States, because immigration statistics tell only a small part of the story. With a 2,000-mile land frontier, thinly settled and lightly guarded, the Mexican usually disdains to pay the ten-dollar visa fee and the eight-dollar head tax that he needs for legal entry into the United States. Saving his money, he just slips quietly over the border, and until we have an alien-registration law, we cannot stop him. Our immigration officers may be able to spot smuggled Europeans and Asiatics coming in from Mexico. But how, without alien-registration cards, can our inspectors spot illegal Mexicans once they lose themselves in the Mexican quarters of our Texas or California towns?

So, the little brown peons keep swarming in and spread far beyond our southern-border states—wherever, in fact, there is a call for "cheap labor." And everywhere the peon brings with him his ignorance, dirt, disease, and vice, which infect cities with slum plague spots, depress wages, and lower the general tone of the community.

Here is what a recent investigator has to say about our latest alien-immigrant problem: The number of those who want the Mexican is steadily increasing. In these days one need not go to the Southwest to meet him. A glance from the car window in Pennsylvania or New York is likely to fall on a succession of blurred olive faces, aligned along the track. In the kingdom of railroad ties a new hierarchy is displacing the Slav; the Mexican is rapidly becoming the railway-track laborer *par excellence*.

"A beet field, its plumed rows suggesting an expanse of sprouting helmets, be it in California or Iowa, Colorado or Wisconsin, is almost sure to produce a crop of Mexicans before the season is over; they are the favorite labor of the sugar growers. In Chicago the Mexican is displacing the Negro in the steel mills and stockyards. European immigration has been restricted, but the cheap-labor vacuum that is thus created is quietly sucking the Mexican out of the Southwest and into the North and East. Soon the man from next door may actually live next door to many of us."[7]

So rapid has been this Mexican "peaceful penetration" that the Mexican immigrant element[8] in the United States today numbers probably at least 1,000,000. Indeed, some estimates run as high as 2,000,000. Furthermore, the Mexican is becoming a "permanent" problem, because he is bringing in his women and tends to stay. Unless something is done, and that right soon, we shall have on our hands another race problem of a very troublesome character. For the Mexican peon is about the most "alien," unassimilable creature that could be imagined. His temperament and outlook on life are absolutely opposed to those of the typical American. Low in intelligence and almost devoid of individual initiative, the Mexican Indian is likewise splendid potential revolutionary material, because he is *a born communist*. "Private property," in our sense of the word, he has never really known. He is a primitive tribesman who has always lived a group life, with everything save a few strictly domestic possessions held in common. Such a being, profoundly alien in blood, ideals, and outlook, can be only a destructive element in our national life. The Mexican must be kept out if grave dangers are to be averted.

Yet the Mexican is merely the nearest of several potential New World immigration problems. There are the West Indies, with several million inhabitants, mostly Negroes and Mulattoes. Already our West Indian Negro immigrants have furnished a large proportion of our most troublesome Negro agitators and revolutionary radicals, as we shall see in later chapters devoted to the Negro problem. Furthermore, south of Mexico lie Central and South America, with a combined population more than three times that of Mexico, or between 45,000,000 and 50,000,000. Most of these millions are Indians, Negroes, or mixed breeds of various kinds—at least, those are the elements that would furnish immigrants to the United States. In view of all this, can any sane person deny that the New World ought to be put immediately on a strict quota basis?

Our analysis of the weaknesses and shortcomings of the present

---

7. Thomson, C. A · "The Man from Next Door," *Century*, January, 1926.
8. The immigrants from Mexico should be sharply distinguished from the descendants of the sparse population which we annexed after our war with Mexico in 1848. These people, whether of Indian or Spanish descent, are mostly small landowners, moderately prosperous, and keeping closely to themselves. They stay at home and rarely enter our industrial life in any way.

immigration situation shows that, while we have made a good start and have evolved a sound line of policy, several steps must be immediately taken if we are to avert dangers of a most pressing nature. We must never forget that immigration is a problem that will always be with us and that will need constant watching to prevent the rapid growth of insidious perils from small beginnings to disastrous proportions. Immigration surely exemplifies the time-honored maxim, "Eternal vigilance is the price of safety!"

And the need for constant vigilance becomes doubly clear when we realize that our immigration policy is threatened, not only by tremendous hostile pressure from abroad but also by persistent enemies at home. Many commercial interests selfishly long for the days of "greenie" labor and hope to see them return, while several numerous and influential immigrant groups in our population are bitterly determined to break down our new immigration policy and open the gates once more to floods of their fellows desperately eager to come to America. Those immigrant groups are largely naturalized American citizens and thus have votes, which they use as clubs on weak-kneed politicians ready to barter away America's future for their own precious political careers. The recent Congress witnessed several attempts to undermine the Johnson Act, and the opposition actually succeeded in postponing for a year the application of the National Origins clause, which is the act's most statesmanlike feature.

Let us examine these two opposition forces in order to gauge their present strength and forecast their future ability to make trouble. First, let us consider the commercial interests opposed to restricted immigration. Here, happily, we find a force that is rapidly on the wane. The "unholy alliance" of vested interests, which was once the chief foe of immigration restriction, has been pretty well dissolved. The steamship companies have about made up their minds that wholesale immigration is a thing of the past and are accordingly adjusting their business along other lines. The fraternity of shady labor brokers who fattened upon the alien immigrant have mostly transferred their talents to other fields. Most important of all, the ranks of the big employers, once almost solid for cheap alien labor, are today thoroughly split, with an ever-larger proportion genuinely converted to the soundness of our present immigration policy and adjusting their business thereto. Of course, we still see plenty of the old "hard-boiled" type. But our best and most far-seeing industrial and financial leaders now recognize that immigration restriction is not only a patriotic necessity but also "good business" in the long run.

The war and post-war period opened the eyes of American employers as nothing else could have done. For five years American industry, suddenly deprived of cheap labor, was as suddenly confronted by the need for unprecedented activity and expansion. Yet the strain was successfully met by better business methods, and American industry found itself on a sounder and more truly prosperous basis than it had been before. The radical unrest of the post-war period was the final touch that completed the awakening of American business to the realities of the situation. It showed that immediate profits might involve total ruin later on; that "cheap" labor was apt to be frightfully expensive labor in the end.

The upshot is that American industry is no longer based on "greenie" labor, "hire-and-fire," gambler" profits regardless of consequences, and other features of the bad old days before the war. Instead, American industry is thinking in terms of efficiency management, labor-saving machinery, and reduction of labor turnover. Never have the relations of capital and labor been so good as they are today. Industrial leaders and labor leaders are "getting together" on a common platform of high output and high wages. Profit-sharing and management-sharing systems for employees, bonuses for special performance, and pensions for long service are creating contented, prosperous, loyal working staffs, glad to do their best and immune to revolutionary propaganda.

And, great as the improvement has already been, the opportunities for further progress in industrial efficiency are even greater. The possibilities of labor-saving machinery in reducing the need for low-grade, unskilled labor are almost limitless. How great the progress along this line has already been can be judged by a recent survey of two competent experts who state that the work done today in the United States by mechanical power would otherwise demand the toil of 3,000,000,000 hard-driven slaves—in other words, a servile mass nearly thirty times as large as our entire present population! Beside this stupendous achievement of labor-saving machinery, what do our remaining needs for unskilled labor really amount to?

Surely, with labor-saving machinery expanding so rapidly, a more efficient use of the human labor we now have should suffice for all really necessary demands. The unsoundness of current pleas for cheap alien labor even on strictly economic grounds is well shown by some pertinent remarks of our present Secretary of Labor, who writes, "There is a persistent demand for relaxation of immigration limitation for economic reasons. The plea is continually made that we need labor, particularly common labor, in order that our industries may be kept fully manned. But it is a fact that many of our industries are already overmanned, and that in many others the substitution of up-to-date machinery and methods would eliminate much of the need for manpower."[9] That our best business brains recognize this and are ready to move along new lines is shown by a characteristic utterance of that well-known business leader, Mr. Edward A. Filene, of Boston, who states, "Employers do not need an increased labor supply, since increased use of labor-saving machinery and elimination of waste in production and distribution will for many years reduce costs more rapidly than wages increase, and so prevent undue domination by labor."

From all this it seems clear that immigration restriction will have less and less to fear from its old opponents, the commercial and industrial interests. The chief adversaries to be reckoned with today and in the immediate future are those immigrant groups (chiefly of Eastern and Southern European origin) that, for their own special reasons, strive to undermine our present immigration law and block further progress.

The power of these groups should not be underestimated. They control a vast number of votes, strategically placed in politically "doubtful" states, and they can thus put heavy pressure upon many congressmen and upon both the great political parties. So active were their lobbies in the last Congress that they did distinct harm, while it is always possible that by a combination of skillful tactics and favorable circumstances, they might *temporarily* undo much of what has already been done.

Let us even suppose that some such thing will happen. Very good. And then, we may quietly ask the triumphant "alien blocs": *What will happen to them?*

For surely, before they travel much farther along their present road, they should, *for their own sakes,* ponder that question long and seriously. Remember: the whole trend of the times indicates that the great majority of Americans have made up their minds that immigration restriction has come to stay—that, indeed, it forms the necessary basis for that national stabilization and reconstruction that most Americans supremely desire. The re-forging of America has begun. America is being re-forged upon the anvil of time by the hammer of the national will. And—any immigrant group or combination of groups that meddles with America's re-forging *is going to get hurt!* Let there be no mistake about it: any temporary successes thus gained will prove to be "Pyrrhic victories" that will be paid for tenfold.[10]

The author has thus far in these pages refrained from citing personal experiences, but he feels that one of them bears too strikingly on this particular

---

9. Davis, *op. cit.,* p. 208.
10. One of the most likely consequences would be a law prohibiting all immigration. Such a bill was actually introduced in the last session of Congress.

matter to be omitted:

I had spent the year 1923 in Europe and the Near East, engrossed in studies of political and social conditions, which put me out of touch with American affairs. Upon my return home at the beginning of 1924, I went to Washington to learn what was going on. One of the first persons I saw there was a good friend of mine who is nationally known as one of the keenest judges of American public opinion. I asked him to tell me what the outstanding feature in the evolution of American public opinion during the past year was. Quick as a flash he answered, "Immigration!"

"I tell you," he went on, "in all my experience I have never seen so general a crystallization of public sentiment about any issue as there has been about immigration restriction. Look at Washington today! What's the 'big story' here? It's the fight over the immigration bill. The opposition lobbies are making a big row. I think they'll lose out, though of course you never can tell. But"—and here his face went grave—"but one thing I do know: the American people are today aroused to a stark, grim determination to slam the doors against wholesale immigration. And if the alien groups who are fighting the bill do succeed in throwing a monkey wrench into the machinery, I pity them, because then you'll see an anti-alien movement in this country that will make the Ku Klux Klan look like thirty cents!"

Well, that's my story. And anyone who will recall the state of American feeling in those days of early 1924 will realize that my friend was dead right. Of course, we know that the bill became law and public feeling subsided—because its alarm had been quieted and its determination had been satisfied. But that determination is today even stronger than it was three years ago, because the new law has conclusively proved the wisdom and the necessity of the policy that was then begun. If now, the subsidence of popular emotion leads short-sighted politicians to heed alien lobbies and weaken the immigration law, not only those politicians but even more the alien lobbies will be in for a very unpleasant surprise. For if the American people once make up their mind that a certain immigrant element or combination of elements is the irreconcilable enemy of our national re-forging, the position of that element or those elements is going to be unhappy indeed. The American people is thoroughly awake to the perils that it escaped by a mere hand's breadth and is today inspired by a deep patriotic passion for national security through the attainment of national unity. Let those who seek to thwart this beware: it is they who will be the losers.

# CHAPTER X
# THE WILL TO NATIONAL UNITY

Thinking America is today in a mood of sober exaltation. Gone is the naive popular optimism of former times. Gone, likewise, are the dark forebodings of reflective minds before 1914 and the dread alarms that beset us during the war and post-war periods. The American people today stand, chastened by a realization of past errors and present difficulties, yet inspired by a further realization that they have found the way to a splendid future. The road before us may be long, but the eye can already glimpse the goal of national security upon the far horizon.

Every true American knows that to ensure those blessings of peace, prosperity, and progress, which are the fruits of national security, he must work for the attainment of national unity. Wherefore, the American people today display a firm *will to unity* that will endure. The task that we have set ourselves may take generations, yet it can and will, be done. For, to paraphrase an old-time jingle, "We *know* where we're going—and we're *on our way!*"

The "Great Awakening," which came with the Great War, has aroused a profound longing for national unity in American minds and hearts—not merely political unity in the formal sense, but even more that solidarity of ideals and culture that are the necessary foundations for real and lasting political stability. As President Coolidge well says, "We have a great desire to be supremely American." And the President significantly continues: "That purpose we know we can accomplish by continuing the process which has made us Americans. We must search out and think the thoughts of those who established our institutions."[1]

This is why Americans are "thinking historically" so much more than they used to. In the days of naive optimism, Americans took the permanence of their ideals and institutions almost as much for granted as they did the sunshine and the air they breathed. But, realizing as they now do that their national heritage is not automatically secure, the American people are studying their historic past and are discovering that its roots go back, far beyond even the achievement of nationhood in the Revolution, to the racial and cultural foundations of the early colonial period. America

---
1. From the President's address entitled: *Thought, the Master of Things*.

is, indeed, a stately growth, with roots striking deep through the centuries. Our America is not a half-formed thing, to be lightly made over at the behest of disgruntled critics; it is a staunch and vital creation, begotten of a picked breed, and nourished by the wisdom, courage, and self-sacrifice of many splendid generations.

"America" is not an area, a government, or a convenience; it is the cultural and spiritual birthright of all true Americans—past, present, and future. And we living Americans, who are its present guardians, are resolved to bequeath this birthright to our children. We know only too well that past errors have impaired the national heritage. But this makes us all the more determined to restore its former potency and to hand it on, improved, to the next generation, who will continue the great task.

Our historical survey has taught us the secret of national unity. That secret is like-mindedness in basic ideals and outlook—which, in turn, is due to basic similarity in temperament and blood. We know the reason why the *like-mindedness* of former times has given place to jarring discords and conflicting attitudes. That reason is: mass immigration, prodigious in volume and increasingly "alien" in character. That, in the last analysis, is why our standards are today so demoralized, and our culture is so distracted and confused. Yet, unhappy as is our present plight, the hopeful thing is that we have at last become keenly conscious of our cultural responsibilities. The American people are awake to the fact that, just as they are always stood ready to defend the national territory against the menace of armed invasion, so they must stand equally ready to defend the national culture, ideals, and institutions against the far more insidious menace of alien "peaceful penetration." That is why the gates of the Republic have been shut to mass migration. And that is also why, despite possible temporary setbacks, the policy of restrictive, selective immigration has come to stay.

The closing of the gates has averted national ruin. It gives us the opportunity to stabilize our national life and to begin the reforging of our national unity. But we should not underestimate the problems that confront us in the accomplishment of our task. Although the immigrant flood is now stopped, it has wrought havoc that the labor of generations alone can fully repair. Its effects have, of course, varied greatly with different regions. The South, the Far West, and much of the Middle West have been almost untouched and have thus remained almost purely American. Furthermore, the immigrant flood came in two sharply contrasted waves—the "Old" and the "New" Immigration, which produced correspondingly different results. The effect of the Old Immigration may be compared to a flood, which leaves behind it a deposit of silt, temporarily disturbing yet soon incorporated into the original soil. The effect of the New Immigration, on the other hand, was that of a destructive torrent, bearing with it quantities of sand and gravel that will impoverish the soil for a very long time to come. Fortunately, its full force was confined to our Northeastern states, but that section will feel the effects for generations.

Bearing these facts in mind, let us examine more closely the difficulties that the immigrant elements of our population present to the attainment of America's national unity. As far back as the beginning of our national life, Thomas Jefferson put the thing in a nutshell when he declared that we must Americanize the immigrant, or the immigrant would "foreignize" us. And one of our leading scientists recently well summarized the problem when he wrote, "We had counted on America changing the foreigner instead of the foreigner changing America. The latter possibility is coming now to loom up in a portentous manner. No nation can be a great nation without a spirit of unity—a certain degree of like-mindedness among its people. It is desirable also that it contain much diversity, but it should be diversity on approximately the same level. An infiltration of a moderate number of people from other countries (not too unlike ours) is a wholesome influence in counteracting the tendency to fixity, which is a natural proclivity of social groups. But carried too far, it would result in making a people a mere hodge-podge of heterogeneous elements."[2]

In our previous survey of the immigrant flood, we emphasized the fundamental importance of the factors of *mass* and *time*, and we contrasted the difference between the gradual arrival of relatively small numbers of immigrants who dispersed among a large Native American population and the rapid influx of vast numbers of immigrants who settled in solid blocks and lived almost entirely out of personal contact with real Americans. These factors of mass and time apply to all immigration and account for the slow assimilation of certain "Old Immigrant" groups, like the German and Scandinavian population blocks of Wisconsin and Minnesota, even though those groups are similar to us in blood and ideals and are thus predisposed to Americanization—as is shown by the rapid assimilation of Germans and Scandinavians in other parts of the country, where they live among "American" surroundings.

Furthermore, *individuals*, even of more distantly related European stocks, assimilate easily when they live among Americans and are anxious to identify themselves with their American neighbors. In America's early

---
2. Holmes, S. J.: *Studies in Evolution and Eugenics*, pp. 209-210 (1923).

days a good many individual Italians, Poles, and other South and East Europeans reached our shores. These individuals were, however, usually persons of education and intelligence, who were able to understand their new surroundings and appreciate what America had to offer them in ways other than merely material. And be it noted, such persons nearly always received a hospitable welcome. Despite what some disgruntled aliens assert, the fact remains that the American people have never shown a spirit of dislike for the foreigner *as such*. What Americans *do* dislike, and dislike most heartily, is the *alien*—either the low-grade alien who disrupts our living standards or the aggressive alien who dislikes our ways and wants to change everything here to suit himself.

To illustrate this, we need cite only two out of many possible examples. Contrast the respective American attitudes toward North and South Italians and toward Sephardic and East European Jews. The North Italians are mostly intelligent, high-grade folk who try to Americanize themselves and who are well-liked everywhere. The bulk of the Southern Italians herd together in "Little Italy's" and are looked down on as "Dagoes." The Sephardic Jews have been an asset to the community since colonial days and never had to complain of any popular prejudice against them until the recent mass immigration of Ashkenazim aroused a strong anti-Jewish feeling, which most unjustly failed to discriminate between different sorts of Jews.

Throughout our early national life, when foreigners were few and when our culture and ideals were as yet intact, America showed a strong power of assimilation. Many prominent citizens of those days bore French, Dutch, or German names, while the names of others reveal a Spanish, Portuguese, Italian, or Slavic origin. Yet these men were all thoroughly "American" in their actions and outlook and would unquestionably have been as indignant as any other Americans at the "hyphenism" and aggressive "alienism" that many immigrant groups today display.

As Brander Matthews well puts it, "This process of satisfactory assimilation persisted up to the middle of the nineteenth century. There were in the United States only a few compact settlements of immigrants from any one country, and most of the newcomers, no matter whence they came, were soon scattered in American communities. The various stocks intermarried, and whatever the parents, the children were Americans, often with little sentimental affection for the remote land from which their fathers had migrated.... Even where a given foreign element was numerically strong, the immigrant was likely to abandon his Native language and to speak by preference his acquired English.... These people had been subdued by what they lived in, and they were anxious to assert their solidarity with the older stock of Americans. They wanted to be us; they accepted our traditions; they acquired our folkways; they shared our opinions and even our prejudices."[3]

On the other hand, even our early history reveals some instances of the stubborn persistence of "mass-alienage," where foreign groups retained nationalistic and cultural self-consciousness. Two striking examples are Louisiana and New Mexico. We annexed Louisiana in the year 1803 and New Mexico in 1848. Yet in neither case have we Americanized the original inhabitants. After a century and a quarter of American rule, the "Creoles" of New Orleans' *Vieux Carré* and the "Cajuns" of the Bayou Parishes still speak French and frankly dislike American ways. As for the Spanish-speaking element in New Mexico, it is almost as "alien" to American culture and ideas as it was when we took over the country three-quarters of a century ago. These two long-standing failures of Americanization may give us useful hints as to what we are likely to encounter in efforts to assimilate some of the immigrant "colonies" that have established themselves so thickly and so firmly in various parts of our Northeastern states—particularly those of South and East European origin, which have practically no natural affinities with American life.

For let us frankly face the unpleasant truth: America's assimilative power has long been on the wane. Let us not deceive ourselves. For many, many years, the vast flood of variegated humanity that poured into America has not been really incorporated into the national life. Of course, great numbers of immigrants have been genuinely assimilated, and many of these new citizens have risen to an honored eminence, which reflects their staunch Americanism and their high value to America. Yet such things, though encouraging, should not blind us to the ominous fact that "alienism," which in America's early days was exceptional, has become so widespread that today a majority of the recent immigrant stocks, *Native-born as well as foreign-born*, have not been genuinely assimilated and are not "Americanized" save in a superficial, formal sense. For the past half-century, America has been suffering from a rapidly growing "hyphenism" and mass-alienage, and only our fatuous optimism kept us from seeing this until the Great War took us by the scruff of the neck and forced us to look the situation squarely in the face. Now that we see things as they are, let no "Pollyanna" optimists delude us into playing the silly old game of drawing up lists of eminent New-Stock citizens and then jumping to the conclusion that millions outside those lists are equally "good Americans."

---

3. Quoted from *The Literary Digest*, September 9, 1922, pp. 31-32.

That is just plain *bunk*. Everyone who has honestly faced the facts knows that the immigrant masses that congest our industrial centers or have settled in blocks upon the land are, generally speaking, not "good Americans." They are still essentially "aliens," who are, for the most part, either indifferent or hostile to American ideals and institutions. America is today confronted with a "mass-alienage" that is not merely passive, but that is becoming increasingly aggressive and seeks, frankly and even exultantly, to attack the existing fabric of our national life. Furthermore, the reflex effect of this alienism has weakened the morale of many Old-Stock Americans and has thereby still further lowered America's assimilative power. That is the plain, ugly truth of the matter, and all real Americans, old stock and new stock, who love *our* America, should close ranks and get together on a common policy and program of action.

The problem of "mass-alienage" in its wider aspect has nowhere been better analyzed than in the writings of Mr. Gino Speranza—one of those New-Stock Americans whose whole-hearted patriotism is the most hopeful aspect of what is in many ways a dark situation. So excellent is his analysis that we would do well to consider it firsthand.

Mr. Speranza begins by emphasizing the shortsightedness of our fathers regarding wholesale immigration. "This nation," he writes, "in all the essentials of its life and character, was grafted upon a historically definite and distinguishable North European or Anglo-Saxon stock. And upon that graft there was developed a definite and distinguishable racial type—the historic American people. . . .

"This does not mean that there is no room within the republic for peoples whose views, beliefs, and antecedents differ from those of the historic American stock. It does mean, however, that when, by the sheer weight of numbers, these peoples bear down too heavily with their cultural differences upon the structure of the democracy, they become a distinctly denationalizing element within the republic. It does mean that when, by combining and solidifying their unlikenesses and divergences from the American civilization, they attempt to impose their dissentient social and political ideas, ideals, and habits, they then become a distinctly disrupting element within the democracy. They are then political and cultural disturbing factors akin to those racial minorities that have threatened, and today still threaten, the life and peace of some of the states of Europe. . . .

"The effect of *mass*, so obvious and impressive in nature, was not considered at all in its workings and consequences upon a distinct civilization and political system developed by a homogeneous people."[4] . . .

Summarizing the alien situation by stating that "one out of every six Whites in this country, today, is foreign-born and belongs to one of thirty different nationalities and has one of thirty different languages as his mother tongue," Mr. Speranza draws the following trenchant conclusions: "It is no answer, and it has become distinctly misleading, to point to our Michael Pupins or our Edward Boks as proof of the desirability of such alienage. The problem is a sociological one; it does not deal with *individuals* but with *masses*; its concern is not with specific successes or specific failures but with *general averages*. Just as you cannot impute the vices and the crimes of a few immigrants to the racial group to which those few belong, neither can you attribute the virtues and the character of a few outstanding 'alien-Americans' to the immigrant stock of which they are a cultural part. The trouble is that New-Stock spokesmen and some Old-Stock 'liberals' recognize the law of averages when it comes to the good qualities of the immigrant; they vehemently deny it or quietly 'side-step' it when his deficiencies are involved.

"It is, therefore, both the 'suddenness' and the massiveness (with the resulting coherence and aggressiveness) of our immigrant-alienage, that *threaten seriously to modify our whole social structure*. And they threaten it, not because of any inherent inferiority or superiority, but because that cohering mass is a mass of social and moral views, customs, ideals, and 'ways' *different* in varying degrees from those of the American people."[5]

This illuminating survey of mass alienage enables us to appreciate another matter that must be carefully borne in mind—the fact that the alienage that America confronts is not a temporary but a *continuing* alienage, which threatens to persist for generations. We usually identify alienage with the immigrant and thus think of alienism solely in terms of "hyphenism"—a preference for the "old country" over America. But, as a matter of fact, that is only the beginning of the difficulty. Of course, many children of immigrants are likewise hyphenates, especially those reared in the larger immigrant "colonies." Yet a much larger number of immigrant children are plainly not hyphenates, since they break away from their parents' viewpoint and scornfully reject the ancestral language, culture, and ideals as "old stuff." But this, in itself, *does not make them Americans*. All too frequently it makes them mere nondescripts, with no ideals, standards, or culture of any kind.

And be it noted: these unfortunate nondescripts are just the ones who are apt to be not merely *un*-American but bitterly *anti*-American. The

---
4. Speranza, Gino: *Race or Nation*, pp. 14, 17, 20 (1924).
5. Speranza, *op. cit.*, pp. 137-138.

reason for this is clear. The nondescript regards America's ideals and culture, like those of his ancestors, as so much "old stuff." Wherefore, our moral standards and social controls irk him and make him restless and dissatisfied. For why should he respect duties and disciplines that we cherish but that to him are meaningless and foreign? And why should he not instinctively dislike these foreign ways and institutions and try to break them down in order to remold America according to his desires?

That is the question that will confront America long after the present immigrants have died and "hyphenism" (in its true sense) has shrunk to minor proportions. Not the foreign-born hyphenate, but the Native-born nondescript, is the real concern of the future. A few keen-sighted observers have already glimpsed this, and somebody has collectively termed our alien nondescripts "The New American." That description is, of course, much too flattering. A more accurate term would be "The Nothing-in-Particular." However, since that would be a cumbersome phrase, let us employ the term "New American"—always recalling its true meaning.

The New American" is a social phenomenon without precedent in modern times. His nearest counterpart is probably the mongrel urban populace of the Roman Empire, which was "Roman" only in name. A clever journalist has aptly described the nondescript elements of our Eastern cities and industrial centers as "American citizens but not Americans." That is just what they are; and so far as the more unassimilable immigrant stocks are concerned, that is just about what many of their children and grandchildren will be, one or two generations hence. We will deal with the "New American" more fully in our concluding pages, when we come to survey future trends and policies. Let us here note the "New American" as an increasing factor in that challenge to our national ideals, institutions, and culture, which America today unquestionably confronts.

This challenge is at present not so much a definite movement as it is a complex emotional trend, ranging all the way from a slight distaste for certain aspects of American life to a deep-seated, malevolent hatred of everything characteristically American. The milder phases of this anti-American tendency are harmless signs of temporary maladjustment on the part of elements destined to harmonious assimilation. Other phases, however, are symptoms of really dangerous alien antipathies, which must be carefully watched.

We must remember that the Great War increased the self-consciousness of all our immigrant groups, while the success of foreign propaganda here during the war and post-war periods has led several European governments to continue their propagandist activities. The distinctly hyphenated attitude of certain immigrant stocks and their persistent efforts to influence American foreign policy in favor of their homelands are too well known to need detailed comment. Such hyphenated activities are, of course, most annoying, but they need not really alarm us, because they inevitably work at cross-purposes and so tend to cancel one another out. What we should watch, however, is the attitude of unassimilated elements on domestic issues, because there the alien groups tend to sink their Old-World differences and line up solidly for common ends. A good example of this is the way that groups that are hereditary enemies in Europe combine in efforts to break down our immigration-restriction laws. Each of these groups would be glad to see the others kept out if it could get its own kinsmen into America. But since this is impossible, they pool their interests in a common "logrolling" program, and we witness an alliance of diverse alien elements on the immigration issue, which could not be formed for any other purpose.

The crux of the whole problem is, however, not specific alien activities but the general spirit of *alienism*, which includes not only the hyphenated groups but also the denationalized mass of "New Americans." This alien spirit is hostile to the very foundations of our national life. Alienism reveals itself in a general attitude of mind that systematically belittles our past, sneers at our present, and hopes for a future when our America shall have been destroyed. *Alienism is America's irreconcilable foe.* That is the plain, ugly truth of the matter, and the sooner we realize it, the better for us.

Let us watch alienism at work. The first thing we notice is the way its spokesmen deny our very nationhood! Some readers may raise their eyebrows at this statement, but if they will read on, they will discover that we are stating a sober fact. Of course, our entire history testifies to the truth that America *is* a nation with roots deep in the past, with long-established institutions, and with distinctive ideals and culture. But all this the spokesmen of alienism blithely sweep aside. With amazing effrontery, they vehemently assert that America is not a true nation but that it is a sort of inchoate mass, still "in the making." Some alienist writers try to make out that even in colonial days America was a mere hodge-podge of many races, and they further imply that America has never been much more than a fluid mixture of immigrant elements.

One phrase especially popular with alienist orators is that "the only real Americans are the Red Indians." That bright remark has been used numberless times by hyphenated speakers, and it never fails to bring a good "hand" from an alien audience. But think of the mental attitude that such a statement implies! Logically, it means that "America" is nothing but a stretch of land, and that the instant a person sets foot on it, he is as much an "American" as anybody else who happens to be here. Why, then, bother about a needless formality like citizenship? Indeed, carrying the idea to its logical conclusion—can there ever be any real "Americans" except Red Indians, since persons of other stocks, though domiciled here for centuries, are as much "hyphenates" as persons who landed only yesterday? To hear some alienist spokesmen, one might think that America had no history, no traditions, no institutions, no coherent fabric of civilization, but that all of us had been dumped down together at Ellis Island a few short years ago. Of course, the idea behind all this is that America is a sort of no man's land—or, rather, every man's land, to which people from every part of the world have a "right" to come and develop a separate group life along any lines that they may see fit. As for American objections, they are instantly stigmatized as "race prejudice" and *"un-American!"*

Americans unacquainted with alienist writings cannot imagine the amazing fables that are today being palmed off as "American history." So grotesque are some of these effusions[6] that to most Americans they might seem to be the work either of madmen or of burlesque humorists. Yet they are neither. They are written with a very practical purpose, and they are gladly received by large circles of readers who want to hear just such things. What such writings do is, of course, to satisfy balked emotions by portraying in an unreal past what authors and audience alike long to see actually happen in the future—the replacement of *our* America by an *alien* "America."

Accordingly, our past is garbled into a glorification of this or that racial element. Even where only a few representatives of a stock can be specifically identified in earlier times, those few worthies are magnified until they almost monopolize "frontstage." And of course, where a group was really present in considerable numbers, they are made out to be nothing less than the whole show. Last but not least, the villain of the piece is always the Native American—or, as alienist writers usually term him, "The Anglo-Saxon." It is he who thwarts their separatist aspirations and crushes them into a mold of national and cultural uniformity. Wherefore, the alienist cry is one of revolt against the "Anglo-Saxon aristocracy" that "rules" America.

This picture of the Anglo-Saxon element as a small ruling upper class does not square with the census figures, which report the colonial and British immigrant stocks as together forming well over one-half of the entire

---

6. For some almost incredible examples, see Gino Speranza's amusing and enlightening article entitled "Playing Horse with American History," *World's Work*, April 1923, pp. 602-610.

White population of the United States. But—what are census reports to the alienist? Is not the Census Bureau probably a propaganda organ of the "Anglo-Saxon aristocracy"? Alienist writers have, therefore, compiled their own statistics, which are certainly interesting, since they usually magnify the size of their respective groups from two to five times as much as the official figures. Indeed, if we consider these private statistics as a whole, we arrive at some startling results. The author has tabulated the numerical claims of a number of spokesmen for non-English-speaking elements and finds that these claims total a trifle more than the entire White population. This gives us a paradoxical America containing not a single individual of English or Scottish blood, to say nothing of the Irish. Indeed, this would logically resolve "The Anglo-Saxon" into a myth, since he must be as extinct as the dodo!

Of course, the exaggerations and extravagances that we have been narrating are found mainly in foreign-language publications not intended for American eyes. When alienism employs the English idiom, it is usually less crude and more careful of its facts. But the alien spirit is there, just the same, and the same general arguments are used. America is described, not as a true nation, but as a geographical area inhabited by a more or less fortuitous collection of people, which is still "in the making." Above all, our past is systematically belittled and assailed. American history is "muckraked" in good, lusty fashion. The colonial period is either ignored or is turned into a racial medley, while the Revolution gives the Anglo-Saxon Fathers of the Republic a splendid chance to buttress their special privileges by erecting such annoying barriers to "progress" as the Constitution and the Supreme Court.

Our winning of the West is likewise taken severely to task. The pioneers, it seems, were rude fellows who messed up matters badly and who destroyed better things than those they brought into being, such things, we presume, including the infrequent clusters of Indian tepees and the occasional river-shacks of half-breed French-Canadian *voyageurs*, which typified the culture encountered by our pioneers. Lastly, to bring the picture down to date, the present-day American is caricatured either as a sour-faced Puritan or as a banal member of the Rotary Club.

Over against this unflattering portrait stands the alien, overflowing with exuberant vitality and cultural possibilities. And, of course, the best thing about the alien is his alienism. It is highly significant to note how alienist spokesmen have soft-pedalled their former slogan of the "Melting-Pot." So long as that slogan could blind Americans to realities and keep the gates open to mass immigration, it was worked overtime. But now that the melting-pot argument is hopelessly cracked, the alienist throws it contemptuously on the scrapheap and no longer disguises his real feelings. Wherefore, the alien is today warmly patted on the back for his reluctance to melt and for his retention of Old-World particularisms even unto the third and the fourth generation.

This viewpoint is well expressed in a recent volume[7] devoted to the various foreign "colonies" scattered so thickly over parts of America. The book states that after a brief period of bewilderment in which many American ways are adopted and the immigrant becomes superficially "Americanized," a reaction sets in, and the newcomers "begin to look with critical eyes at everything. They compare, weigh, and measure, and nine times out of ten they return to their own life, accepting only reluctantly what they must."[8] According to this book, the country is in for a prolonged "friction and elbowing"; yet out of this "tremendous travail," the descendants of the immigrants "will form and build something new, something that has never been before at any time in history anywhere in the world." And what will this marvelous novelty be like? It will be "not a nation"—(Oh, dear, no; perish the thought!)—"but groups of individuals whose bond will be fitness to live in that particular part of the country where they will have settled."[9] If this is not whittling America down to the vanishing point, we are greatly mistaken.

That alienism is developing a definite philosophy and body of doctrine is shown by a very revealing book that appeared a short time ago, entitled *Culture and Democracy in the United States*. The significance of this volume is heightened by the antecedents of its author, Horace M. Kallen. Doctor Kallen is an Ashkenazic Jew, born in Silesia near the Polish border, but brought to America when only five years old. He took full advantage of America's educational opportunities and proved to be a brilliant scholar. A Harvard graduate and Ph.D., he has specialized in philosophy and English literature, making his mark in both fields. Indeed, the volume that we are now considering is dedicated "to the memory of Barrett Wendell: poet, teacher, man of letters, deep-seeing interpreter of America and the American mind, in whose teaching I received my first vision of their trends and meanings."

---

7. Bercovici, Konrad: *On New Shores* (1925).
8. Bercovici, *op. cit.*, p. 15.
9. Bercovici, *op. cit.*, p. 17.

Surely, we have in Doctor Kallen a man surrounded by American influences since early childhood, thoroughly educated in American schools and in one of America's leading universities, the disciple of a characteristic American man of letters, and endowed with a keen intellect, for good measure. Now, what do we find? We find an arch-champion of "hyphenism," who exemplifies the alien spirit better than any other of its spokesmen! Doctor Kallen is a striking example of what we have already emphasized: that high intelligence in immigrants may be combined with a temperamental make-up so different from ours that assimilation is absolutely impossible. Despite his keen, analytical mind, Doctor Kallen simply cannot pierce to America's deeper realities. He is temperamentally as unadapted to America as a fish out of water. Profoundly ill at ease, he protests against *our* America and cries for radical change according to his unsatisfied desires.

The doctor certainly leaves us in no doubt as to where he stands. His first words are a challenge to our very nationhood. "This book," he says, "is a study in the psychology of the American *peoples*."[10] In Doctor Kallen's eyes, our population resolves itself into a miscellaneous lot of hyphenated groups, the largest and most influential of which is at present the Anglo-Saxon. He rejects scornfully the term "Native American" and lumps together all persons of British blood, recent arrivals or descendants of first colonists, into one group, the "British-Americans"—who are as hyphenated as everyone else. Doctor Kallen thus reveals himself not only as an unassimilated alien who refuses to be assimilated but also an alien who denies that there is any "America" to which he can be assimilated. America, he contends, is not a nation, nor can it ever be a nation. And that, be it understood, is something that greatly rejoices the doctor's heart, because he has his own idea of what "America" should be. This fond goal he calls "Cultural Pluralism."

Let us follow the doctor's chain of argument. Since hyphenism is ineradicable, and since the population is bound to remain an assortment of widely varying racial and cultural groups, why not anticipate the inevitable, give up our national delusion, and enthrone hyphenism as our rule of life? There being no "fear" (*sic!*) of the formation of an "American race," why not systematically encourage and develop ethnic and cultural divergencies, thereby turning America into a small-scale replica of the whole world and all mankind?

Naturally, this would relegate the "British-Americans" to a very minor back seat, because the doctor obviously has a poor opinion of the Anglo-Saxon's intellectual and cultural qualities; but of course, since the Anglo-Saxon

---

10. Italics mine.

is so inferior, a back seat is just where he belongs. Doctor Kallen would, to be sure, retain the English language—as a convenient business code and a useful medium of communication between the various culture groups. But English would be merely a convenience, since each group would cherish its own language and would have no further use for anything characteristically American, except as our old traditions and ideals might be preserved inside the humble culture group of "British-Americans." The English idiom debased to a sort of *lingua franca* and a loose, ill-defined administrative union, would be the only vestiges surviving from *our* America if Doctor Kallen could have his way.

And, in place of our vanished America, there would appear the majestic outlines of the doctor's "Pluralistic America." Let us describe it in his own words: "Its form would be that of a federal republic; its substance a democracy of nationalities, co-operating voluntarily and autonomously through common institutions in the enterprise of self-realization through the perfection of men according to their kind. The common language of the commonwealth, the language of its great tradition, would be English, but each nationality would have for its emotional and involuntary life its own peculiar dialect or speech, its own individual and inevitable aesthetic and intellectual forms." After a bit more description, the doctor sums up Ins Pluralistic America as "a multiplicity in a unity, an orchestration of mankind."[11]

Now understand, gentle reader, that we are here dealing, not with an isolated crank, but with a highly intelligent man who unquestionably voices thoughts and feelings shared, in greater or lesser degree by several million persons living among us today. Doctor Kallen's book is a frank expression of that aggressive alienism that is mustering its forces and formulating a clear-cut challenge to our national life. Furthermore, we must also realize that alienism is sympathetically regarded by certain so-called "American" elements, such as mushy sentimentalists, half-baked "liberals," extreme internationalists, and revolutionary radicals eager to welcome anything that tends to upset the existing order.

That the challenge of alienism strikes at the very vitals of American life, there can be no doubt. For surely, the disintegration of national unity into anything like a "Pluralistic America" would mean, not an "orchestration of mankind," but a hellish bedlam. As Brander Matthews aptly remarks in his review of Doctor Kallen's book, "The United States would become a racial ragbag with a linguistic crazy-quilt. . . . If the United States were to legally recognize the 'free diversification of groups no less than of individuals,'

---
11. Kallen, *op. cit.*, p. 124.

centrifugal force would soon shatter the union, and chaos would come again, as it has in the Balkans, where the cultural groups are forever flying at each other's throats.[12]

Now, in the light of all this, it must be clear that we need a well-considered, effective policy toward the alien problem. And we should formulate such a policy, not because there is today any real likelihood of alienism's triumph, but because we ought to solve this vexatious problem with as little disturbance as possible to America's progress and with as little pain as possible to the alien elements themselves.

To the author it appears that the first thing to do is to make it absolutely plain to the alienist leaders that their schemes are vain dreams which can never be realized and which, if persisted in, will merely involve them and their deluded followers in all sorts of misfortune. Alienism had only one real chance—mass immigration. The alienist leaders know this—which is the reason why they are today fighting desperately to break down our immigration-restriction law, or at least to prevent an alien-registration law that would enable our government to detect smuggled aliens and expel undesirable intruders. The American people are, however, so alive to the situation that the alien campaign against our immigration policy will almost certainly fail. As yet the alienist leaders have not quite given up hope. But when they do have to admit to themselves that our gates are finally shut, half the fight will ooze out of them, and they will be in a much more amenable mood. With the supply of recruits cut off, the aggressive alien elements, even though fully organized, would bulk small beside the balance of our 100,000,000 White population and could therefore never make more than local trouble.

Local troubles there surely will be. Some of our Northeastern states may be in for serious times. Yet such difficulties will be localized and will not stop the reforging of America as a whole. In fact, those local alienisms may serve a useful purpose by keeping Americans consciously to their task. The Great Awakening roused the American people to keen national consciousness and gave them their present will to national unity. The persistence of alienism here and there should be enough to prevent the American people from being lulled into false security that would result in fresh misfortunes. We Americans have today come to realize through bitter experience that there is no "substitute" for *patriotism*—"that sentiment of solidarity, that passion for common action, that love of the things which are our own and the life we

---

12. Matthews, Brander: "Making America a Racial Crazy-Quilt," *Literary Digest International Book Review*, August, 1924.

live with and among our fellows, the custom and habit of everyday existence, and those deeper springs of action, self-sacrifice and devotion to something greater than ourselves; greater, indeed, than the sum of us all."[13] And, in the exalted realization of these truths, our will to unity should deepen with time and grow more resolute from the very oppositions that it may encounter.

Yet the *will* to unity, however indispensable as the vital basis for national reconstruction, is not, of itself, enough. This emotional force must be wisely guided and must express itself in intelligent action according to existing realities. We must avoid a recurrence of anything like wartime hysteria, with its panic fears and its program of instant "100-percent Americanism." That hysterical phase, however regrettable, was probably inevitable, because to the excitement of foreign war there was added a sudden popular awakening to the hitherto unrealized menace of hyphenism and mass alienage at home. With scant opportunity to think or plan, it is not strange that public opinion thereupon jumped to measures of crude repression and equally crude "Americanization."

Such methods, however, are not only silly; they tend to defeat their own objective as well. An alien browbeaten into taking out citizenship papers, or an alien-minded American citizen forced to kiss the flag and buy Liberty Bonds, may thenceforth adopt an outward semblance of 100-percent Americanism. Yet at heart he will probably be more bitterly "alien" than ever, and he will be confirmed in that large category of persons who are "American citizens but not Americans."

What we need, therefore, in order to accomplish our task of national reconstruction with maximum efficiency and minimum friction, is a well-considered policy, informed by an exact knowledge of facts and pursued with full realization of the time factor involved. Alienism should be regarded not as an organic unit but as a complex grouping of elements some of which are merely temporary while others are deep-seated. Obviously, our policy should be flexible enough to deal with these various elements, according to their respective natures. Furthermore, what their natures really are can be better ascertained with time and experience.

The time factor cannot be too strongly emphasized, because we Americans are apt to be impatient and want quick solutions. We must realize that in alienism we are confronted by a problem that cannot be quickly solved. To incorporate into our national life the millions of unassimilated aliens who now dwell among us is a task that, even at best, will take two or three generations. Indeed, it may be that certain elements can never be genuinely

---
13. Abbott, Wilbur C.: *The New Barbarians*, p. 240 (1925).

absorbed. But that is something that time will prove and that can then be specially dealt with in the fuller light of experience.

Detailed discussion of national reconstruction will be deferred to our concluding chapters. Here let us confine our attention to the national will to unity and its attitude toward alienism.

The keynote of our policy toward the alien problem should be frankness and firmness, combined with patience and sympathetic understanding. The alien should be convincingly told that our will to unity is inflexible, that aggressive alienism will be effectively combated, and that anything savoring of sedition will be sternly dealt with. But the alien should also be assured that we neither intend nor desire to force him into an artificial "Americanization" nor to persecute him because he clings to ancestral ways. And we ourselves must never forget that alienism is, in the last analysis, a state of mind, which cannot be suddenly abolished even by the alien himself, but which can gradually fade to the extent that the alien is temperamentally fitted to absorb our viewpoint and appreciate our ways.

Finally, let all parties realize that the problem is, at bottom, one of *difference*, for which no one is morally to blame. We Americans have built up *our* America, and we cherish it so supremely that no one should honestly blame us for our resolve that it shall be kept "American." Of course, that is no reason why the alien should like our America, and no moral turpitude should attach to him if he voices his discontent. Let him speak freely, so long as his words are not incitements to illegal and seditious activities. Let us be patient with his impatience and sympathetic with his unhappiness at maladjustment to American surroundings. Let us do our best to help the alien Americanize himself. But, first and last, let us make it unalterably clear that *our* America is going to fulfill its national destiny.

# CHAPTER XI
# THE DILEMMA OF COLOR

No question has been more beclouded by abstract theorizing than that of the relation between nationality and race. And nothing is more encouraging than the way public opinion is coming to a truly realistic attitude, based upon knowledge of facts. What has furthered this attitude is, of course, modern scientific discovery, especially in biology, psychology, and sociology. Today, as never before, we possess a clear appreciation of the basic realities underlying both nationality and race. We are, therefore, in a position to deal wisely and constructively with the problems presented by the interaction of these two factors.

What is the test of nationhood? It is unquestionably the sense of *belonging together as a nation*. Without such an instinctive community feeling, you may have a government, but you will not find a true national life. Now let us carry the matter one step farther. What causes this community sense? It is what sociologists term "consciousness of kind"—an instinctive recognition that we are the same general sort of people, with the same basic ideals and attitude toward life. Only thus does a population possess that *like-mindedness* that is necessary for mutual agreement and harmonious cooperation. But, to carry the matter still farther, like-mindedness springs from similarity of temperament, which, in turn, depends on similarity in blood.

Here, then, is the connecting link between nationality and race. Our survey of America's past has already strikingly revealed the need for a racial basis to true nationhood. We saw that America was founded by a blend of closely related North European stocks, who evolved institutions, ideals, and cultural manifestations that were spontaneous expressions of their ethnic temperament and tendencies. And the overwhelming weight of both historical and scientific evidence proves that only so long as America remains predominantly North European in blood will its institutions, ideals, and culture continue to fit the temperament of its inhabitants and hence continue to endure. We analyzed the disturbing influence produced by the influx of other European stocks and saw that immigration restriction was vitally necessary to our national and cultural self-preservation.

Despite the serious consequences produced by this immigration, however, our survey left us optimistic regarding America's future. It did so for two reasons: (1) because America is still mainly North European in its racial make-up; (2) because most of the immigrant stocks are racially not too remote for ultimate assimilation. The East and South European elements now among us aggregate less than 15 percent of our total White population, and (for reasons that we shall later discuss) it seems unlikely that they will increase relatively faster than the North European elements. Therefore, it is probable that most of them can eventually be absorbed into the nation's blood without such alteration of America's racial make-up as would endanger the stability and continuity of our national life.

But what is thus true of European immigrants, most of whom belong to some branch of the White racial group, most emphatically does not apply to non-White immigrants, like the Chinese, Japanese, or Mexicans; neither does it apply to the large resident Negro element, which has been a tragic anomaly from our earliest times. Here, ethnic differences are so great that "assimilation" in the racial sense is impossible. The non-White elements in our population thus constitute a special problem that requires separate treatment. For surely, if we desire to retain that like-mindedness that is the true basis of nationhood, we should absolutely refuse to spread through the blood of the nation racial strains so different that they would undermine our ethnic foundations.

At the very start of our discussion, let one point be understood: here, as elsewhere in these pages, we shall not go into the question of racial superiority or inferiority but will confine ourselves to the matter of *difference*. And we do so because, for our present purpose, the question of relative racial values is not really involved. This book deals with a specific problem: the maintenance and the harmonious evolution of *our* America. For the great majority of Americans, that is an issue of vital importance. Hence, even though it could be conclusively shown that a certain stock was superior to us in some ways, nevertheless, if that stock is so different from us in temperament that its incorporation would threaten to disrupt *our* America, we should still refuse to receive it on grounds of self-preservation.

That is likewise the reason why we should not only exclude non-White immigrants but should also forbid the intermarriage of resident non-White elements with our White population. For even if we entirely disregard the weight of scientific evidence, which clearly tends to show that crosses between White and non-White races are biologically undesirable, we must be guided by one fact that has been scientifically determined beyond all doubt—the fact that such crosses produce highly *disruptive* effects.

The great racial divisions of mankind are very old and well-established. Each race, despite wide internal variation, forms a generalized type possessing a complex pattern of closely linked physical, mental, and temperamental characteristics, which have evolved through long ages of natural selection that have eliminated disharmonic variations and produced a relatively smooth-working psycho-physical whole.

Now the interbreeding of such widely differentiated racial types disrupts both patterns and produces hybrid offspring who are more or less disharmonic. Again, the subsequent interbreeding of these first hybrids disrupts still further, breaks apart more and more of the linked characteristics, and ends in a population that displays an almost infinite range of variation instead of the relatively restricted, harmonious range that occurred in the original racial types. To be sure, some of these new variants may be desirable, as others are undesirable. But one thing is certain: stability and harmony are hopelessly gone, and in their place reign bewildering variety and uncertainty. The effect of such biological changes on national life is surely obvious. The results are clearly shown in the chronic political and social instability of Mexico and the Caribbean republics, whose populations are largely hybrid mixtures of Whites, Indians, and Negroes, in varying proportions. And the example of our Southern neighbors has been enough to convince most Americans that such hybridization in the United States must be prevented, since none of the difficulties involved in maintaining White race-integrity can outweigh the national and social disruption that hybridization would certainly entail.

Thus, national self-preservation, rather than abstract considerations of race values, underlies our traditional policy of White integrity, usually known as the *color line*. A good proof of this is the way persons with a clear perception of race values endorse the marriage ban against all non-White races. Few well-informed Americans today consider the Chinese or Japanese as "inferiors." Yet well-informed Americans are almost as much a unit against free intermarriage with Chinese and Japanese as they are against intermarriage with Mexican peons or Negroes, who are usually classed as inferior stocks. The reason for this general marriage taboo is that, consciously or instinctively, most Americans realize that, in either case, such racial changes would ensue that *our* America would be foredoomed to pass away. The color line will, therefore, not be abolished but will be resolutely maintained as a cardinal principle of our national life.

Thanks to our Asiatic-exclusion laws, the Chinese and Japanese elements in America will never be more than local Pacific Coast problems. Again, the recent wholesale influx of Mexican peons will probably be taken in hand before it becomes a really serious matter. But one major race problem remains. The Negro has been with us from the first; he was the basic cause of our worst national disaster—the Civil War; and he now numbers over 10,500,000—nearly one-tenth of our total population. The Negro is at once the most chronic and the most acute of our national problems. The Negro problem has been so mishandled in the past that it is today far worse than it normally would have been. To be sure, the last few years have seen a certain lessening of race tension, but that is probably only a superficial phase. Beneath the surface, explosive forces are at wor, which, unless dealt with promptly and constructively, will cause fresh crises and may produce a frightful tragedy.

Because of past errors and blunders, the race problem needs to be considered *by both Whites and Negroes* in a thoroughly frank and realistic way. Throwing old arguments at one another will get us nowhere. Neither should we expect to evolve any "solution" to the problem. Logically, there are only two "solutions": one, the extinction or expulsion of the Negro; the other, his incorporation with the White population. But it is worse than useless to consider the present application of either alternative, since that would instantly rouse the fiercest passions, which might provoke an immediate explosion.

However, there remains a middle ground on which the best minds of both races can, and should, meet for a frank exchange of ideas. To us, it seems that the wisest policy would be to formulate a real *modus vivendi*—a genuine method of "getting along together" as a temporary experiment to last, say, for a generation. During that period each race should develop its own life, mutually recognizing the color line as a symbol not of "superiority" or "inferiority" but of *difference*. With the allaying of White fears of persistent attacks on the color line many of the social discriminations that the Negro most resents could be relaxed, and in the easement of tension that would ensue, the experiment of mutually willed "bi-racialism" could be fairly tried out. If, after anything like a fair trial, the experiment should break down or be seen to be unworkable in the long run, the racial situation would have been maintained substantially unaltered, and the extreme alternatives would remain. To Negro objectors we may point out that it is they who have the most to gain by attempting some such experiment, because if present conditions continue to drift without a real attempt at mutual accommodation, an extreme solution will probably be precipitated, and that solution might be something very like the wholesale expulsion or destruction of the Negro population. If this seems an extreme statement, we will ask the reader to suspend judgment until he has followed our analysis of the explosive forces now gathering, as we shall present it a little later on.

The "race question," as we today understand the term, dates really from the Civil War. Before the war there was, of course, a slavery problem, but hardly a race problem in its present sense. The Negroes were then a servile caste, sharply fenced off by law as well as custom from the White population. Even the group of "Free Negroes," though exempt from slavery, had the legal status of "freedmen" rather than of full-fledged citizens. This special legal status of the Negro, slave or free, was the formal expression of a traditional American attitude toward race. From early colonial times public opinion had been practically unanimous in its determination to preserve White race integrity by a strict color line. Legal intermarriage being forbidden, racial intermixture was confined to illicit sexual relations between White men and Negro women, the Mulatto offspring always being considered Negroes. The color line is unquestionably the oldest and most firmly established of American policies. It has also been thoroughly successful in its primary objective, because for three hundred years it has maintained White race integrity even in places where Whites have been a minority among a dense Negro population.

Nothing is more certain than that the Fathers of the Republic intended America to be a "White man's country." They showed this unequivocally by restricting naturalization to "free White persons."[1] We must clearly distinguish between the Fathers' attitude toward slavery and toward race relations. We have previously observed that most of the Revolutionary leaders deplored slavery and hoped to see it extinguished by some gradual process of law. But, while a few keen minds like Jefferson foresaw grave difficulties in adjusting the Negro's post-slavery status, no man of any standing then considered for a moment that the color line should ever be abolished.

In previous chapters we saw how the egalitarian principles of French radical thought gradually engendered an American radical group that not only demanded the immediate abolition of slavery but also denounced the color line and championed race amalgamation. This confounding of what were really two distinct issues (slavery and race relations) produced the most disastrous consequences. More than any other factor, it brought on the Civil War, while after the war, the policy of the radical Republicans caused the

---

1. After the Negroes were legally endowed with citizenship, the Federal naturalization law was amended to include Negro immigrants as entitled to naturalization. But the Supreme Court has decided (U. S. vs. Bhagat Singh Thind) that this amendment did not include other non-White races, and that therefore only Whites and Negroes are eligible for naturalization to American citizenship.

colossal blunder of "Reconstruction."

We have already analyzed Reconstruction's tragic effects on White America. Let us now consider its even more tragic effects upon the Negro. For the Negro was the real victim of that insane experiment. The Radicals who tried to impose Black rule and racial equality on the South defied basic realities and betrayed an amazing lack of elementary common sense. Had Lincoln lived, "Reconstruction" would have been averted, because Lincoln possessed a statesmanlike grasp of the true situation. But Lincoln's assassination opened the floodgates of partisan passion and precipitated a series of disasters that afflict us even today. And, as already remarked, the Negro has been the worst sufferer. For Reconstruction gave the Negro a thoroughly wrong start. Instead of completing his emancipation, Reconstruction imprisoned the Negro within a vicious circle from which he has never been able to escape. That vicious circle is an attitude of mind wholly at variance with the realities of his situation. And surely no graver misfortune can afflict a people, because it literally blinds their vision and renders them incapable of seeing how to cope with their problems.

What the newly emancipated Negroes needed above everything was a wise and kindly friend to show them where they then stood and whither they should go. Abraham Lincoln would have been just the man for the task, because the Negroes worshipped him as their liberator and would have held his word as law. That great mass of freedmen was as helpless as a pack of children set down in a strange world. How they should be started was, therefore, of paramount importance because, once started, sheer momentum would carry them wherever they were headed, whether toward good or ill.

The position of the freedmen would, at best, have been a difficult one. These primitive folk, suddenly released from slavery, possessed only two really valuable assets—good health and the goodwill of their former masters. Under slavery the Negro had been so valuable a chattel that, despite many instances of abuse, his physical welfare had been usually looked after. In parts of the South the Negro death rate in slavery days was actually less than that of the Whites, while Federal army medical records of the Civil War show that the Negro recruits averaged high in physical fitness and freedom from disease. Thus, however ignorant and backward, the newly emancipated Negroes enjoyed a physical vigor which, if conserved and productively used, might have transformed them into a contented and moderately prosperous peasantry, considering the easy living conditions that then prevailed in the South. What would have aided such a transformation more than anything else would have been the goodwill of their former masters. And this the

Negroes at first possessed, because most owners had felt a personal as well as a pecuniary interest in their slaves, and because these kindly feelings had been quickened by the loyalty and good conduct of the slaves on the plantations during the Civil War.

The collapse of the Confederacy was, of course, followed by a breakdown of the social system based on slavery. The emancipated Negroes generally quit work and wandered about in irresponsible vagabondage. Yet the situation at first had in it nothing of a menacing character. The Negroes, delirious with joy, were like children on a holiday, and beyond much petty pilfering there was little crime or disturbance. The Southern Whites realized this and viewed the proceedings with half-amused exasperation rather than with genuine anger or alarm. If Lincoln had lived, he could undoubtedly have appealed to the best men of the South and could have worked out a system (such as we know he had in mind) by which new social controls could have been established that would have guided and trained the freedmen, through a period of tutelage, for a stable position in American life. Mistakes would undoubtedly have been made and friction engendered. Yet a sound course would have been set, and the nation's best minds, North and South, could have cooperated in friendly fashion for constructive ends.

But alas! Instead of this wise policy, there came—"Reconstruct!" The first consequence of that tragic blunder was to destroy good relations between the races in the South and thus to deprive the freedmen of the sympathetic aid of their former masters. The Negroes turned to their new friends, the Northern politicians and the agents of the Federal Freedman' Bureau, many of whom were extreme radicals who taught the Negroes to look on the Southern Whites as tyrant foes, preached social equality, and made the Negroes all sorts of rash promises typified by the legend of "forty acres and a mule." And on top of all this came the disfranchisement of the Whites, the elevation of ignorant freedmen to political power, and the terrible ten years of veiled race war which ended in the collapse of Reconstruction and the triumph of a fearfully embittered White South.

From that prolonged ordeal the races emerged deeply estranged. Goodwill was gone, hatred and fear having taken its place. And the Negro was the chief sufferer by the change. Those first formative years after emancipation, which might have set him on the upward path, had been worse than wasted. Instead of developing habits of industry and thrift, by which alone his future could be assured, the Negro had been living in a fool's paradise of privileges and hopes, which now collapsed like a house of cards, leaving him bewildered and helpless. We were about to add—"disillusioned," but, unfortunately, this was not the case. If the Negro really had been disillusioned, it would have been a hopeful sign. But so deeply had he drunk of the heady wine of "natural rights" and "God-given franchises" that he still clung to the mirage of his fool's paradise, hoping against hope that his Northern friends would put into his hands things that he had proved unable to hold and unfit to use. Instead of learning the indispensable lesson of self-help, the Negro had been merely confirmed in his old servile attitude of dependence on others. Instead of working diligently for what he wanted, the Negro continued to despise labor, and, feeling that the world somehow owed him a living, he expended his efforts in appeals to the sympathy of Northern friends. His own leaders did nothing to show him where he stood, because until the appearance of Booker Washington in the nineties, not a single Negro of any standing did more than bewail his fate or voice bitterness and hate.

Thus, for thirty years after emancipation, the Negro population slid steadily downhill. Of course this was not universally the case, because a minority struggled against the trend and succeeded in rising in the social scale. Slavery had held all Negroes on about the same level. Freedom enabled the more industrious and capable to rise in economic status and in self-respect. Yet if freedom let the capable rise, it also allowed the incapable to fall. And unfortunately, this sifting process dropped many more than it raised. The bulk of the Negro population vegetated on a low level of shiftless poverty, while the dregs sank far below their former slave-level to jungle depths of almost bestial savagery. An ominously large degenerate Negro element appeared—criminal, depraved, and diseased. Utterly unable to adapt themselves to a civilized environment, these sinister waste products were slated by Nature for elimination by her usual thorough methods. In the process, however, they caused grave social disturbances, because it was these vicious, criminal Negroes who were mainly responsible for the rapes and other felonies against Whites, which enormously inflamed race-hatred and stimulated the lynching evil.

The retrogression of the Negro population was clearly revealed by its increasing proneness to disease. During the decades after emancipation, the Negro rapidly squandered his patrimony of health and vitality. From being one of the healthiest groups in America, as the Negroes were during slavery, they soon became the most diseased. Bad living conditions and widespread sexual promiscuity scourged the Negroes with many grave ailments, especially tuberculosis and venereal diseases. Their waning vitality presently showed in a startling reduction of their rate of increase. At the close of the Civil War, the Negro population numbered about 4,500,000. For a while the emancipated Negroes bred with tropical fecundity, so that by 1880 they had increased to over 6,500,000—a gain of nearly 34 percent. But by 1890 their rate of increase dropped to 14 percent; by 1910 it had dropped still further to 11 percent, while the last census (1920) showed a gain of only 6.5 percent. To be sure, in 1910 the Negro death rate, which in the preceding decades had been enormous, showed a decided improvement, which was maintained by the census of 1920. But that factor was more than offset by a steady decline in the birth rate. Everything seems to portend that the Negro's former high fecundity will not return. According to the census of 1920, the Negro population is increasing only one-third as fast as the White (6.5 percent as against 16 percent), and the weight of expert opinion predicts that the Negro element will henceforth be nearly stationary, if it does not absolutely decline. The present-day tremendous Negro exodus from the countryside to the cities and industrial centers of both North and South must tend to check Negro fecundity. In almost all American cities Negroes die faster than they are born. Since the cityward tide is composed mostly of young Negroes, or Negroes in their early prime, the sterilizing effects of city life on the race as a whole should become more and more pronounced as time goes on.

Few competent observers consider the prospects of the Negro population, taken as a whole, to be particularly bright. The sifting process that began with emancipation is continuing inexorably. A minority of Negroes have so adjusted themselves to their environment that they have attained economic well-being or even wealth. But the bulk of the race is still shiftless and improvident, while the vicious, criminal residue is distressingly large. The leadership of Booker Washington in the middle nineties did arrest the rapid downward trend that had continued since emancipation. Booker Washington's gospel of self-help and self-respect through honest work did an enormous amount of good. He told his people frankly that unless they got busy and made the most of their opportunities, they would find even their present chances gone and would end in hopeless racial bankruptcy. Booker Washington's solemn warning that the Negro must save himself and must adjust himself to American life or be inexorably scrapped by Nature as she scraps all organisms that cannot adapt themselves to their environment produced an immediate effect. Someone has said that Booker Washington changed a *crying* race into a *trying* race." Certainly, from the mid-nineties to the present day, the number of successful Negro farmers and artisans, which before then had been actually declining, has been increasing in a most hopeful way.

Yet the results of the "Tuskegee Movement," headed by Booker Washington until his death and now ably continued by his successor, Doctor Moton, should not be overestimated. What the Tuskegee movement did was to rouse the able minority to a sense of reality and give them a gospel of hope, which enlisted their best efforts. It is this minority (and it is a large minority) that has been making real progress. But the majority of the race seems to have continued to drift, still immersed in its old delusions, and today tends to listen to false prophets of violence and race-hatred whose call, if followed, will lead the Negro to destruction.

The fate of the American Negro will probably be decided within the next twenty or thirty years. If the Negro hearkens to his revolutionary leaders, race tension will rapidly increase and will culminate in an explosion that must end in the Negro's defeat and probable ruin. If race relations improve, the next few decades should show whether the Negro can make a place for himself in the fabric of American life.

One thing seems clear: the Negro is not going to die out by natural causes in the near future. Even if the bulk of the race should so fail to meet the increasingly exacting requirements of our strenuous age that it must eventually be weeded out, the process of elimination would take several generations. A group numbering over 10,500,000 is not going to disappear overnight. Therefore, we need not here discuss the arguments for or against the Negro's ultimate elimination by natural selection, because this book deals with practical problems of the present and the near future, not with remote eventualities. Thus, the race question will be an important factor in any program of national reconstruction. The Negro is here, with his peculiar racial temperament, which, being inborn, will not change, although specific traits may be either so stimulated or so inhibited that a workable adjustment to American life can be made.

The outstanding feature of American Negro-dom today is the presence of two sharply contrasted schools of thought: one striving for a peaceful adjustment within the existing scheme of things, the other demanding the immediate abolition of the color line and threatening race war or revolution at the first likely opportunity if this demand be not acknowledged. Of course, both groups are minorities, the bulk of the Negro population not being clearly affiliated with either. However, the fact that these rival groups are as yet relatively small minorities should not blind us to their significance. The whole trend of the times is making the Negro more conscious of his situation and his problems. In the near future we shall probably see the

Negro population definitely ranged under these two banners, since there is no third party in sight. Furthermore, the line-up may come suddenly, because the Negro is temperamentally crowd-minded and easily swayed by leadership that appeals to his emotions. The Negro is extremely susceptible to crowd contagion. That is one reason why the recent massing of Negroes in cities is politically so important. Twenty years ago, the Negroes were mostly a rural population scattered through the South and largely out of touch with one another except locally. Today more than 4,000,000 Negroes are city dwellers—over one-third of the entire Negro population. These urban Negroes live in the closest possible group contact and are thus highly susceptible to crowd contagion. Add to this the development of a Negro press, numbering hundreds of newspapers and periodicals of every kind, and we can realize how rapid would be the evolution of Negro public opinion and how unexpectedly political movements may arise that might sweep the Negro masses into line.

Let us first examine the radical minority, which demands the abolition of the color line and is ready to risk race war or social revolution to attain its ends. We have no desire to be alarmist, but we believe that, today at least, the radicals are getting far more recruits than the moderates are obtaining for their program of a peaceful, evolutionary adjustment of race relations. Who, then, are the Negro radicals, and on what elements can they especially rely?

Today, as formerly, the strength of the Negro radicals is in the North. There is nothing new about the present radicals. They are the lineal successors of those Northern free Negroes who in slavery times sat at the feet of the White radical abolitionists and there imbibed the doctrines of racial equality and amalgamation. Since those free Negroes were largely Mulattoes, they were peculiarly susceptible to the appeal of such doctrines. During Reconstruction, many of them went South to be leaders to the freedmen, and they in fact often held political office and played an important part in the Reconstruction regime. The downfall of Reconstruction sent them promptly North again, accompanied by many Southern Negroes who had been politically active and who had, therefore, become marked men to the victorious Southern Whites. Bitter and disillusioned at the failure of their hopes, these exiles kept up an agitation that, however vain as regards the South, did enlist most Northern Negroes in their ranks and thus maintained an organized radical group.

For many years this radical group declined in importance. Until the great northward migration of recent times, the Negro population of the

North was small and was economically losing ground before the competition of European immigrants, who ousted the Negroes from many lines of work that they had traditionally held. The appearance of Booker Washington in the mid-nineties dealt the Northern radicals a heavy blow. The Tuskegee movement appealed so strongly to the more able Negroes of the South, anxious to find some way of adjusting themselves to the realities of their situation, that they turned away from radical insistence upon abstract "rights" which could not be obtained to Booker Washington's hopeful gospel of self-help and good relations with their White neighbors for the furtherance of mutual economic interests.

The Northern radical Negroes were furious. They denounced Booker Washington as a traitor to his race and called the supporters of the Tuskegee movement "White folks' niggers" and other unpleasant names. The Northern radicals kept up an organized opposition, headed by a number of leaders of oratorical and journalistic ability, including such well-known radicals as W. M. Trotter and Doctor Dubois. Nevertheless, down to the Great War, their influence was confined mainly to the relatively small Negro population of the North. In the South, where dwelt the great majority of the race, articulate Negro opinion tended to favor Booker Washington and his moderate counsels.

The Great War, however, dramatically changed the situation and led to an acute crisis in race relations. The stoppage of immigration caused a tremendous demand for Native labor, and a vast migration of Negroes from the South to the Northern industrial centers soon produced a large Negro element in the North, earning good wages and thus laying the economic foundations for a prosperous group life. Unfortunately, bitter friction arose between the newcomers and the White resident workers, while the sudden expansion of Negro quarters in Northern cities led to further race friction and social disturbances of the gravest kind. Meanwhile, the wholesale drafting of Negroes into the army and their shipment to France (a country with no color line) produced a new aggravation of the racial situation. Finally, the general unrest and the wave of revolutionary agitation that marked the close of the war completed the embroilment of race relations. The upshot was a racial crisis throughout America, of unparalleled magnitude, culminating in terrible urban riots and in serious agrarian disturbances in parts of the South.

Now all this was grist for the radical mill. Accordingly, the war and post-war periods witnessed a rapid growth of radical influence and prestige. The death of Booker Washington, in 1915, had been a heavy loss to the moderates, and though they managed to hold their ground, the radicals not only established their ascendancy among the Negro newcomers in the North but also made notable gains in the South.

The growing strength of the radicals is shown by the widening circle of their leaders. Before the war, the radical Negro movement was essentially a Mulatto movement. Of this, Doctor Dubois is a good example. Doctor Dubois is a light Mulatto, and he typifies the intense resentment felt by such persons at the color line which debars them from full incorporation with the White race. Since the war, however, many full-blooded Negroes have joined the radical camp, not merely from desire for social equality but also because they believe the breakdown of the color line would remove economic handicaps to the Negro's material advancement.

Another factor that should be noted is the role played by foreign-born Negroes in the radical movement. Claude McKay, known for his poetry and his Bolshevism, is a Jamaican. From Jamaica, likewise, came Marcus Garvey, who started out as a believer in race war but who later became convinced that this would mean the American Negro's annihilation and so evolved his dramatic "Pan-African" idea for the return of the Negroes to their ancestral homeland.

To the radical Negroes and Mulattoes, we must also add certain White radicals, especially the Communists and other revolutionary agitators. Moscow sees in the Negro a useful tool for its plans of Bolshevizing America and is therefore doing everything possible to bring on a racial explosion here.

Such is the officers' corps, which is today mobilizing the Negro radicals into what they hope will be an efficient army for the grand assault on the color line.

Only those who read the Negro press and periodicals can have any idea of the violent and inflammatory propaganda that has been going on since the war. A few Negro radical publications are well edited, notably *The Crisis*, the organ of Doctor Dubois, who is a highly educated man of genuine literary talent. Most radical publications, however, descend to mere rant and diatribe. Yet, whether expressed in polished periods or in cheap vilification, the spirit is the same. Always there is the same insistence upon "natural rights," the same angry rejection of compromise, and the same threats of race war or social revolution if radical demands are not speedily and fully granted.

The general temper of this radical Negro propaganda, together with a warning note as to its probable consequences, is admirably stated by Professor Dowd in his recent study of the Negro problem. Says Professor Dowd: "The Northern (Negro) papers are more radical and more bitter than those of the South. With a few exceptions they are extremely partisan and discuss political issues, especially those concerning conditions in the South, with such passion as to destroy candor and the capacity to form a judgment related to facts. Their attitude toward the White South is that of frenzied hatred and vengefulness. They see in the Southern White man only a monster of iniquity who deserves condign punishment for his sins against the Negro. They profess to believe that the White South is endeavoring, with might and main, to reduce the Negro again to a state of slavery. They denounce very justly the lynchings and other injustices to which the Southern Negroes are subjected but scorn to credit the White South with any worthy endeavor or achievement on behalf of the colored population. Any evidence of improvement in the status of the Southern Negro seems to be actually unwelcome to them as diminishing the fuel for the flame of malice. The Northern (Negro) press seeks, above everything else, to inspire the Southern Negroes with a hatred of their White neighbors, and to a large extent it has succeeded in doing so. Consequently, it looks with disfavor upon the movement for cooperation in the South between the two races. The rabid Northern (Negro) press needs to learn that in cultivating hatred between the races in the South, it is doing the same for the races in the North."[2]

Referring to violent Negro publications exemplified by W. M. Trotter's organ, *The Guardian*. Professor Dowd writes:, "Trotter's newspaper and others of like kind throughout the North keep up an incessant tirade against what they call race prejudice, totally oblivious of the fact that they exhibit more of it than any other class in America. If any Southern White editor should carry on a campaign of abuse of the Negro half so full of narrowness, malevolence, and ignorant prejudice as is characteristic of a large section of the Northern Negro press, he would be universally condemned by Southern sentiment. The Trotter type of newspaper is blind to the fact that, in inflaming the passions of the Negro against the Southern Whites, they are at the same time kindling race animosities in the North and are driving all Whites and Blacks into opposing camps. It is amazing that the race that has the most to lose from race prejudice should be the most deliberate and aggressive in stirring it up. The rampant type of Negro would do well to take the hint thrown out by the Chicago *Tribune*, to wit: 'The Blacks form less than 10 percent of the population of the United States. They have less than one-tenth of a ghost of a show if the relations between White and

---

2. Dowd, Jerome: *The Negro in American Life*, p. 353 (1926).

# The Dilemma of Color

Black become bitterly hostile.'"³

Such warnings have apparently fallen on deaf ears, for the radical propaganda keeps right on, oblivious to, or defiant of, probable consequences. As far back as the close of the war, Doctor Dubois announced in *The Crisis*:

"We return.
We return from fighting.
We return fighting."

In the autumn of 1919, Doctor Dubois sounded the keynote of radical extremism by exclaiming editorially, "We have cast off on the voyage which will lead to freedom or to death!" At the same moment, another leading radical publication, *The Messenger*, edited by two young Negro college graduates of pronounced revolutionary leanings, came out with an uncompromising demand for full social equality, particularly stressing "sex equality."

The furious rage at the color line voiced by many Negro radicals is nowhere more strikingly revealed than in the following stanza from a poem by Claude McKay entitled *White Houses*:

"Your door is shut against my tightened face,
And I am sharp as steel with discontent,
But I possess the courage and the grace
To bear my anger proudly and unbent.
The pavement slabs burn loose beneath my feet,
A chafing savage, down the decent street,
And passion rends my vitals as I pass,
Where boldly shines your shuttered door of glass."⁴

Claude McKay is the most notorious member of that group of firebrands who are today busy spreading the sparks of a racial conflagration. Stigmatizing the United States as "a cultured hell," McKay has expressed the wish that the whole White world might be swallowed by the earth or go up in smoke. Accompanied by a notorious White radical, Max Eastman, he has made a pilgrimage to Moscow, where he received a tremendous ovation and, amid scenes of wild enthusiasm, made the most incendiary speeches against

---
3. Dowd, *op. cit.,* p. 517.
4. Quoted from the collaborative volume edited by Alain Locke, entitled: *The New Negro,* p. 134 (1925).

America. Other Negro radicals have gone to Moscow and have returned here. One of them recently organized a Communist Negro labor group. There also exists in America an ultra-radical Negro secret order called "The African Blood-Brotherhood." Undoubtedly Bolshevik money (and plenty of it) has been, and is being, spent in America for revolutionary propaganda among the Negro population. At the present moment a number of young American Negro radicals are in Russia, where they are being carefully trained as Bolshevik apostles to their race.

Such is the radical Negro movement—a movement not only supported by a considerable portion of American Negrodom but also stimulated by foreign-born Negroes, by certain White revolutionary radicals, and by the powerful Bolshevik propaganda directed from Moscow.

Now we do not wish to be alarmist, and in our next chapter we shall show that notable factors of conciliation exist which, by the wisdom and good sense of the best elements of both races, may well evolve a compromise program that will ensure social peace for at least a generation and that may evolve into a lasting system of racial adjustment. But peace will not come of itself. Clear thinking and constructive action on both sides can alone check those malevolent forces today, preparing a great racial explosion. For the good of both races, therefore, let us speak plainly and not mince our words.

First and foremost, *the color line is going to stay*, and every attack upon it will merely result in its being made stronger and stricter in its details. To threaten White America as the Negro radicals are now doing is useless, because no disasters that White America could possibly undergo would, in its opinion, outweigh the supreme disaster that White America would certainly undergo by the loss of its race-existence. There are enough Negroes in America to tinge us all with Black blood. Since the Negroes form nearly one-tenth of the population, we are *statistically* light Mulattoes. The only thing that keeps us from being *biologically* Mulattoes is the color line. And the overwhelming majority of White Americans, North, South, East, and West, will risk anything *and will do anything* rather than see White America become a Mulatto America. With a few exceptions, White Americans would prefer to die, to see their children dead, and to have their race perish from off the face of the earth rather than jeopardize the birthright of even their remote posterity.

Such being the practically unanimous attitude of White America, the agitation and menaces of the Negro radicals are nothing short of madness—for themselves and their race. At present, the average White man either knows little about them or declines to take them seriously. But the stronger and more successful their propaganda becomes, the more the Negro radicals are awakening among the Whites a passion of racial self-preservation that, if thoroughly aroused, will stop at nothing. The Negro's position would become simply intolerable, and an impossible situation would automatically explode into race war.

Once again let us emphasize the fact that drift is the most perilous of policies. Both races must resolutely face the situation, or it will ultimately face them in very real and terrible fashion. The American Negro today stands at a critical parting of the ways. Not only are the more capable and ambitious elements attaining a distinct material well-being, but the race as a whole is awakening to a self-consciousness never before known. In the Negro quarter of our big cities there is developing a well-marked community life. Harlem, the Negro section of New York, has become a real Negro capital, the spiritual center of the race, where many interesting cultural forms express in poetry, music, and the arts those emotional gifts that the Negro undoubtedly possesses and that he may fruitfully develop for his own happiness and the enrichment of the world's cultural store. And this the Negro can do by remaining himself and evolving his own race-life.

Will he do so? Or will his aroused self-consciousness and vaulting ambitions cause him to follow leaders who urge him to reject a separate race-life and seek to mingle his existence with that of a race that resolutely refuses to merge its race-life with any other? If the Negro tries to do that, his material advancement and awakened self-consciousness will merely lead to his undoing.

Such is the "dilemma of color" that today confronts us. Is there a way out? Let us see.

# CHAPTER XII
# BIRACIALISM: THE KEY TO SOCIAL PEACE

IN THE PRECEDING CHAPTER OUR analysis of the "dilemma of color" led us, seemingly, to most pessimistic conclusions. The Negro radicals' insistent demand for the abolition of the color line and the uncompromising refusal of White America to make any concessions that might spell amalgamation appeared to result in a deadlock whose logical end was race war.

However, we then remarked that this was not the whole story; that other factors existed which hopefully modified the situation and which might eventually lead to a constructive adjustment of race relations that, while maintaining the color line, would yet give adequate scope for the Negro's growing self-consciousness and desire for advancement. To a consideration of these hopeful, constructive factors, let us now turn.

The impression probably made upon most readers of Negro radical literature, even when they know little about the race problem, is one of distorted unreality. Such readers instinctively feel that the facts presented are not all the facts and that the intense emotions voiced by radical writers are not shared by the majority of the Negro population. If the incidents of oppression and injustice featured in radical journals were typical, and if all, or even most, Negroes felt the same burning flame of revolt, the racial situation would everywhere be simply intolerable. The South, especially, would be a searing volcano of racial strife, and even though the Negroes might not at present venture armed revolt, both sides would generally recognize that race war was inevitable and would be actively preparing for the great explosion.

Now every sensible person knows that this is not the case. It does not need first hand knowledge of the South to recognize that conditions there are, generally speaking, peaceful and stable. For every Southern community that gets into the newspapers, there are a dozen tat have no serious racial troubles. Despite much minor friction and occasional outbreaks of violence, the races manage to get along tolerably well, cooperate sufficiently to ensure sound material progress, and evince much evidence of genuine amicability and mutual regard. The last few years, especially, have witnessed in the South an unprecedented degree of racial harmony and desire for friendly cooperation. Surely all this would be impossible if conditions were anywhere nearly as bad as Northern radical Negroes make out.

Let us, therefore, survey the Southern situation as it really is, and let us hear what the Southern Negro himself has to say. It may be that we shall discover many harmonizing factors and constructive ideas that Northern Negro radicals either deride, minimize, or ignore.

The cardinal fact of Southern life is the color line. The color line, which Northern radicals denounce as intolerable and untenable, has in the South become the recognized foundation of society, accepted in practice by the vast majority of both races as part of the natural order of things. Out of the chaotic uncertainties of the Reconstruction period, the South has evolved a clear-cut system of racial segregation. From birth to death the color line functions efficiently to keep Black and White in their respective social spheres. As infants, they are born in different parts of their native city, town, or village. In childhood and youth, they are educated in separate schools and colleges. As adults, they work largely in non-competing lines and seek recreation in different restaurants and places of amusement. On Sundays they go to separate churches. In travel they occupy separate railroad cars and put up at different hotels. Finally, when they die, they are embalmed by different undertakers and are buried in separate cemeteries. Everywhere racial contacts are systematically minimized; every year racial segregation becomes more pronounced and is more frankly recognized by both races as the basic fact of Southern life.

Furthermore, this system of racial separation is as firmly established by law as it is by custom and public opinion. The Supreme Court has definitely ruled that race segregation does not violate the Fifteenth Amendment of the Federal Constitution, so long as its action is mutual. In other words, if Whites and Negroes are equally forbidden to intrude on the respective spheres assigned to the other race, there is no legal "discrimination." Therefore, the South's social system accords with the basic law of the land and cannot be upset by any adverse Federal judicial ruling.

One point of great significance is the fact that in those parts of the South where race separation is most clearly defined, race friction is least in evidence. A good example is the city of Charleston, South Carolina. In this ultra-Southern city, situated in the heart of the "Black Belt," segregation is unusually thorough. Yet Charleston, with its great Negro population, has never had a race riot or other serious racial trouble. The worst racial outbreaks have usually occurred where race relations had not been well defined and where the rougher elements of both races were in close contact with one another. Indeed, that is one of the reasons why sensible Southern Negroes recognize the beneficial effects of segregation on themselves. Wherever low-down, rowdy Negroes and low-down, rowdy "White trash," full of bad liquor and looking for trouble, are thrown together, there are bound to be fights that may grow into race riots from which the whole community suffers. Nearly all sensible persons, without distinction of color, realize that the less the races touch at their lower levels, the better for both.

The truth is that, instead of moving toward race war, as Northern radicals assert, the general trend in the South is away from race war and toward a stable adjustment of race relations. During Reconstruction, things were at their worst. Since then, the situation has been steadily improving. When Reconstruction collapsed, the Negroes at first simply bowed to superior force. But in the half-century that has since elapsed, the bewildered mass of freedmen has evolved a group life of its own that offers material rewards and social satisfactions inside the Negro community. Southern Negrodom is today a well-differentiated social system, with its own professional and middle classes and with a richly diversified social life. Ambitious young Negroes can now satisfy their desire for a career without running up against the color line. There are good opportunities to acquire money and reputation on their own side. That is one of the main reasons why most able, thoughtful Negroes in the South today belong to that moderate party that believes in good relations with its White neighbors and a working out of racial adjustment through mutual understanding.

To Booker Washington, the launching of a genuine moderate movement is primarily due. Before his rise to leadership, Southern Negrodom had vegetated in the bewildered, embittered disillusionment into which it had been plunged by the collapse of Reconstruction. It was Booker Washington who not only awakened the best elements of his own race to courage and hope but also showed the White South that there were sensible, intelligent Negroes who had renounced vain dreams and were ready to go forward on a basis of existing realities. Booker Washington's famous Atlanta address, delivered in the year 1895, marks a new epoch in Southern life. His memorable phrase was, "In all things purely social we can be as separate as the fingers, yet one as the hand in all things essential to mutual progress."

The way that phrase electrified both races showed that the time was ripe for the best minds of both races to evolve something better than war cries like "Social Equality!" and "Keep the Nigger Down!" In fact, the generation that has elapsed since the Atlanta address has seen a remarkable clarifying of thought in the South on the race question. Nearly all forward-looking White Southerners today believe in Negro education and welcome the

Negro's economic and cultural advancement. As a recent Southern writer well says, "There is now a much more substantial agreement on many of the so-called Negro problems than there has been in the past. Doctor Edgar Gardner Murphy, writing in 1904, said, 'Because no ten men have ever yet agreed as to what we shall do, the Negro presents something more than a task; he presents a problem.' The lapse of twenty years has marked a genuinely encouraging tendency to dispel this disagreement. Not ten, but ten thousand men agree that the Negro must have equal justice in the courts, must receive training for life in the complex democracy of the United States, must be instructed and safeguarded in the preservation of health, and must receive a square deal in economic life. This substantial agreement is rapidly replacing the intellectual confusion that followed the Civil War."[1]

This statement undoubtedly reflects the present attitude of the intelligent White South. The policy of race separation does not imply an intention to degrade the Negro. The idea is not to assign the Negro a lower place but to accord him a *different* place, based upon the fact that the two races are so different that, despite incidental hardships, social separation is in the best interests of both.

Again, the White South today realizes that an ignorant, poverty-stricken, degenerate mass of Negroes is at once a social menace and an economic handicap, which should be remedied by education and fair treatment. And by "education" the South no longer means merely manual training. The old idea that "education always spoils a Negro" has been pretty well discarded. Intelligent Southerners now discriminate between education's primary and secondary effects. They know that while a smattering of "book learning" may upset an ignorant Negro's balance and make him hard to deal with, the trouble there is not education *per se* but superficial education. What the South insists upon is that Negro education shall include character-building and shall exclude radical teaching that produces bitterness and vain discontent. Where Negro education is sound and constructive, it is warmly welcomed and assisted by the White South. Tuskegee Institute is a good example. This creation of Booker Washington has the hearty sympathy of White Southerners and is helped by them in every way. Under the wise guidance of Doctor Moton, Booker Washington's successor, Tuskegee remains the headquarters of the moderate, constructive forces in American Negro life.

That Doctor Moton is inspired by Booker Washington's spirit can be seen by the following characteristic remarks uttered a short time ago. Addressing a Negro audience, Doctor Moton said, "I want to give you some

---

1. Woofter, Thomas J.: *The Basis of Racial Readjustment*, p. 1 (1925).

good advice. There are many things we can learn from the White race to our profit. A member of the White race is never ashamed to admit that he is a White man. I know one race that seems to think that God cursed them when He made them Black. Don't let anybody fool you into believing that God cursed the Black race. Don't feel that you have to apologize to every man you meet because you have got a Black face.

"The White man can beat me at being a White man, but I can beat him at being a Negro. I am proud of my race. There is no race in history that has made as much progress in the last sixty years as we have made. Don't be ashamed of your race. Everybody respects an American because Americans believe in America. To respect your own race means that you will get respect from other races. If we do not respect ourselves, we can be sure that other people won't respect us. Self-respect begets self-respect. Let's show the White race that we believe in ourselves."[2]

Self-respect and a frank facing of realities increasingly characterize the more able and intelligent Negroes of the South. If the Negro population were not continually stirred up by Northern radical propaganda, it is probable that the best elements of both races would by this time have evolved a stable basis for the adjustment of race relations. Sensible moderates like Doctor Moton realize that race separation is not an abnormal fiat arbitrarily imposed, but that it is a social phenomenon produced by the co-existence of two widely different races on the same territory. The natural instinct that sociologists term "consciousness of kind," and which appears in animals as well as in man, inevitably tends to make each type flock by itself and normally causes it to find greater satisfaction in association with its fellows. Thus, intelligent Southern Negroes accept race separation, not merely as a necessity or as a helpful method of averting social friction, but also as the wisest and best arrangement for both races in the long run. Therefore, they do not object on principle to legal measures of segregation but require only that such measures shall apply equally and shall not be unfairly or humiliatingly administered. For example, they do not object to separate Negro schools. What they ask is that Negro schools shall be good and adequate. Again, they do not denounce separate railway coaches but do criticize the lack of Pullman and dining-car facilities. If existing discriminations in such matters were fairly adjusted, the policy of racesegregation would be genuinely accepted by the most influential elements of Southern Negrodom.

The very real advantages to be gained by a separate race-life become clear when we consider what the Negro has already gained by his tacit

---

2. Quoted from *The Negro Year-Book* for 1925-26, p. 76.

acceptance of race segregation in the South. If the Southern Negroes had followed radical counsels and had stubbornly rebelled against the color line, they would either have been long since crushed in a hopeless race war or would today be vegetating in general misery. By accepting the situation and making the most of their opportunities, a considerable section of the race has risen to material well-being and has evolved a satisfactory group life. Booker Washington saw this clearly when he wrote, "The division of the races is an advantage to us as a people, insofar as it permits us to become the teachers of our own people. No better discipline can be given to a people than that which they gain by being their own teachers. They can have no greater opportunity than that of developing within themselves the ideals and the leadership that are to make them not merely in law but in fact the masters of their own fortunes."[3]

On the larger aspects of the subject, Dowd makes some very pertinent comments. "What would happen to the Negroes in the South," he writes, "if they were not segregated? They would have to compete in every occupation with the Whites; they would find the door of opportunity practically closed to them in all the higher walks of life. It would rarely happen that a Negro could secure a position as a teacher in a school, as a pastor of a church, or as an editor of a paper. There would be no Negro doctors, dentists, lawyers, actors, or singers. Even in the unskilled trades they would have to compete with the White man.

"What does the Negro gain by segregation? He finds in the South a large field of employment open to him with little or no competition from the Whites. In other words, segregation enables him to lead an easier and less strenuous existence, which ensures him a diminishing death rate and a higher birth rate; also, it enables him to resist the downward pressure into poverty, vice, and crime. Above all, segregation builds up cooperation and race pride and, by diminishing the incentive to imitate the Whites, tends to bring out in the race its special aptitudes and geniuses. The progress of mankind can be best advanced by each race's developing the genius and culture peculiar to it instead of striving to imitate another.

"Segregation enables the Negro to find among his own people as many opportunities in the higher walks of life as are found among the White people. He may be a merchant, banker, doctor, lawyer, dentist, schoolteacher, college president, pastor of a church, editor of a paper, actor, musician, officer in a lodge, and so forth. In many Southern states there are more Negroes holding high positions in professional life than in the entire

---
3. Washington, Booker T.: *The American Negro of Today*, p. 67.

territory of Brazil, where segregation has largely broken down as a result of racial intermixture."[4]

Furthermore, wise Negro leaders realize that a stable adjustment of race relations based on mutual goodwill is necessary in order to give the still backward Negro masses a chance in the increasingly strenuous competition of American life. Such leaders know that the time is coming when there will be a White man or woman available for every job in the land. When that time comes, the average Negro will need not only to be efficient enough to hold a job but also well-liked enough to get a job at all. Thus, friendly relations with their White neighbors will become more, rather than less, important to the Negro as time goes on.

Nothing is more significant than the way Negro public opinion in the South not only tends to accept social segregation but also positively dislikes the very idea of racial amalgamation. Having built up a satisfactory group existence, Southern Negrodom is increasingly content to lead its own race life. Indeed, throughout the United States, North as well as South, racial intermixture is today decidedly on the wane. This is true of both legal and extra-legal contacts. Even in the North, where marriage between Whites and Negroes is legally possible, such unions (always infrequent) are now very rare. Mostly between the lowest elements of both races, these marriages almost invariably lead to tragic consequences. The few interracial marriages that have occurred between educated persons have been perhaps the most tragic of all, because both parties have been promptly ostracized alike by reputable Whites and Negroes, and they have therefore become outcasts, cut off from social standing of any kind.

Legal marriage has, of course, always been a negligible factor in racial intermixture. The chief factors have been extra-legal concubinage and casual sex relations between Negro women and White men, usually termed "miscegenation." Now the interesting fact is that miscegenation is also rapidly decreasing. It has, indeed, been decreasing steadily for the past fifty years. The patriarchal situation under slavery and the free-and-easy conditions after emancipation, which favored miscegenation, have disappeared. Except in a few rural backwaters of the South, where old customs persist, cohabitation with colored girls is considered disgraceful by White public opinion. No White man who values the respect of his community can afford to let such conduct be known. And among respectable Negro circles, likewise, the birth of a Mulatto baby by a White father is considered a misfortune and a disgrace. Most miscegenation at present takes the form of casual sex contacts,

---
4. Dowd, *op. cit.*, pp. 475-476.

in the cities and towns, between debauched colored women and vicious White men. Obviously, factors like venereal disease and abortion render the number of children from such sources comparatively few. Therefore, it seems clear that race mixture in America is falling to relatively minor proportions. On this matter, it may be interesting to note that the same thing is occurring in South Africa, which has a color problem very similar to our own. In South Africa miscegenation, once widespread under the patriarchal conditions of Boer slavery, has now almost ceased.

The momentous importance of all this is surely obvious. If the influx of White blood into the Negro population stops (as it has today apparently almost stopped), the whole nature of the race question will gradually change—and change for the better. What principally embitters race relations is the Mulatto. It is the Mulatto who is the explosive element in the race problem, because it is he who longs for "social equality" and amalgamation with the White race, to which he is partly allied in blood. We have already seen that the Northern radical movement is essentially a Mulatto movement. A certain number of full-blooded Negroes are found in the radical camp, but it is a significant fact that many of them are actuated more by economic than by racial considerations.

The genuine Negro realizes that he is different from the White man and is usually content with the society of his fellows. Naturally easy-going and good-natured, the Negro rarely harbors bitterness over abstract matters like "social equality." If he is fairly treated and enjoys a moderate share of the good things of life, he is certainly not likely of his own accord to risk present well-being by dubious and dangerous efforts to gain theoretical "rights."

However, as already remarked, the Negro is highly emotional and easily swayed by crowd contagion. This is why the character of his leaders is so important. Skillful Mulatto agitators can sweep impressionable Negroes off their feet and get them to do things that they themselves would never think of doing. As a recent writer well says, "Our colored population may be likened to a huge mass of high explosive—a product composed of a comparatively inert ingredient mixed with a small amount of highly explosive 'sensitizing agent,' the detonation of which causes a violent explosion of the far larger mass of the normally non-explosive ingredient. And the explosive element of the race problem dynamite is the Mulatto."[5]

Since the Mulatto, and especially the light Mulatto, is the real challenger of the color line, any diminution in his numbers, while it might not make much immediate difference, would profoundly ease race tension as time

---

5. Gregg, W. W.: "The Mulatto—Crux of the Negro Problem," *Current History*, March, 1924.

went on. And the weight of evidence clearly indicates that light Mulattoes are rapidly decreasing. On this point the census figures are especially revealing. These figures admittedly indicate only roughly the proportion of White blood in the entire colored population, since many dark Mulattoes are classed as full-blooded Negroes. But the census returns do give us a good idea of the number of Mulattoes with one-half or more than one-half of White blood. Up to the census of 1910, the number of Mulattoes steadily increased. In that year, 2,151,000 persons were enumerated as Mulattoes—nearly 21 percent of the entire colored population. But the census of 1920 showed only 1,660,000 Mulattoes—an absolute decrease of nearly 500,000 and a relative decrease to 15.9 percent of the total colored population. Whatever their minor inaccuracies, these figures undoubtedly portray the general trend. In this connection, the author may remark that when he visited Tuskegee last year, he noted the relative scarcity of light Mulattoes among the student body, drawn as it is from all parts of the South. One of the older members of the faculty informed the author that the proportion of light Mulatto students had been diminishing for years and was markedly less than it had been a decade before.

The decrease of light Mulattoes in the colored population is due not merely to lessening miscegenation but also to the fact that light-Mulatto families average fewer children than darker Mulattoes and Negroes. This may be partly caused by relative infertility, as has been often alleged, but it is also caused by social reasons. Light Mulattoes are most attracted by city life and are most apt to imitate White living standards. Such persons likewise feel their anomalous racial status so keenly that they often do not care to bring children into the world. As a result of all these factors, light Mulattoes are today rapidly decreasing, and everything indicates that this decrease will continue.

On the other hand, the number of dark Mulattoes is probably increasing through intermarriage or cohabitation between Mulattoes and Negroes. If this process continues at its present rate, the colored population may ultimately come to consist mainly of dark Mulattoes, with relatively few full-blooded Negroes and with almost no Mulattoes of the lighter shades. This would, however, ease race tension almost as much as if the colored population were pure Black, because dark Mulattoes usually have the Negro temperament and are so clearly differentiated from the Whites that they rarely feel the "near-White" Mulatto's keen desire to cross the color line.

Another hopeful aspect is the fact that not even the light Mulattoes are a unit in bitterness and stubborn hostility to racial separation. Taken as a whole, the Southern Mulattoes do not share the radical ideas of their Northern fellows. Under slavery the Southern Mulattoes were the aristocracy of Negrodom and evolved a group life of their own that satisfied their social desires. This situation still persists in many parts of the South. In conservative Southern cities like Charleston and Savannah, the light Mulattoes form a social caste that holds itself apart from the rest of the colored population. In New Orleans, especially, Mulatto society is highly complex, with various grades that are carefully maintained. This caste arrangement, which was general before the Civil War, did not favor the interests of the colored population as a whole, since it made the Mulattoes indifferent to the lot of the Negroes and created jealous antagonism between the two elements. But it certainly did ease race tension, because it gave the light Mulattoes a satisfying social status and thus lulled their instinctive discontent at the color line.

Reconstruction threw the Southern Mulattoes into profound mental and emotional confusion. They listened eagerly to the doctrines of social equality and amalgamation preached by Northern White and Mulatto radicals, and for a while most light Mulattoes actually hoped to cross the colorline and escape further connection with the Negroes, whom they secretly or openly despised. But the collapse of Reconstruction showed the Southern Mulattoes that this was impossible. There followed a most painful period of disillusionment and readjustment. Some Mulattoes went North in despairing rage. Others, though remaining in the South, never really accepted the situation and continued to eat their hearts out in vain bitterness. This type of Mulatto today heads the Southern radical element, which is in close touch with the Northern radicals and which goes as far as it dares in fomenting race friction and spreading radical propaganda.

The Southern radical group is, however, relatively small. Most Southern Mulattoes have either fallen back on the old caste status, finding thereby a measure of social satisfaction for their balked racial desires, or, throwing in their lot with the Negroes, they seek material advancement and social prestige within the larger group life of the colored race. Booker Washington is the outstanding example of this latter type of Mulatto, and his attitude has had a profound effect in welding the different elements of the colored population. Most Southern Mulattoes today consider themselves members of the "Negro race." They live *inside* Negrodom and have definitely merged themselves with the Negroes for mutual advancement and common aims. Renouncing their former dream of crossing the color line, these Mulattoes have found present contentment and a satisfying future. Their social and psychological status being fixed, disillusionment and bitterness have faded, and they are usually as averse to radical incitements as are moderate-minded Negroes.

The Northern Mulattoes thus remain, today as formerly, the core of the radical movement. Their bitter, fanatical temper is due chiefly to their social and intellectual past. The Northern Mulattoes have never enjoyed a real group life of their own. Too few in numbers to form a well-established society like that of their Southern fellows, their early conversion to the extreme abolitionist doctrine of race amalgamation made it psychologically impossible for them to desire to form one. How could they put forth social roots when their hope was to lose their identity by merging themselves with the White world?

But this hope was vain, because the White North refused to receive them, as uncompromisingly as did the White South. In the North, the color line was drawn differently, but it was drawn hard and fast, just the same. The Civil War made no real change in the situation. The radical Republicans of the Reconstruction period, like the extreme abolitionists before the war, were a mere handful—and even these White radicals did not practice what they preached, since, with a few rare exceptions, they refused to permit racial intermarriage within the circle of their own families.

Thus, for a whole century, the Northern Mulattoes have been leading a most unhappy and uncertain existence. They have been literally suspended in a vacuum, allied to both races, yet really belonging to neither. The Northern Mulattoes refuse to be Negroes and cannot be Whites. The upshot is a tragic sense of loneliness and isolation, which causes the pessimistic, despairing note so often voiced by Northern Mulattoes and perhaps best exemplified by the earlier writings of Doctor Dubois, with their anguished cry from "behind the veil." Unhappier than the traditional "man without a country," the Northern Mulatto feels himself a man without a race. It is this morbid psychosis that largely accounts alike for the Northern Mulatto's despairing bitterness and for his fanatical determination to smash the color line. His entire outlook on life reveals an abnormal attitude that is not found elsewhere in our colored population.

This morbid introspection and intense preoccupation with their own special status accounts for a fact that we noted at the very opening of this chapter—the distorted unreality with which Northern radicals (mostly Mulattoes) view the whole race problem. Such radicals may pose as champions of the Negro race and may be careful to call themselves "Negroes." Yet even a slight knowledge of facts will enable the reader of Northern radical literature to discern that these propagandists are thinking in terms of a special problem—the deracialized Mulatto—and that they are seeking to use the Negro masses for Mulatto ends. Many of these Northern radicals hardly know the South at first hand and have never come in genuine contact with the Negro masses—whom they secretly despise as inferiors. Northern Mulattoes who have actually gone South and mingled with Negro life have often been frightfully disillusioned. One of the most pessimistic books ever written about the Negro is from the pen of an educated Northern Mulatto[6] who went South to be a leader of his people and returned North to frame against them an indictment of a most sweeping and scathing character.

The attitude and agitation of the Northern Mulattoes are resented by many Negroes and by many Southern Mulattoes as well. The Northern radicals who are forever bemoaning their fate and inveighing against the color line are often termed *"hate-to-be-Negroes"* by other members of their race. Indeed, some Negro radicals, though working along the same general lines as the Mulatto radicals, object strongly to Mulatto assumptions of superiority and assert that the genuine Negro, rather than the Mulatto, best knows what the Black race should do and is best fitted for leadership. One well-known Negro radical exclaims, "We, whose brains are still unbastardized, must face the frank realities of this situation of racial conflict and competition."[7] Marcus Garvey's "Pan-African" movement is exclusively a Negro movement and is frankly anti-Mulatto.

Here, again, the general trend seems to indicate that in the future the deracialized Mulatto radical will not be as influential as he is today or has been in the past. As already stated, light Mulattoes are decreasing in number. Furthermore, the recent northward migration, while temporarily strengthening radicalism, should ultimately weaken it by so expanding the Northern colored population that it can evolve a socially satisfying group life like that of the South. Under such circumstances, the Northern Mulattoes would tend more and more to merge themselves with the rest of the colored population, thereby losing their isolation psychosis and the bitter passions that it engenders.

Our survey of the deeper trends of the race problem thus leads us to decidedly optimistic conclusions. The color line works so effectively that miscegenation is rapidly decreasing and should soon become negligible. The policy of race-egregation is being steadily confirmed and is no longer objected to on principle by a large section of the Negro population. Lastly, the Southern majority of the colored population has evolved such a satisfactory

---

6. Thomas, W. Hannibal: *The American Negro (1901)*.
7. Harrison, Hubert H.: *When Africa Awakes*, p, 46 (1920).

group life that it is becoming indifferent to radical agitation.

Yet such trends, however hopeful for the future, should not blind us to dangerous possibilities of the present. While race relations in the South are steadily improving, radicalism is growing among the newly transplanted Negro masses in the industrial centers of the North. In the previous chapter we analyzed the present radical movement and saw that it was not merely a local growth but that it was also being cleverly fostered by Bolshevik and other influences of the most sinister kind. The Northern Negro population must today number fully 2,000,000 and is still increasing by migration from the South and, to a lesser extent, by immigration from abroad. The great Negro quarters of New York, Chicago, and other Northern cities are caldrons seething with ideas and emotions which, by the power of mass contagion, may engender sudden and startling developments. The American Negro is passing through a critical transition stage of awakening self-consciousness, which may turn out for good or for ill.

All this makes it highly necessary that the best minds of both races should meet frankly and evolve a program of racial adjustment soundly based on facts and capable of handling critical situations. Fortunately, such a process of conscious race adjustment has already begun in the South. Let us see what has been accomplished and how it may be extended and amplified.

The movement for bettering race relations by organized effort began shortly before the Great War, through agencies like the Southern Sociological Congress, the University Commission on Southern Race Problems, and the study groups of the Y. M. C. A. These agencies included many eminent Whites and Negroes, with emphasis being laid on the study of facts. The idea was not to attempt any immediate formulation of "solutions," but to analyze the material and psychological factors involved, thus laying a firm basis of ascertained knowledge and developing a truly scientific approach to the larger problems of racial adjustment.

The war temporarily interrupted these investigations, while the wave of unrest and race friction that followed the war temporarily worsened the racial situation. But the very crisis that had arisen revealed the necessity for further action. The terrible urban riots in the North, the widespread disturbances in the South, and the general growth of Negro radicalism acted like a stimulating challenge to the best minds of both races.

Accordingly, in the year 1919, a general conference was held at Atlanta, Georgia, attended by representative Whites and Negroes from all parts of the South. The conference resulted in the establishment of the celebrated Commission on Inter-Racial Cooperation. This Commission is a permanent organization with headquarters in Atlanta, which directs and coordinates the efforts of state and local committees functioning all over the South. The organization has proved a great success. Today over 800 county committees, composed equally of Whites and Negroes, are on the job improving race relations. The idea is to tackle trouble at the start—not merely before it gets acute, but almost before it begins. Furthermore, the Commission deals with larger aspects of race relations like schools, public health, slum conditions, and so forth. The Negro representatives are able to state what they consider to be legitimate grievances on specific points and can discuss matters with their White colleagues in a friendly, open-minded way. Theoretical, controversial issues are taboo. The system of racial segregation is tacitly accepted by both sides as axiomatic, their joint efforts being directed to a practical betterment of conditions within the bounds of the existing social order.

Another harmonizing factor is the excellent work that is being done by Southern women in promoting better race relations. Numerous women's organizations, White and colored, have established helpful contacts with one another and are cooperating on questions of mutual interest such as education, child welfare, and public health. Here, also, controversial topics are excluded by mutual consent.

The combined effect of all these conciliatory agencies is enormous. In the first place, it creates a general atmosphere of friendliness and sympathetic understanding, which is the prerequisite of real progress in racial adjustment. Of course, the individual contacts of Whites and Negroes have always been, on average, much more amicable than outsiders imagine. Except as between their rougher elements, the individual members of both races ordinarily display instinctive tact and good manners toward one another. If this were not so, racial friction would everywhere be acute, and conditions would be intolerable.

What the organized agencies for racial cooperation are doing is to mobilize all this diffused goodwill for community service. They also impress upon individuals the importance of their individual attitude and conduct on community life. Throughout the South, innumerable Whites and Negroes are realizing as never before what a rich harvest they will reap, individually and collectively, by ordinary tact, consideration, and fair dealing, even in their most casual relations. A rude word or a harsh look, when wholly uncalled for, may do lasting harm. This, by the way, is a point that needs to be emphasized in the North even more than in the South. The average White Southerner instinctively knows how to get along with Negroes much better than Northerners do, and the Negro just as instinctively senses the

White man's feeling toward him. The Negro normally respects and likes "quality folks." What riles him is the attitude of the low-class White, without breeding or good manners, whom the Negro (quite rightly) does not respect.

Yet here again outsiders must not think that "White trash" can treat Negroes as they like. The better-class Southern Whites have always looked out for respectable, well-meaning Negroes. Anybody who wantonly picks on a "good Negro" in the South is usually stopped in short order by other White men. The "bad" Negro, or the radical agitator, who tries to "start something," finds trouble—and plenty of it. But the unoffending Negro is rarely mishandled, and when he is, he usually gets justice from the White authorities.

What the South needs, therefore, is chiefly a better enforcement by the White community of good manners toward the Negro on the part of low-class Whites, thereby avoiding most of those needless affronts which, however petty in themselves, are, as Doctor Moton well says, "gravel in the Negro's shoe, small in size, but capable of inflicting great discomfort and impeding progress."

Another great service rendered by organized agencies for interracial cooperation is their bridging of the psychological gulf that opened between the races after the Civil War. In slavery times the races were in close touch and understood one another. After emancipation, the races drew steadily apart, especially at their higher levels. Social relations, in the ordinary sense of the word, being impossible, educated Whites and Negroes could not meet, and each group was therefore almost totally ignorant of the other's attitude. The various interracial organizations that have been established now permit the best minds of both races to meet, exchange ideas, and understand respective viewpoints in an atmosphere free from embarrassment or constraint. Thus, while racial segregation keeps the races apart on their harmful lower levels, organized cooperation is drawing the races together on the helpful higher levels for mutual service and without engendering social friction or rousing racial ill-feeling. Indeed, doubting Thomases of both races are being clearly shown that mutual respect, goodwill, and genuine understanding are entirely consistent with the policy of racial segregation.

The basis of interracial cooperation has been so soundly laid that the time has come for a further step. The best minds of both races should attempt to arrive at a frank understanding about the fundamental question of racial relations and should try to formulate a definite policy that will have their mutual assent and support. This can best be begun in the South, but it should eventually be extended to the North so that throughout the country there will be a general agreement on aims and methods.

Of course, we do not mean that a program should be forthwith launched, complete in all its details. But we do mean that a definite beginning should be made because, although race relations are today unusually good in the South, Negro radicalism is dangerously active in the North and is exerting ominous subterranean pressure on the Negro population of the South as well. Beneath a seemingly fair surface, explosive factors are at work. The favorable conditions now prevailing should therefore be constructively employed.

Now, the only policy that seems to have a chance of success is that which may best be termed *biracialism*—a parallel evolution of White and Negro race-lives, biologically distinct, yet bound together by mutual interests and co-operating amicably for common ends. To enlist the support of the best elements of both races for an equitable biracial system, mutual concessions will be needed. Yet, provided the two groups agree on the basic principle of race separation, such a system can be worked out with fairness to both.

First of all, let us see what biracialism is not. Biracialism is not discrimination; it is separation. Biracialism does not imply relative "superiority" or "inferiority"; it is based on the self-evident fact of *difference*. No sensible person can deny that the Negro and the White man do differ widely, not only in physical appearance but also in temperament and outlook. Those Negroes who believe in their race should not object on principle to an arrangement that would permit the American Negro to remain himself and develop his special aptitudes. The formula of difference surely offers a common ground on which Negroes and Whites can meet without loss of self-respect and without raising controversial issues of merit or demerit in regard to which individuals of either race may entertain varying opinions.

Furthermore, biracialism is not caste. The two systems should be sharply distinguished from one another. Caste stratifies the population in horizontal layers, thereby preventing individuals from rising in the social and economic scale. Under slavery, the Negroes were a lower caste. The Northern Mulattoes are still virtually a caste, debarred in practice from a satisfactory economic or social status. On the other hand, the colored population of the South already enjoys a rudimentary form of biracialism, under which individuals can rise freely to high economic and social levels. Unlike caste, therefore, biracialism draws one vertical line through society, from top to bottom, and then allows individuals to rise as high as their talents will take them, on their side of the line.

Our survey of the way racial segregation has undoubtedly benefited the colored population of the South by enabling them to develop a satisfying group life and to give their talented members a wide range of opportunities shows what the Negro has already gained by a rudimentary, tacit form of biracialism. The drawbacks to the present situation are due chiefly to the fact that biracialism is as yet unacknowledged and incomplete. Under a perfected biracial system, the line separating the races would be straight and logical. The present situation is partly a biracial and partly a caste arrangement. Politically, for instance, the line today runs horizontally, the Southern Negroes being, in that particular respect, a disenfranchised caste. Again, some of the legal and customary measures of segregation are framed or administered with an emphasis that would be uncalled for under a stable biracial system genuinely agreed to by both races. If the Negro will consent unreservedly to the biracial principle, he will find that most existing anomalies can be rectified by the cordial co-operation of his White neighbors.

Every Negro should ask himself one searching question: *What does he really want?* Does he desire fuller and freer opportunities for self-development within his own group life, aided thereto by the goodwill and assistance of the Whites? Or does he, after all, crave social equality and racial amalgamation? One thing is certain: he cannot have both these alternatives.

Furthermore, until the biracial principle has been so firmly established that the White man feels a sense of genuine security for the maintenance of his race integrity, the Negro cannot enjoy the full benefits of biracialism. Therefore, every Negro who recognizes that biracialism is sound and advantageous to himself should not merely give it his passive assent but should work actively for its definite establishment. Some Negro leaders are today ready to take the step, but their position is a delicate one. The emotional legacy of the past is strong, and radical agitators continually strive to discredit moderate spokesmen by emotional harangues accusing the moderates of "selling out to the Whites." All intelligent Negroes should resist the emotional incitements of radical propagandists by frankly facing facts.

Every sensible Negro ought to realize that White America, North and South, is unalterably opposed to race amalgamation. And the reason why this opposition is unalterable is because it is based, not upon the doctrine of White race superiority, but upon the unchangeable fact of race difference. The Negro should recognize that the problem of Black and White is only one phase of a much larger problem—the relations of all the primary races of mankind. For instance, White Americans do not usually believe Chinese and Japanese to be racially their inferiors. Yet the very persons who cordially admire Orientals for their capacities and achievements are firmly opposed to intermarriage with them. Every Western state that contains a considerable Oriental element in its population has laws prohibiting the marriage of Orientals and Whites, while custom amplifies law by drawing a definite color line. Therefore, even if the Negro should make such economic and cultural progress as to definitely disprove present ideas about his innate inferiority, the situation would be basically unchanged. The Negro would still be racially so different that White America would continue to feel that it must preserve its race identity, which it regards as an infinitely precious heritage. In fact, every attack on the color line merely results in its being made stricter and harsher and hinders the trend toward interracial cooperation.

Unless the American Negro wishes to embark on a desperate gamble in which the odds against him are practically hopeless, his only alternative is a genuine understanding with White America. And the logical culmination of such an understanding is biracialism. Forward-looking Negroes should remember that under a biracial system their perfect-group-life would be so increasingly satisfying that they would feel less and less desire to lose their identity through amalgamation with the White world. The desire today felt by many educated colored persons for "social equality" is largely due to the fact that they do not find adequate social and cultural associates within their own group. The Negro's cultural advancement under the favorable conditions of a stable biracial system would soon do away with such balked emotions. Culture solidifies races, intensifies racial self-respect, and stimulates race pride in the best sense of the word. It is because the White man possesses a wealth of cultural achievement and tradition that he prizes so highly and guards so jealously his racial identity. To term this deep-seated instinct of racial self-preservation mere "race prejudice" is nonsense. What the Negro should do is frankly to respect the White man's feeling as a natural and legitimate attitude and then so cultivate his own capacities that he will evolve a race-life that he will want to protect. When the Negro does that, he need not bother about amalgamation or inferiority, because these matters will have settled themselves. The Negro will no longer want to amalgamate, and the White man will accord him full respect.

Thus far we have been considering how biracialism would affect the Negro and why intelligent Negroes who accept the idea should work actively for its establishment. Now let us look at the matter from the White man's point of view. Here, fortunately, we find no serious obstacles to enlisting the hearty support of the best White elements. Nevertheless, we must realize that, on the White side also, much must be done. The entire legal and customary code of race segregation should be thoroughly overhauled so as to minimize friction in every feasible way. Certainly, the policy must be purged of every taint of discrimination. Negro schools must be adequate; Negro travelling accommodations must be good; Negro sections of cities and towns must have satisfactory municipal improvements. All this will require a vast outlay of money, which will spell higher tax rates. But White men must realize that such pecuniary sacrifices will be a cheap price to pay for enduring interracial harmony. Unless the Negro recognizes that segregation is based upon fairness and justice and is in no sense a cloak for oppression and exploitation, he will never assent to biracialism, and segregation will remain a policy imposed by one race and opposed by the other.

Assuming that the forward-looking elements of both races do agree in principle to biracialism, they will still have a big job on their hands converting the masses of their respective groups to a truly constructive attitude. Negro leaders will have to wean their fellows from the emotional appeals of radical propagandists, while White leaders will have to instill good manners into low-class Whites and will also have to fight White demagogues who preach race hatred. As previously stated, the establishment of the bi racial system should normally begin in the South but should be extended to the North as rapidly as possible. In its application the system will have to be extremely flexible, since conditions vary widely in different parts of the country. Indeed, attempts to elaborate details at the start should be avoided, and specific applications of the biracial principle should usually be tested out by practical experience. The current Negro migration northward, however, helps the general establishment of biracialism, because the race problem has ceased to be a sectional matter. With its large Negro population, the North is coming to understand what the race question really means. Faced as it is with an imperative need for adjusting race relations, the North will appreciate the significance of biracialism as it otherwise could not do.

One of the first points in the biracial program to be established on a national scale is the general legal prohibition of racial intermixture. Not merely intermarriage but all sexual contacts between the races should be legally forbidden under heavy penalties in every state of the Union. This legal sanction of the color line is necessary for the creation of that sense of White security that is vital to interracial harmony. A nationwide ban against interracial marriage would be no real loss to the Negro, since, even in those Northern States that now permit it, marriage between Negroes and Whites is very rare, is disapproved by most Negroes, and almost always ends tragically. As for sexual relations outside marriage, their legal prohibition under severe penalties would tend to remove one of the grievances today most strongly resented by Negroes—the lack of protection for respectable colored women against the advances of vicious White men. To be sure, such a law might be used by unscrupulous colored women to extort Blackmail. Yet in most cases the White man who put himself in a compromising situation would deserve little sympathy. On this whole matter of miscegenation, the Southern White woman can do much. As a voter, she can help put drastic laws on the statute book, while on the jury she can see to it that offenders do not escape their just deserts.

Perhaps the most thorny problem in the whole field of racial adjustment is that of politics. The horrors of Reconstruction are still fresh in Southern minds, and the relation of the Negro to politics must be very delicately handled, lest passions be aroused that would bedevil the whole situation. Probably not much can, or should, be attempted at present. The South is certainly going about things in the right way by first remedying specific economic and social abuses and by laying the bases of interracial understanding but going slow on ticklish political matters. The Negro is, of course, disenfranchised in the South and has practically no voice in politics. In one sense, though, things are better than they were after Reconstruction, because Negro disenfranchisement is at least today accomplished by legal means, whereas formerly it was done by violence and fraud, which chronically inflamed racial passions. This so lowered the tone of Southern politics that better-class Whites abandoned the political arena to self-seeking party hacks and violent demagogues. With legal stabilization, the South's political tone has improved. The caliber of present-day Southern political leaders is vastly improved.

The keynote of Southern political life is White supremacy. And its legalized status has certainly had much to do with the remarkable material progress of the last generation, which has resulted in "The New South." Political stability, social security, economic prosperity, and cultural advancement have interacted happily and have benefited the colored as well as the White population.

Nevertheless, the steady rise of the colored people in education and material well-being will eventually necessitate changes in the present political situation. Sooner or later the intelligent, progressive elements of the colored population must have some way of participating in political life, or a very dangerous state of tension will ensue. Forward-looking Whites and Negroes should, therefore, face facts and try to find a practicable way out of the difficulty.

One point, however, might as well be understood at the start: White supremacy must be safeguarded. The White South will never submit to Negro rule—open or disguised. All theoretical arguments on this matter are mere wastes of breath, since they ignore basic realities. On this point Dowd hits the nail on the head when he writes, "Experience has shown that both races cannot govern jointly in those (the Southern) states. The White people believe that they are better able to govern than the Negro and are determined to do it. They propose to do it by some lawful means and have adopted lawful means of doing it. If every Negro in South Carolina and Mississippi could read and write and understand all the constitutions in the world, the White people would not allow them to control their governments, and in this respect, they are not different from the White people of any other state. If a majority of the people of California were Japanese, the fact that they could read and understand would not have a feather's weight against the determination of the White people to govern that state at all hazards. Or, if a majority of the people of Massachusetts were Negroes, the Whites of that state would no more submit to Negro rule than the people of South Carolina or Mississippi. They would prefer to retain White supremacy by some lawful expedient, but if that did not work, they would control it by any expedient that would work. Save by force of arms, no colored race is ever going to govern any state in this republic. This fact is fundamental to any discussion of the Negro problem."[8]

Offhand, it might seem as though we were facing a hopeless dilemma. Yet here, again, biracialism suggests encouraging possibilities. Since Negroes and Whites cannot be thrown together politically in anything like equal numbers without causing intolerable friction, the obvious alternative is to segregate them politically as they are segregated socially. Other countries, notably Austria and New Zealand, have already tried political segregation with beneficial results. These nations have instituted the system known as "curial voting," by which different racial groups are assigned a certain definite ratio of local offices and parliamentary seats. What individuals shall fill these offices depends on the verdict of the respective racial groups, who divide into parties and have political campaigns inside their group borders, just as we Americans now have our primary contests inside party lines. If such a system should be established in the South, the Negro population of each state would be assigned a certain proportion of local offices and legislative seats.[9] Thereafter, the Negroes could divide into parties, enjoy all the thrills of political campaigning, and get as much political experience

---
8. Dowd, *op. cit.*, pp. 107-108.
9. The apportionment need not be on a basis of population.

as their White fellow citizens, without in the least changing the ratio of White and colored officeholders and legislators. This is done today in New Zealand, where the native Māori element is politically segregated from the White population. The system would not conflict with the Fifteenth Amendment, because its racial effects would be mutual: a White man could no more vote for a Negro than a Negro could vote for a White candidate. How, then, would this differ from our present primary system, where a voter must register either as a Democrat or a Republican and can vote only for the primary in which he is registered?

Understand: curial voting is not advanced as a panacea for the South's political ills. It is merely cited as a suggestion to indicate how the political situation dovetails into the general racial situation and how biracialism may be applied to politics as to other phases of race relations.

In this whole subject of race relations we must avoid the seductive lure of plausible "solutions." About the worst way to try and "solve" a problem is to impose a mechanical device, no matter how ingenious, which disregards facts and popular sentiment. "Reconstruction" is a classic example of the tragic results of that method.

The great thing in apparent dilemmas is to get the best minds of both sides to meet, study the facts, and try to reach some general agreement on the basic realities of the situation. Given a friendly atmosphere and a genuine desire to get somewhere, it is surprising how constructive ideas develop and how practical methods are invented that nobody had thought of before. If intelligent men can only agree as to where they want to go and then want it hard enough, they are apt to get there—somehow.

That is the way in which the whole question of race relations ought to be approached. Racial adjustment should be visualized, not as a program but as a process, evolving normally as the joint product of the wisdom, foresight, and common sense of the best elements on both sides. And biracialism seems to be the only policy that offers a real chance for stable and amicable race relations.

Yet we should frankly realize that biracialism is not a perfect "solution." Even at best, it will not entirely eliminate race friction, though it should reduce it to a minimum and thus exorcise the dread specter of race war. Again, biracialism implies a partial renunciation of the ideal of national unity. Its justification lies in the fact that it safeguards White race integrity, which nearly all White Americans believe to be the sole basis for any national life worth having. . .

Biracialism is frankly an experiment. Yet it is an experiment that should be earnestly and loyally undertaken by both races for a period long enough to test out its practicability—say, one or two generations. For this, there are two reasons. The more immediate reason is that, even if biracialism should not prove to be permanently satisfactory, it would at least give us social peace during the critical decades that lie just ahead, in which the American Negro will awaken to full self-consciousness and will attempt his economic and social adjustment to American life. If social peace is not maintained, and if the field is left open for radical extremists, the Negro will not have his chance to adapt himself to American life, because there will probably be a racial explosion that would almost certainly result in his being either thrust down into a hopeless caste status or forcibly expelled from America. If, however, social peace can be maintained for the next generation or two, the Negro will have a chance to adapt himself, and in the light of what will have happened, the best minds of both races should then be in a much better position to judge what had best be done.

We have no desire to usurp the future, still less to essay the role of prophet. Yet we may perhaps suggest one possible eventuality—the ultimate colonization of the American Negro, either in his African homeland or in some other area outside the United States. The idea is, of course, not new. The present Republic of Liberia, on the west coast of Africa, is the result of a colonization project undertaken nearly a century ago. (Now, nearly two.) For generations many eminent men, Negroes as well as Whites, have thought, and today think, that colonization is the only real solution to our race problem. Thomas Jefferson and Abraham Lincoln, for instance, were firm believers in colonization. At present a school of thought exemplified by the "White America" movement[10] strongly urges that colonization be immediately undertaken, while on the Negro side Marcus Garvey's "Pan-African" movement proclaims that the Negro has no future in America and asserts that his only hope lies in a return to his ancestral home.

Now it may well be that something like this will eventually take place. We have already seen that the Negro's prospects in America are far from bright. It is by no means certain that the bulk of the race can adapt itself to the increasingly strenuous requirements of American life. If this proves to be so, the American Negro may himself come to realize that his only chance of survival lies in removal to an environment more suited to his racial aptitudes, especially since he is already the spiritual and cultural leader of his race and is thus fitted for leadership among more backward African peoples.

---

10. The thesis for immediate colonization is best stated by one of the leaders of the "White America" movement, Earnest S. Cox, in his book, *White America* (1923).

Colonization should, therefore, be seriously pondered and should always be kept in mind as a possible solution. But at present it is scarcely a practical matter. Most Negroes are today strongly opposed to the idea, while White America is not prepared to undertake the task and to undergo the profound economic readjustment that the removal of our great Negro population would entail.

Biracialism thus appears to be the only feasible policy for our time. It offers a hopeful *modus vivendi*—a way of getting along together, which appeals to sane idealism and gives adequate scope for the practical efforts of both races. Above all, if given a fair trial, biracialism should ensure social peace during the American Negro's critical transition period of self-discovery and self-realization.

# CHAPTER XIII
# THE SCOPE OF THE TASK BEFORE US

OUR ANALYSIS OF THE NEGRO question completes our survey of the specific obstacles confronting America's will to national unity. Mass alienation and color are the two main problems in the task of national reconstruction. The difficulty and duration of that task must be frankly faced. We are only at the beginning of America's reforging. The most critical period lies ahead and may not reach its climax for another ten or twenty years. Thereafter, the worst should be over, although national reconstruction will probably not be complete for two or three generations.

However, ultimate success is practically certain, while the gravest obstacles will be localized. Our Northeastern states are unquestionably in for troublous times. They contain not only the bulk of our unassimilated aliens but also most of the Negro radicals, and these refractory elements may form a close alliance—as they already show signs of doing. It is even possible that in certain Northeastern states the activities of disaffected or seditious elements might create local situations calling for federal intervention.

Yet such local situations, however grave, would instantly mobilize all loyal America, whose united intervention would be quick and decisive. It is this overwhelming preponderance of the real America that must always be remembered, no matter how dark local conditions may appear. For let us never forget: America is still American—*and is going to remain American.*

Does anyone doubt this? Then, look at the facts: Our White population is approximately 100,000,000.[1] Nearly one-half of that total (about 49,000,000) is of the old colonial stock. Most of the colonial stock is of English or Scottish blood, and the balance is of closely kindred North European blood, which has been completely assimilated. Of this, Theodore Roosevelt is a good example. If ever there was a typical American, it was "T. R." Yet Roosevelt's ancestry was Dutch, French Huguenot, Scotch-Irish, and German. His genealogy shows no English strain. But Roosevelt was American through and through and had a supreme contempt for "hyphenates"

---

1. According to recent official estimates, the White population of the United States is somewhat over 100,000,000. However, we will take this conservative and handy figure as the basis for our calculations. By underestimating the mass of the White population, the significance of the numerical data is heightened rather than diminished.

of any kind. Thus we have as the cornerstone of our national life the huge block of the old colonial stock, 49,000,000 strong, all of closely kindred North European blood, and welded by many generations of common existence into a thoroughly homogeneous American unity. Now add to the old colonial stock another great mass of North European blood, numbering between 36,000,000 and 38,000,000. These are the "Old Immigrant" elements—English, Scotch, Irish, German, Scandinavian, Dutch, and a few others of minor importance. The great majority of these elements, especially the second and third generations in America, are completely assimilated, while those who are not yet fully Americanized are so basically like us in blood, culture, and outlook that their eventual assimilation is only a matter of time. Certainly, none of the "Old Immigrant" elements is genuinely antagonistic to our basic institutions and ideals. Thus, of our total White population, over 85,000,000 are of North European blood, for the most part thoroughly American, and all Americanizable in the near future.

The only refractory elements in our White population are found among the 14,000,000 of the "New Immigrant" stocks from Southern and Eastern Europe or Western Asia, together with our 1,000,000 French-Canadians, who are on average an intensely clannish, unassimilable folk. These 15,000,000 of diverse origins constitute a tough problem for assimilation. Some elements seem to be incurably alien to American life. Others, however, are more promising, while many individual members of all these stocks have proved happy exceptions to the rule and are today good Americans. The refractory, unassimilated elements constitute a serious problem mainly because they are so solidly massed in certain sections of our Northeastern states.

Besides its 100,000,000 Whites, America contains between 12,000,000 and 13,000,000 non-Whites, of whom 10,500,000 are Negroes, 1,500,000 are Mexicans,[2] 200,000 are Orientals,[3] and 250,000 are American Indians. The Negro is the only non-White element that constitutes a serious problem. In a sense, the Negro problem is more dangerous in the North than in the South, because the prevalence of Negro unrest and radicalism in our Northern cities coincides with that of the disaffected alien elements.

Our balance sheet of population thus gives a decisive numerical preponderance to what we may term the real Americans. And this preponderance in numbers is heightened by a still greater preponderance in power, wealth,

---

2. As previously stated, the size of the Mexican element is most uncertain, various estimates placing it at from 1,000,000 to 2,000,000. We have adopted the medium figure of 1,500,000 in our calculations.
3. Mostly Japanese and Chinese, with a sprinkling of Hindus, Koreans, Filipinos, etc.

and prestige. Even in sections where the "American" element is a minority, it heads the community and really controls the situation even when political offices are held by representatives of unassimilated stocks. In such cases, American control may be veiled, but, on essential matters, it is effective just the same. Furthermore, the American element steadily strengthens itself by absorbing those individuals who are converted to the American point of view from the unassimilated groups.

In the heterogeneous community life of our Northern cities, we do find a certain number of American renegades who make common cause with the disaffected alien elements. A few Native Americans are notorious as avowed revolutionists, and such persons have been especially active in promoting an alliance between alien and Negro radicals. Yet for every American who goes over to alienism, probably fifty persons of alien origin become good Americans. Slowly but surely, America absorbs those who are temperamentally attracted to our ways and who are intellectually fitted to comprehend what America means. Even in the most unpropitious quarters a selective process is at work, sifting those capable of Americanization from those who cannot or will not Americanize.

Not only are the "New Immigrant" elements today mostly massed in the Northeastern states, but they will probably remain thus localized. They won their way into American industry solely because they were cheap labor. The Native American and "Old Immigrant" workman was, on average, more intelligent and more efficient than the South and East European "greenie," but the greenie supplanted them owing to his lower living standards. Now that greenie immigration is stopped, the whole situation is changed. The erstwhile greenies settled in America are greenies no longer. They eat meat, smoke cigarettes, go to the movies, wear "classy clothing," and aspire to steam-heated flats, radios, and motorcars. All this means that they require as good wages as the cheaper grades of American labor because they themselves have been "Americanized" in the superficial, material sense, even though they are far from being Americanized in the deeper sense of conversion to our culture and ideals. In other words, they have lost their former economic advantage; they possess no superiority in intelligence or efficiency, and there is no reason why they should spread beyond those regions where they have settled and where they form part of the local labor supply.

Furthermore, the "New Immigrant" elements appear destined to remain in the cities and industrial centers. With a few exceptions, they seem ill-adapted to American agricultural life. America's agricultural system is based upon the yeoman farmer, cultivating a good-sized holding, averaging from 50 to 150 acres, with a minimum of hired labor and a maximum of machinery. Now this system appeals to the individualistic North European immigrant. It does not suit immigrants from Eastern and Southern Europe, who are much more gregarious in temperament and who have been used to a typical "peasant" existence in compact village communities with small-scale, intensive agriculture. Accordingly, as pioneers or as single-family units in a settled American countryside, the "New Immigrant" stocks have done badly. American methods are strange, while the sense of isolation from their compatriots is depressing to them. Thus, even where the old folks stick it out, the children usually quit the farm and drift back to industrial urban life. Only where South and East Europeans have settled in groups and formed compact rural "colonies" have they really taken root. The Poles are the best example, many localities in rural New England and New York State having been transformed into "Little Polands." Yet these are, after all, exceptions to the general rule. Broadly speaking, even in our Northeastern states the countryside remains Native American, reinforced by numerous North European immigrants who like our agricultural life and soon become typical American farmers.

This confinement of the "New Immigrant" stocks not merely to our Northeastern states but also to the cities and industrial centers of those states, is a point of great significance, because it sharply limits their prospects of future increase by reproduction. The tremendously high birth rates of newly arrived immigrants at first led many observers to predict that these prolific aliens would in a few generations constitute a majority of our population. So they might if unrestricted immigration had permitted a continual mass influx which would have broken down our living standards and established an alien working class existing on a low economic plane. But the closing of the gates to mass immigration has changed everything. The "New Immigrants" already here have been too few in number to lower permanently our living standards, and in the general rebound to higher wage scales that followed immigration restriction, these elements have benefited with the rest of our working-class population. And their rapid acquirement of new economic wants spells a corresponding decrease in their production of children. The best way to check the fecundity of any stock is to raise its standard of living. No race is exempt from that economic law. Social customs and religious beliefs may check the process for a time, but they cannot long avert it.

Now our vital statistics show that the immigrants themselves lower their birth rate as soon as they adopt American living standards, while the second generation usually has a birth rate almost identical with that of its American neighbors. In rural "colonies," isolated from American ways, birth rates often continue high in the second or even the third generation. But, as we have already seen, the "New Immigrant" stocks will remain mostly city dwellers. There they will continually acquire new economic wants, stimulated by matters like systematic advertising and the lure of urban pleasures; and the higher they rise in the economic and social scale, the slower their rate of increase will become. Indeed, where economic and social advancement is especially rapid, the "New Immigrant" stocks often seem more prone to "race suicide" than Native Americans. Because of these social reasons, therefore, combined with certain other factors that we will shortly consider, the "New Immigrant" elements are unlikely to increase substantially faster than the rest of the population, and since immigration restriction has cut off their foreign source of supply, they will probably never constitute a larger proportion of our general population than they do today. Just as the Negro's former tropical exuberance of reproduction has been repressed by the action of social forces, so the "New Immigrant's" first reproductive expansion is being slowed down to very modest proportions.

Of course, there is a pauper and defective class among the "New Immigrant" stocks, which has no economic or social standards and which therefore breeds recklessly on a low level of poverty and squalor. But this is just as true of the pauper and defective class among Native Americans, North European immigrants, and Negroes. Whatever their racial origin, these unfortunates form an abnormal group and constitute a special social problem whose treatment lies outside the scope of this book.

Continuing our survey of the "New Immigrant" elements, let us analyze some other factors that bear upon their racial future in America. The first checks on their early fecundity were scarcity of women and bad living conditions. Some immigrant groups were composed almost wholly of males. Since intermarriage outside the group was rare, it follows that even where the birth rate of their women was high, their number was so small that the group rate of increase by births was insignificant. This is notably true of the Greeks and Balkan Slavs, who are today decreasing in America by death and by return to their homelands. On the other hand, this factor does not apply to elements that, like the Jews, came by families, with a high percentage of women and children.

The factor of bad living conditions affected all the "New Immigrant" elements. Even the Jews, habituated as they were to ages of urban existence, suffered from those aspects of American city life to which they were not accustomed. The bulk of the "New Immigrants," being country-bred peasants, suffered severely from the bad effects of slum surroundings and industrial labor. In many cities and factory towns the death rate of the alien elements has averaged several times as high as the death rate of the American residents, thus offsetting the high alien birthrate.

This check on alien increase is, to be sure, being steadily minimized by measures of public health and by charitable agencies. Indeed, in New York City, the infant death rate of some of the "New Immigrant" elements is today less than that of the Native Americans. But, as already remarked, the newer checks of raised living standards and social desires cut the alien birthrate faster than sanitation cuts the death rate, and so more than offset the increase due to saving children who would otherwise have died.

Furthermore, measures like public health, private charity, and social service can only slightly counteract the effect of other deep-seated factors, which we will now consider.

The first of these factors is climate. South European immigrants, especially, are not well fitted for the rigorous winters of our Northeastern states. Accordingly, South Europeans suffer much from lung and throat diseases, as well as from temperamental depression due to climatic causes.

Even more important than climate are the psychological strains involved in adaptation to American life. This applies strongly to all the "New Immigrant" elements, since it is they who differ most widely from us and thus find it especially hard to adjust themselves to American conditions. Secretary Davis does not overstate matters when he writes, "The adjustment to American life means nervous strain. It means a heavy tax on all one's physical and mental stamina. It is a testing process, sometimes quite extreme; it is a trial by fire of the kind of human material that has newly come to the Republic. Here quality counts. Here good stock stands up under the strain. Here weak heredity leads to cracking under the stress and pressure of our highly organized, driving life. Here good blood tells in the capacity to take on new habits and to replace old ones, to adjust to a new community, to recognize new laws and customs, and to become, in a sense, a new person. Here, in high-pressure America, the man or family of weak stock demoralizes."[4]

The results of psychological overstrain are tragically revealed by the high rate of nervous troubles and insanity among the "New Immigrant" stocks, while the combined effects of overstrain and faulty social adaptation are shown by the way the children of such immigrants lose their moral balance

---

4. Davis, Honorable James J.: *Selective Immigration*, p. 110 (1925).

and fall into vice and crime. The gangsters, gunmen, prostitutes, and other social derelicts of our Northern cities are largely sons and daughters of immigrants, who have lost their ancestral standards without acquiring our ideals.

The "New Immigrant" stocks are thus undergoing an intensive process of selection, which is weeding out the more unfit and unassimilable elements. Of course, this temporarily involves much individual suffering and also much social disturbance, since these human waste products will make a deal of trouble before they are eliminated. But in the end it should greatly simplify the problem, because those who survive will tend to be just those best fitted for harmonious incorporation into American national life. Meanwhile, the process of elimination will still further limit the increase of the "New Immigrant" stocks.

This is a matter of local as well as of national importance. In our survey of the alien flood, we noted how in certain regions, especially New England and New York, the "New Immigration" threatened to drown out both the Native American and "Old Immigrant" inhabitants. We saw that the Native Americans of those sections were failing even to reproduce themselves and that the "Old Immigrant" stocks were barely holding their own, whereas the "New Immigrant" elements were rapidly increasing. Our conclusion was that, *unless other factors should become operative,* the Native American and "Old Immigrant" stocks in those parts of the United States would be wholly replaced by "New Immigrant" stocks.

Well, we now see that total replacement is not inevitable, because other factors have come into play! What was "socially sterilizing" the Native American and "Old Immigrant" stocks of New York, New England, and other parts of the Northeast? It was the steady inpouring of low-standard aliens who were undermining the economic and social foundations of American life. No racial blight had suddenly fallen upon the older inhabitants. They were sound, healthy folk who wanted families but who declined to bring children into the world unless they could give them a fair start in life. Their "sterility" was thus due to an abnormal social factor—mass immigration. Now that this unhealthy situation has been remedied, the very normalization of economic and social conditions that checks the fecundity of the "New Immigrant" elements should stimulate the fecundity of the Native American and "Old Immigrant" stocks. In other words, what spells birth control for the former should mean *birth release* for the latter.

This is all the more likely when we remember that the "sterility" of the Native American and "Old Immigrant" stocks in New York and New

England is a strictly local phenomenon. Over the rest of the country, they both maintain healthy growth. One of the outstanding features of the 1920 census was the steady increase of the old colonial stock throughout the West and South, which showed that it was a sound and vigorous element with no signs of racial decline. And even in New York and New England, where conditions are the most unfavorable, the old stock only just barely fails to reproduce itself. It would not be surprising if the census of 1930 should reflect the beneficial results of our immigration-restriction laws and should show that in New York and New England the old stock was at least holding its own.

These facts should greatly hearten all true Americans, especially those who have long been waging an apparently losing fight for the maintenance of American ideals in localities especially threatened by alienism. The turn of the tide has been so recent that many persons are unaware of it and still regard the future with gloomy foreboding. Such persons should wake up to the fact that the tide has turned. So long as the gates stood open to mass immigration the future looked gloomy indeed. Feeling themselves literally drowning in the alien flood, patriotic citizens in the "submerged" areas spoke despairingly of the "vanishing American" and often fell into deep pessimism. A decade ago, one of our most eminent patriots, Madison Grant, concluded a book, significantly entitled *The Passing of the Great Race*, with the solemn warning that unless the alien flood was stayed, the Native American would "become as extinct as the Athenian of the age of Pericles and the Viking of the days of Rollo."[5]

That, however, was ten years ago. Today Americans everywhere should realize that pessimism, though formerly justified, no longer squares with existing facts. The Native American is not "vanishing"; on the contrary, he is increasing at a good' healthy rate and can absolutely control the situation. All he needs, to ensure national reconstruction, is to keep the gates shut and evolve a sound Americanization policy. Of course, there will be a troublesome transition period. Yet this period, while long and difficult from the standpoint of the individual, will be merely an episode in the life of the nation. In other words, Americans should take the long rather than the short view, should face present problems with a confident smile, and should get busy reforging America.

This confident optimism will be especially helpful for those Americans who live in regions like New York and New England, where alienism is

---

5. Grant, Madison: *The Passing of the Great Race*, p. 263. This book, the first edition of which appeared in 1916, made a great sensation and played an important part in America's awakening to national and racial realities.

most deeply entrenched. These Americans might as well recognize that they will have to bear the brunt of the conflict with disaffected, alien forces and that they have a long, tough job on their hands upholding American ideals, culture, and institutions. Although the general trend is now upward, conditions in some localities will probably continue to get worse for at least another decade and may lead to very critical local situations.

Yet, however grave local conditions may become, the men on the spot need never lose faith and courage if they will but lift their gaze to America as a whole. Such persons should regard themselves as outposts of a mighty and invincible army, numbering many millions—even tens of millions. As a matter of fact, even in the most unfavorable localities the "American" element should normally contain not only the Native stock but also the best of the "Old Immigrant" stock, plus an increasing number of individuals from the "New Immigrant" stocks who have been genuinely converted to Americanism. Thus the "American" element, even where it is distinctly in the minority, should be able to control the local situation by its superiority in brains, prestige, and morale. Under normal circumstances, therefore, no state in the Union should ever fall into the grip of alienism.

But, for the sake of argument, let us assume the worst. Let us suppose that sometime within the next ten or fifteen years a combination of unusual circumstances and a weakening of local morale should throw not merely one but several of our Northeastern States into the control of disaffected elements bent on using their power for aggressive, un-American ends. Would not the local Americans then be in real danger? Yes, they certainly would. And, in the larger sense: *what of it?* Should not every American worth his salt be as ready to face danger from internal enemies as from foreign invaders? Surely, every American who might be exposed to such a situation should realize that the crisis would be brief, because all loyal America would instantly take a hand in the game and would finish it in short order.

Let Americans "on outpost" remember the vast reservoirs of loyal America—the strong men of the Middle West, the eagle-faced men of the Sierras, and the quiet, watchful-eyed men of the South. There they are, in their millions and tens of millions, going about their business and serenely confident of the future. Yet those millions are one in love and devotion to their America, and if a crisis "on the outposts" ever arose, they would march and settle the matter with the thoroughness that Americans always display when a really big job has to be done.

Such words may sound alarmist. In one way they are, and in another way they are not. They may be considered alarmist, in the sense that they suggest what, *as things are now going,* is highly improbable. But they are not alarmist insofar as they depict what would almost certainly have happened if the situation today was what it was only a few years ago. Down to the closing of the gates to mass immigration, America was headed straight for social and racial war. If the alien flood had poured in for another ten years, conditions would have become desperate. Our Northeastern States would have been swamped by the immigrant tide, and mass-alienism would have grown so self-confident and aggressive that it would have made a determined bid for control.

But if anybody imagines that loyal America would have submitted to the destruction or radical transformation of its ideals and institutions, that person is mistaken. Loyal America would not have tolerated the triumph of alienism in a single State of the Union, and theoretical considerations like "majority votes" would not have altered by a feather's weight its grim determination. The upshot would have been an elemental clash of wills, which would almost certainly have been decided by force of arms. Loyal America would have probably won, but the Northeast would have been a hotbed of disaffection for generations, and the rebellious alien masses might never have been really Americanized.

The closing of the gates has almost certainly averted any such catastrophe. But the dread of *what might have been* should be neither forgotten nor glossed over. On the contrary, it should be frankly stated and should be driven home to the consciousness of every patriotic American. America was saved, not by good luck or drift, but by a determined act of the national will. And only vigilant determination can hold what has been gained.

Furthermore, Americans should realize that although a general disaster has been averted, a great problem of mass alienism remains. The presence of disaffected alien masses, concentrated in our Northeastern States, not only spontaneously engenders trouble but also incites other disaffected elements like Negro radicals and Native-born revolutionists to courses that they would never dream of pursuing if mass-alienism did not exist. As time goes on, all these disaffected or seditious elements are bound to draw together for common ends, and under certain circumstances, such as a foreign war, they might make serious trouble. The realization of such potential dangers should spur all true Americans to undertake the task of national reconstruction without delay so that the dangers may be minimized or eliminated in the shortest possible time.

A clear understanding of what should be done would at once produce two very beneficial, albeit highly dissimilar, effects—it would heighten

American morale, and it would weaken the morale of the disaffected elements. We have already emphasized the importance of morale for Americans facing aggressive alienism. But surely, nothing could more quickly undermine alienism's aggressiveness than the disillusionment of its hopes. Already we see signs that alienism's keenest-sighted champions begin to realize that the tide has turned against them. Much of their present bitterness is probably due to their secret sensing of that unwelcome fact. Their angry attacks on our immigration-restriction policy and their furious opposition to an alien-registration law are desperate attempts to stay the trend of the times. Once they are decisively beaten on those cardinal points, their aggressive spirit will be proportionately weakened, although we may expect stubborn resistance even to the inevitable, because this opposition is so deep-seated.

How deep-rooted alienism is in the more unassimilable immigrant stocks is explained by Professor Abbott in his treatise on this subject. "Let us not deceive ourselves," he writes, "these newer additions to our numbers are inheritors, not founders. They come into a land subdued and civilized, into a social and political system alien to their previous experience, and with much of which, outside of its material benefits, many of them have no sympathy. They often jump a thousand years of progress in crossing the Atlantic; they come from the Middle Ages into the twentieth century, and the telephone is not more of a novelty to them than representative government. Their memories are of ancient wrongs, not ancient rights; their standards are those of other times as well as those of other places. Their skies change but not their minds. Their heroes are not American, nor are their traditions, habits, customs, institutions, much less their ideas of government and their language.

"Why should not some of these men wish to shatter the whole scheme of things and 'remold it nearer to the heart's desire'? Our ancestors brought with them their conceptions of government and their standards of morals and conduct. Why should these newcomers not do the same? That is, in fact, precisely what they are trying to do. That is the root of the whole problem. We have admitted the people of Eastern and Southern Europe. . . . And we face the problem of alteration in the theories and practices of government from the same direction."[6]

Professor Abbott also analyzes the natural alliance between alien and Native-born revolutionary radicals in the following lines: "All revolutionary leaders have striven to abolish the past, in whole or in part; for this is the essence of revolution. But in this case the situation is more striking. For

---

6. Abbott, Wilbur C.: *The New Barbarians*, pp. 225-226 (1925).

many of these newer arrivals, their own past is one that they are only too anxious to forget; a past to be remembered, if at all, not with pride but with shame. The past of the United States is unknown or dismissed as unimportant by them. In it they had no part; it can make no appeal to them. But they have as much future as any of us, and that future they think they should determine for themselves (and for the rest of us) according to their theories as to how society should be organized and administered, not to have it determined for them by laws and customs and traditions that they had no share in making and whose principles and standards are either unknown or repugnant to them, of whose experience they are ignorant or contemptuous, or both. This is the real danger of the concurrence of the revolutionist and the immigrant."[7]

The susceptibility of the "New Immigrant" stocks to revolutionary agitation is a factor that, however unwelcome, must be clearly recognized. Their historic background is not one of ordered liberty, but of despotic oppression countered by veiled sedition and occasional revolt. Their legendary heroes, from Russia to the Balkans and Sicily, are brigand-patriots who kill tyrants, despoil the rich, and reward the poor. Such worthies, though quite natural in their time and place, are hardly civic models for the land of Washington and Lincoln. As for the Ashkenazic Jews, we have already seen how their long past as an aloof and persecuted sect gave them an instinctive dislike for established governments and for the very idea of nationality, and how this makes them highly receptive to revolutionary propaganda and theories of internationalism.

Now add to all this the fact that East and South Europeans are naturally gregarious, temperamental folk, and we can understand how prone they are to crowd contagion and how easily they can be swayed by leaders of the emotional type. These are just the sort of people whom our Native-born radicals are looking for. Radicalism has never made much of a dent on the thinking of either the old American or "old immigrant" stocks. But radicalism has established itself solidly among the newer elements of our population. Radicalism in America is today composed chiefly of East and South European followers, with leaders partly of alien and partly of Native origin, who have pooled their efforts for common ends.

We should therefore frankly recognize that certain immigrant groups are temperamentally predisposed to radicalism. However, we must not make the mistake of thinking that every member of those groups is a born revolutionist. Many individuals of such groups have proved conclusively that they

---

7. *Ibid*, pp. 229-230.

have accepted our ideals and are staunch Americans. Such persons should be received into full fellowship with us. The man or woman who displays the strength of character and independence of thought required to rise above ancestral training and group prejudices is just the sort of person who makes the best kind of American. Such persons should be welcomed, neither patronizingly nor effusively, but quietly and sincerely, as one of ourselves.

Once more let us emphasize a point that we have previously stressed—assimilation is a longtime, complex matter. Crude "Americanization" methods and sweeping judgments are alike worse than useless. We must keep an open mind and a flexible policy if we intend to do better than muddling through with a maximum of friction and a minimum of constructive results.

How complex the problem presented by each immigrant group is and what different attitudes exist within group borders is shown in the following analysis by our present Secretary of Labor: "In any great foreign-city group you will find three characteristic mental attitudes. You will find people, mostly the old-timers, who cling tenaciously to Old World customs, traditions, and language. You will find people who are hard at work trying to adjust themselves to America as they find it, wanting to become Americans in spirit and in truth. And you will find people who sit around telling each other what a sink of iniquity America is and how much better it would be if they could reshape it according to their heart's desire: a paradise without police, law, or work."[8]

Such widely contrasted types clearly require correspondingly different treatment. Those immigrants who are sincerely trying to become Americans are obviously no "problem." All we have to do is to hold a friendly attitude toward them and make it easy for them to learn our language and acquire our ideals through night schools, civic centers, and other public or private Americanization agencies. And that is about as far as organized Americanization of adult immigrants should go. Anything savoring of coercion should be carefully avoided. This is especially true of citizenship. Far from urging aliens to become naturalized, we should tell the alien that we do not want him to become a citizen until he feels himself to be an American. Citizenship should be the end, not the beginning, of Americanization. To urge or force citizenship upon the immigrant makes him despise it and gives him a pretty poor idea of America.

As for the "old-timers," as Secretary Davis calls them, who cling tenaciously to their ancestral ideas and customs, they should be left alone. We ought to state convincingly that any adult individual who wants to remain

---

8. Davis, *op. cit.*, 124.

an alien can stay an alien and will be allowed to go his own way so long as he minds his own business and does not make trouble.

With the children, of course, it is different. They should be made to attend either the public schools or private schools conducted in English and imbued with American ideals. Yet even the children, when they reach maturity, should not be harassed if they show that they are still alien in spirit. We might as well realize that, in the last analysis, the alien must *Americanize himself.*

Fortunately, our immigration-restriction policy has checked the growth of mass alienism. Alien "colonies" will long persist in our Northeastern cities and will probably persist still longer in certain rural districts. But the foreign source of supply has been cut off, and alienism, in its primary "hyphenate" sense, will thus diminish in the course of time.

The most troublesome phase of the problem is not the foreign-born "hyphenate," but the American-born nondescript who has lost his ancestral heritage without acquiring American culture and ideals. This type, whom we have satirically termed "The New American," is a real problem that is destined to become more serious as time goes on.

The presence among us of a vast nondescript mass, with no genuine loyalties, traditional roots, or cultural and idealistic standards, is a real menace to our national life. Not only do such persons fall easily into vice and crime; they are also the most inflammable sort of revolutionary material. All history proves that men must have ideals and standards to live by, or they fall prey to chronic bitterness and discontent. These "New Americans" growing up in our midst, who despise their fathers and sneer at us, are far more aggressively "alien" than are the hidebound "old-timers" who speak no English and have no contact with Americans. For the alien immigrant, however incomprehensible or repugnant America may be to him, he can content himself with a negative protest, consoling himself by withdrawal into the haven of his group, language, and traditions. But his "New American" children, discarding these things, have no such refuge. Accordingly, they tend to voice their discontent in a positive fashion, by seeking to change their American environment and mold it according to their liking.

That is what the "New American" wants to do, and with him we may include the more restlessly disaffected among the foreign-born immigrants, who have the same attitude and ambitions as the alien-minded Native-born. But such persons soon make an annoying discovery—*the "New American" runs up against Old America!* However eloquently he may dispute it, the disaffected alien encounters the stubborn fact that America is not "in the making," but that it is substantially *made*. He quickly finds that he is a newcomer in an old and well-established social order, with traditions, institutions, and ideals rooted in centuries of growth, and with a resident population deeply attached to their America and determined to continue it along traditional lines.

But, insofar as he is temperamentally unadapted to this America, the alien's discontent merely increases, and his balked emotions extend his resentment from ideals and institutions to the Americans themselves. Here we discover the psychological basis of that bitter, aggressive challenge of Alienism both to Americanism and to the Native American, which we previously noted. Here, also, is the basis of that alliance between the disaffected aliens and the Native radicals, which is today in the process of formation. We may as well face the fact that a coalition of disaffected, seditious elements already exists and is probably going to get closer in the near future.

Here is a clash of antagonistic wills that can neither be averted nor compromised. And it is high time to say so frankly, instead of trying to dodge or cover up the issue, as is so often attempted. Granting that such opposed aims and viewpoints exist, the best way is to trot them out in the open, where they can be clearly seen, studied, and comprehended. Everybody would then know just where he stood and where the other fellow stood as well. By trying to hush matters up, the situation becomes mysterious, and rumor takes the place of reality. That is bad for both sides. Loyal Americans, overestimating the danger, may be driven to panic measures of unnecessary severity. On the other hand, the disaffected elements, misreading the national will, may be tempted into courses upon which they would never venture if they were better informed.

Above all, let us have done with the sentimental homilies on "prejudice" and "intolerance" that we so often hear these days. On this point a recent writer speaks with such refreshing candor that we cannot do better than quote him.

Says this writer: "It may be as well for us to ask ourselves what tolerance really is and why we have become intolerant. The latter of these questions is, unfortunately, easy to answer. We are no longer a homogeneous people. There are some fourteen million aliens among us, whose ideals are not ours. Where we seek to Americanize them, they tell us in their foreign tongues that the country is as much theirs as ours and that they propose to remain themselves, to remain European, and even to Europeanize our social, moral, and political state of affairs. When we protest, these people accuse us of intolerance. And they are not beside the mark in doing so, for clearly, we do not tolerate them as they are. But, on the other hand (a thing not often mentioned), *they do not tolerate us:* our literature, art, morals, habits of life, our ideals, religion, traditions, and the Republic we have created. There is no mistaking their feelings in the matter, for they tell us in plain words, in editorials, in books, in plays, and in political addresses that they don't like us and our ways. We reply in as plain. And, as I have indicated, this growth of mutual intolerance has come about because our fundamental ideals are at variance.

"To cover the whole immense and complicated state of affairs with a word, we are no longer 'like-minded.' And this, I take it, is the gravest mischance that can befall a people. Hence, and quite inevitably, the spirit of extremism, of unrest, of dissension, of dislocation, which, under a calm surface, is continually in evidence. . . .

"But what is tolerance? It is founded, no doubt, on a sense of justice and the spirit of moderation. Things, it will be agreed, dear enough to the American heart of the past! But the word and what it represents are not very accurately understood. It must be remembered that tolerance is not indifference. It is not the spirit that permits any and everything because it values nothing. Tolerance has its limits. We do not call a man intolerant who refuses to have his house burned down or his wife taken from him. And just so, we Americans have in the past been intolerant of some things. When our deeper ideals were violated, we took action. . . .

"It may be said that when a people are like-minded, the ideal aims not being too far apart, they tolerate much, though not all. But we are no longer like-minded. We are at variance. And accordingly, the wise and moderate among our Native-born people are themselves forced into intolerance. They are ready, or not far from being ready, for extreme action. ... It is useless to wring our hands and ask how it happened—useless to blame ourselves or the stranger within our gates. We have simply to admit that this is the state of affairs and apply what remedy we may be able to apply."[9]

Indeed, the writer of this admirable essay goes on to strike an even deeper note. Giving his essay the significant title of *The New Secession,* he very justly compares the attitude of our disaffected aliens with that of the Southern extremists before the Civil War. "These various foreign races," he says, "have really created in their mass a spirit which is in no wise different from the spirit of secession. They are here; they are with us; we have one state and one fate, *but they have seceded in spirit,* and they think it as right

---

9. Mitchell, Langdon: "The New Secession," *Atlantic Monthly,* August, 1926.

and reasonable as did John C. Calhoun."[10]

The writer of that essay might have gone still farther and stated that the new spirit of secession is far deeper-going than the old. We, who in these pages have surveyed the tragic past, know that North and South, while bitterly divided on certain issues, were yet basically one in blood, culture, and ideals. How much more profound is the gulf that today opens between loyal America and our disaffected aliens!

Then, is the answer war? No. But why not? Because the new secessionists are too few and too dispersed to have any hope of success in an appeal to arms. Let us not mince words! That is the answer. If the disaffected elements in America numbered one-half of our population, instead of one-tenth,[11] we should today be headed for a convulsion that would make the Civil War look like child's play. We have averted that catastrophe by our closing of the gates, and so long as we keep the gates closed, we are reasonably safe. But should we ever be insane enough to reopen the gates to mass immigration, America would be foredoomed to a social and racial war of the most horrible character.

Fortunately, America's awakening to national and racial realities has been so thorough that a reversal of our present immigration-restriction policy is practically unthinkable. The American people today display an aroused national consciousness and a firm will to national unity. Alienist attacks will merely strengthen the national will and lead to stronger measures of national unification. That we shall eventually attain our goal, there can be no reasonable doubt. The only question that remains is how it may best be done.

Now the only sound way to approach the problem of national reconstruction is through plain-speaking and common sense. For the past ten years the American people have felt that something was wrong. More and more, Americans have realized the challenge of alienism to American national life. But the dawning realization was so unwelcome that most persons disliked facing the issue and tried to evade it or hush it up. The upshot is that public discussion has hitherto been almost monopolized by emotional extremists on both sides, who have beclouded the issue with passion and

---

10. *Ibid.*
11. Of course, it should be understood that by no means all the "New Immigrant" elements are disaffected. A considerable minority are already good Americans, while a still larger number are either partially assimilated or at least not actively dissatisfied. One-half would probably be a liberal estimate of those who are aggressively disaffected. The balance of the disaffected or seditious elements in America is made up of Negro radicals, a small percentage of "Old Immigrants," and a sprinkling of Native American radicals of the "redder" shades. Adding all these disaffected elements together, they cannot possibly total more than 10,000,000 or 12,000,000 in other words, between 8 and 10 per cent of our total population.

have inflamed popular fears by making the situation seem more alarmingly perilous than it really is. Goodness knows, the problem is serious enough; yet the survey that we have made in these pages shows that there need be no hysterical alarm about the present or undue apprehension about the future.

Wherefore: away with the conspiracy of silence which has hedged the question about with reticences and taboos! Let the wise and clear-sighted discuss the issue openly and acquaint the public with the facts of the case. That is the only way to quiet popular fears, allay rising passions, and evolve a sane, informed public opinion.

Let us see why this is so. A clash of antagonistic wills exists today. A deep-going issue confronts us, which must inevitably cause much friction and heart-burning in the process of settlement. But a great deal of unnecessary friction and resentment could be eliminated at the start if both sides mutually comprehended the motives underlying their respective attitudes. One thing should be clearly understood: no moral blame attaches to either side. The alien ought to realize that there is nothing inherently brutal or tyrannical in our determination to preserve our America and to reforge our national unity. But we should likewise realize that the alien desires to transform America, not because of innate "cussedness" or sinister malevolence, but because of temperamental and intellectual urges perfectly natural in themselves. The issue is, therefore, not "righteousness versus wickedness" or "superiority versus inferiority," but simply *difference*. Of course, men may differ so profoundly that a deep-going conflict is inevitable. Nevertheless, that conflict can be conducted on a high plane, with mutual respect and even with personal regard.

Such an attitude is certainly possible in the present case, because anything like civil war is practically excluded owing to the unequal strength of the opposing forces. Since the disaffected elements in America are too weak to succeed by force of arms, the blood-madness that destroys reason in wartime should never bedevil the situation. If, therefore, instead of standing off and hurling verbal brickbats at one another, the intelligent minds of both sides will face facts and discuss matters on the basis of existing realities, friction will be minimized, and popular passions will be kept within bounds.

Discontented aliens should realize that, however much they may dislike America as it now is, their only hope of effecting any changes is by persuading Americans that such changes are desirable from the American as well as from the alien point of view. Sensible Americans realize that present-day America is not perfect. Indeed, broad-minded Americans welcome genuine criticism as a helpful, stimulating factor that portrays our civilization from new aspects and thus enables us to detect shortcomings to which we may have been blind or of which we may have been insufficiently aware.

But alien critics must likewise respect our thoughts and feelings. They must realize that some of the things that to them are incomprehensible or repugnant may to us be treasures that we do not intend to forego. And (they may as well understand this once and for all) we Americans of the North European stocks intend to have the last word. It is our blood that wrested America from the wilderness and the savage, won its freedom, and built up its civilization. That civilization is now three centuries old. The dissatisfied aliens are, after all, but a small minority newly come into a mature and well-established national and social order. The "New American" must recognize the stubborn fact of Old America. However much he may dislike some of its aspects, he must come to realize that these can be altered only by mutual consent. We older Americans will not be browbeaten into scrapping one jot or tittle of our handiwork until we are convinced that it should be done.

Another thing that discontented aliens should realize is that by allying themselves to other disaffected elements, like Native-born radicals (as many of them are now doing), they are entering upon a course of conduct highly dangerous to themselves. For if loyal America ever makes up its mind that the national life is really threatened by a combination of disaffected, seditious elements, it will strike quickly and hard. Such repressive measures would be unfortunate for America itself, because the resulting bitterness would retard progress toward national unity. But the worst sufferers would, of course, be the disaffected elements, whose situation would be a most unhappy one. Meanwhile, the only persons who stand to gain anything by anti-American activities are the radical agitators, who thrive on stirring up discontent. Sensible aliens, however, should be too wise to let themselves be used as catspaws by false prophets who would lead them to their undoing.

The dissatisfied alien might just as well make up his mind that America is going to remain substantially what it is in blood, ideals, culture, and institutions. Certain adjustments the alien may be able to bring about by a friendly understanding with his American neighbors. But if he is to be contented and happy here, he must adjust himself to America rather than expect America to adjust itself to him.

If the dissatisfied alien cannot reconcile himself to this and finds American life intolerably distasteful, he is always at perfect liberty to go elsewhere. That is, indeed, what is happening on a fairly large scale. Every year witnesses the departure of thousands of aliens who make no secret of the fact that they dislike America and are glad to be gone. The pleasure is mutual, for we are thereby rid of many recalcitrants who would make much trouble if they stayed. In course of time, as America's national reforging proceeds, the whole atmosphere of American life will probably become increasingly distasteful to alien-minded individuals, and emigration of such persons should steadily relieve us of many unassimilable elements.

As for the unassimilables who remain with us, their number ought gradually to diminish with the passage of time. Silently but surely, the assimilative power of American life must inevitably absorb all who dwell in it, except those who by temperament and conviction are decidedly antagonistic and unadaptable. Furthermore, we should realize that, as America reforges its national unity, its assimilative strength will increase and become as powerful as it was in earlier times. A generation hence ,America, as a whole, should be substantially reforged. Alienism will still linger here and there but its remaining strongholds will be like isolated islets, steadily worn away by the solvent action of the surrounding sea.

As already stated, the critical transition period will be the next ten or twenty years. For the next decade, at least, alienism will probably be vociferous in protest and agitation. Whatever feels itself menaced struggles desperately to avert the danger, and our national awakening is a far graver threat to alienism than alienism is to America. For America, alienism is today a serious problem, but on alienism, the national will has pronounced a sentence of death. Thus, alienism frantically seeks to avert its doom and will continue to struggle while life remains. Yet, as time passes and it grows weaker, alienism's last struggles will become a matter of no practical importance.

Such is the general trend of events that should normally occur during the coming half-century. America's reforging is apparently certain. But we can speed up the process by wise effort or retard it by unwise action. In the preceding pages we have considered the scope of the task of national reconstruction that lies before us. Let us now survey the task itself, together with its logical culmination in a happy and glorious future.

# CHAPTER XIV
# REFORGING AMERICA

EVERY TRUE AMERICAN SHOULD BE glad to be alive today. For he is privileged in being able to share in the greatest enterprise since Independence—the reforging of America! Difficulties? Surely. But what of them? We know what they are. We know how to surmount them. And we have already begun to do so. A happy national future is practically assured. Our job is to make it come soon.

Immersed as we are in the immediate present, it is hard for us to discern the deeper trend of the times. Perhaps only those who have closely followed public affairs for a considerable series of years can fully appreciate the momentous change *for the better* that has occurred in the past decade. Yet all persons who reached maturity before 1914 can, on looking back, recall to some extent the ominous symptoms that then troubled the national life. Such persons must vividly recall the shock of the Great War and the popular awakening to national and racial realities that followed. Out of that stern time a new America emerged. The story of this new America has not yet been told, though our children will find it a stirring tale.

However, we know enough about present-day America to realize that it differs from the America of 1914 fully as much as the America of 1870 did from America before the Civil War. Happily, while the America of 1870 had changed for the worse, our America of today is vastly improved. Indeed, not since the nation's youthful days before 1850 have America's prospects been so bright as they are right now. We have already seen that the Immigration Restriction Act of 1924 marks the second great turning point in our national life. And we must remember that this momentous event was no chance happening but was rather the deliberate enactment of the national will, the decision of an enlightened national consciousness that will endure.

The most hopeful aspect of present-day America is its idealism. The reckless, short-sighted materialism into which America plunged after the Civil War has been succeeded by a staunchly patriotic spirit. Furthermore, this patriotic idealism is as sound as it is fine. Our very blunders and misfortunes have taught us lessons that neither we nor our descendants are likely to forget. Thus, if our optimism is more restrained than that of our forebears, we are not liable, as they were, to be beguiled by high-sounding, sentimental sophistries. With broader experience and fuller knowledge, we feel ourselves trustees of an infinitely precious legacy, bequeathed to us by our fathers and destined for our children, to whom we are in duty bound to hand it on, improved. "America" is, in the highest sense, a spiritual unity, composed alike of the dead, the living, and the unborn. We living Americans are therefore links in a vital chain, and we are charged with high responsibilities both to the future and to the past. Now that we know our duty, we shall not fail therein.

For we living Americans are a mighty host, endowed with ample strength, intelligence, and vision. Loyal America consists not only of the old stock but also of every soul from the newer stocks who believes in America's ideals and institutions. Some of the best and truest Americans are men and women who, though born in other lands, are one with us and have, by a sort of spiritual adoption, become joint heirs of our past and coworkers for our common future. These fellow citizens (in the real sense of the word) rejoice in the thought that the living foundations of the Republic are solidly laid in the great mass of the old stock, nearly 50,000,000 strong, who are the enduring basis of our national life.

Let false prophets of hyphenism and sedition remember those 50,000,000! For not only do they contribute one-half of all the White blood in America, they also furnish brains and leadership out of all proportion to their numbers. In every field of endeavor, whether it be agriculture, business, literature, politics, or science, the old stock displays its intellectual and constructive ability. Statistical studies have shown that, in proportion to its numbers, the old stock in different parts of the country furnishes from three to ten times its numerical quota of eminent men.[1] Today, as in the past, leadership remains chiefly in old-stock hands.

Furthermore, despite minor sectional and local differences, the old stock is everywhere profoundly one in ideals, culture, and outlook. Scientific research has proved the striking homogeneity of the old stock in all parts of America,[2] and this similarity of physical type is reflected in a corresponding likeness of temperament and attitude. As a qualified expert on the subject writes, "Hence it comes about (no American needs to be told) that the great central, inspiring, and controlling element of the American population over a domain of three million square miles is singularly homogeneous

---

1. On this point see the statistical studies made by Doctor Frederick Adams Woods, summarized in his paper entitled "Racial Origins of Successful Americans," *Popular Science Monthly*, April, 1914.
2. See the anthropometrical survey of the old stock mode by the Smithsonian Institution under the direction of Doctor Ales Hrdlicka, previously referred to in these pages.

and singularly at one in ideals. Any intelligent stranger from New England entering the home of a well-to-do family selected at random in a far Southern state would, upon inquiry, find a similar origin and the existence of opinions, hopes, and principles varying from his own only to the extent that might be expected as a result of a different climate and a different environment. He would find, also, exactly the same language, varied only by a slight local accent. Were he similarly to enter a farmhouse in Iowa, he would be likely to find the descendants of respected citizens of his own state, or even county, a century ago; and they probably would exhibit among their household goods some prized bits of furniture or silver that were brought over by the Pilgrims or made in colonial days. In such households is found the old national spirit, and here, also, the traditions of the past. They are substantially the same in this basic national stock, whether its members be resident in New England, the far South, or the far West."[3]

Such is the old American stock, which today numbers practically one-half of our entire White population and which the last census shows to be increasing at a normal, healthy rate, except in a few of the Northeastern states. If now we add to the old stock the many millions of the "Old Immigrant" stocks who have been completely assimilated and the increasing minority of "New Immigrant" stock that has genuinely accepted American ideals, we need not worry about America's ultimate future. Now that the gates are closed to the alien flood, America can stabilize its national life and can steadily reforge its racial and cultural unity. Slowly but surely, we will become again what we once were—an essentially homogeneous, like-minded people.

One of the most hopeful portents for the future is the fact that we can already discern the first foreshadowings of a cultural renaissance in America. In preceding pages, we surveyed America's first cultural flowering and showed how it was the normal consequence of the fusion of kindred stocks, resulting in the evolution of common standards, which, in turn, expressed themselves in harmonious forms of literature and art. We likewise saw how this early cultural flowering was prematurely blasted by the fires of civil war and the blight of alien factors. Nothing is more certain than the blighting effect of alien forces on a nation's cultural life. The abstract merit of intruding foreign cultures will not avert the blighting effects. It is not a matter of superiority or inferiority, but of *difference*. Indeed, the more admirable an alien culture is, the more tenaciously its bearers will cling to it and seek to

---

3. Rossiter, William S.: "Who Are Americans?" *Atlantic Monthly*, August, 1920. Mr. Rossiter was long an official of the Federal Census Bureau and is a recognized authority on our population problems.

perpetuate it, and the sharper will be the struggle between rival standards that will ensue. The increasing pressure of alien cultures is the reason why America's ideals and standards have become increasingly uncertain for the past few decades. That is likewise the reason why our literature has been so confused and our art forms so chaotic. If the alien influx had continued much longer, not only would there have been a general breakdown of ideals and standards, but we might never have been able to re-create a truly national culture but would have remained culturally and spiritually "Balkanized."

Happily, this disaster has been averted. The national soul is today thoroughly aroused, and the alien influx has been stopped. For the first time since the Civil War, the American people are consciously one in spirit, while at the same time the degree of cultural isolation needed to reweld its weakened standards and traditions.

And the significant point is that, from the very moment of the "Great Awakening," the nation's cultural life began to show signs of new vitality. Beneath the cultural confusion, which still persists, and despite the loud clamor of disaffected aliens, we can discern the signs of a genuinely American cultural growth.

In this connection the author believes he should cite an interesting conversation that he had recently with a prominent architect of his acquaintance. This man fully shared the author's ideas regarding American conditions. Furthermore, he had long been impressed by the way in which the national awakening was being reflected in his professional field. Nothing, said he, better reveals the national spirit than the state of its architecture. Now, we know that down to the Civil War, our homes and public buildings alike expressed a harmonious national culture. But after the Civil War, American architecture slumped like everything else. And as time passed and alien factors increasingly intruded, American architecture became more and more confused. The seventies and eighties were architecturally a howling wilderness of post-mansard, neo-gothic, and other monstrosities. The nineties specialized in the "gingerbread" style and in homes with Queen Anne fronts and Mary Ann backs. The opening decade of the present century saw better copying of foreign forms, but no distinctively American architectural developments.

Then came the "Great Awakening." And American architecture woke up along with the rest. The past decade has witnessed truly remarkable achievements in our magnificent temples of business and education, our splendid country homes, and other lines. We are today evolving a whole series of distinctively "American" forms that truly express the national spirit and that therefore possess creative feeling and real beauty. Architecturally, America is finding itself once more. And the same thing is true, in greater or lesser degree, of nearly every phase of America's cultural life. Thus culturally, as well as racially and spiritually, alienism is being slowly but surely mastered. A stormy transition period in American culture still lies before us. Yet ultimately American culture will win out.

Let one thing be clearly understood: our goal is a distinctive national culture, just as it is a distinctive national stock, institutions, and ideals. Loyal America rejects absolutely the concept of a "Pluralistic America," Balkanized into a haphazard assortment of diverse racial and cultural groups. And loyal America rejects equally the idea of the "melting pot"—the fusion of all existing elements into a mongrel mass devoid of outstanding, dominant qualities.

When Americans say "assimilation," they mean *assimilation* in the true sense of the word—the complete absorption of the foreigner into the national life. We Americans frankly insist that the foreigner shall accept our basic ideals and viewpoint before we will admit him to anything more than a formal civic status. If he wishes to obtain full social recognition as "one of us," he must demonstrate to our satisfaction that he *is* "American" in spirit as well as in clothing and other externals. With all its inconveniences, we prefer a slow process of genuine assimilation to a rapid process of fusion, which would break down our characteristic national life and would merge our identity with that of alien, discordant elements.

Genuine assimilation must necessarily be an *individual* matter. Individuals of foreign origin can outgrow their alienism and become really Americanized. But how, pray, can you "Americanize" a group?

Now, most Americans instinctively sense the true nature of assimilation. They prove this by their social attitude, which is often much sounder than their words might seem to indicate. Many a worthy citizen who is forever preaching "Americanization" never dreams of taking an unassimilated alien into the bosom of his family. And this social attitude of Americans is, on the whole, a good thing, because it means that we are admitting to intermarriage only those individuals who show distinct capacity for assimilation. In this way, notwithstanding a steady infiltration of foreign blood, our racial and national identity will be kept substantially intact. Broadly speaking, only those who are relatively like us in mental and temperamental make-up will mingle their blood with ours, while genuinely "alien" strains will be prevented from perturbing our stock with their discordant qualities.

The bitter criticisms of American "exclusiveness" and "snobbishness," which disgruntled aliens often utter, are thus really left-handed compliments to our sound racial instinct. Imagine what would happen if we did not feel as we do. Suppose that by some strange temperamental transformation our attitude should be suddenly reversed, and the unassimilated alien masses should be admitted to close social intimacy and general intermarriage. Such wholesale admixture with even the alien minority now among us would profoundly disturb our racial identity and hence permanently alter our national and cultural existence, whereas the racial incorporation of even large numbers of assimilable individuals, spread over a relatively long period, will produce no such disturbing effects.

Furthermore, we should realize that during this same period, while the more assimilable elements are being absorbed, the most unassimilable elements will tend to be eliminated. In the previous chapter we saw that many aliens today feel so unadapted and discontented that they voluntarily quit America, either for their homelands or for other countries that they deem more congenial. In the long run, we shall thus get rid of a considerable proportion of the most unassimilable and dissatisfied elements in our population.

And even those unassimilable elements that remain may be largely eliminated by various causes. It is a law of nature that any organism, animal or human, that fails to adjust itself to its surroundings tends to be weeded out. We have seen how the nondescript types of our Northern cities fall prey to vice, crime, and general moral instability. Under such unfavorable circumstances their future seems far from bright. Some observers believe that the bulk of these urban nondescripts will be eliminated in a comparatively brief period—say, two or three generations. Since there is little likelihood of extensive intermarriage between them and the older stocks, they will thus constitute a temporary social phenomenon that will eventually disappear, leaving only a few permanent traces in our future population.

One thing is certain: so far, America shows no signs of being a "melting pot." Careful statistical studies have shown that nowhere does the old stock intermarry much with the newer immigrant elements. Such unions as do occur are mostly between Americans and persons of immigrant groups that are racially akin. The old stock mixes freely with newcomers of British blood and with English-speaking Canadians. Intermarriage is less common, though still relatively frequent, between the old stock and persons of other North European nationalities like the Scandinavians, Germans, and Dutch. But unions of the old stock and the newer immigrant elements from Eastern and Southern Europe are comparatively few and do not appear to be rapidly increasing. Finally, each of the immigrant groups tends to intermarry within itself. This strong tendency toward what is known as "assortative mating" is evident at every social level. For example, a recent study of the parentage of college students shows that even where the parents were of different national origins ,they were almost invariably of kindred racial stocks.[4] We should, of course, realize that the ordinary census reports are misleading, because they class all Native-born individuals of Native-born parents under one head, with no distinction of national origin. However, the special investigations that have been made prove beyond question that most of the unions recorded by the census as between the Native-born and persons of foreign birth or foreign parentage are marriages of individuals having the same national origin. It is safe to conclude that, generally speaking, the rule is that "like tends to mate with like." Thus, only where individuals have become so "like" us that they are practically indistinguishable from us will intermarriage readily take place. In short: the "melting pot" is a myth, clearly opposed to facts.

Furthermore, the "melting pot" idea is not only false biologically; it is equally false as regards culture, standards, and ideals. A moment's reflection will make this clear. How, pray, can you "melt" and fuse even two distinct, well-established languages (to say nothing of twenty or thirty!) into a new synthetic speech? It simply can't be done. How can you fuse two or more different moral ideals whose very nature it is to be absolute and mutually exclusive? Again, the thing cannot be done. The only result of "harmonizing" even two distinct ideals would be to break down both and leave no moral sanctions whatsoever. Lastly, how can you fuse two or more patriotisms? Try it, and you get a loose cosmopolitanism, with no real loyalty of any kind.

The whole "melting pot" theory is absurd. Whether applied to human beings, languages, cultures, or ideals, it gets you nowhere—unless your objective is a chaotic mass in which everything distinctive has been cancelled out by the mutually destructive action of disharmonic, antagonistic forces.

That is what general *fusion* means. The only practical alternative is *assimilation*—the absorption of all assimilable elements into *one* of these human stocks, languages, and cultures. This does not mean that certain new traits, words, ideas, or cultural forms may not be harmoniously incorporated during the process of assimilation. But it does mean that the dominant, assimilating factor must survive, must retain its identity, and must emerge from the absorbing process essentially itself.

---

4. Holmes, Professor S. J.: "The Nature of So-called Mixed Marriages among the Parents of College Students," *Journal of Heredity,* August 1926.

So much loose thinking and sentimental substitutes for thought have obscured the true meaning of assimilation that the realities of the process should be frankly faced by both the American and the unassimilated foreigner. The matter is nowhere better stated than by Professor Fairchild, a leading authority on immigration problems, who writes, "It must be confessed that the implications with reference to the stranger within our gates are rigid and harsh enough. It is he who must undergo the entire transformation; the true member of the American nationality is not called upon to change in the least. The traits of foreign nationality that the immigrant brings with him are not to be mixed or interwoven. They are to be *abandoned*. The standard to which he must conform has already been fixed by forces quite outside himself, quite outside any individual, Native or foreign; fixed by all the factors—topographical, climatic, racial, historical, and fortuitous, which have worked together to make the American nationality what it is. A harsh situation, indeed! But a situation the harshness of which is determined not by the inclination or wish of any person or group of persons but by the inherent qualities of human nature and social organization. It can therefore not be eliminated by any sentimental aspiration, however generous or altruistic. If our nation is to be preserved, we must all, Natives and foreigners alike, resign ourselves to the inevitable truth that unity can be maintained only through the complete sacrifice of extraneous national traits on the part of foreign elements. There is no 'give-and-take' in assimilation."[5]

That is the plain truth of the matter. The foreigner must abandon everything distinctly alien to American life if he is to be genuinely assimilated. It is he who must make practically all the sacrifices. The crucial question, which, in all fairness, we may suggest that he should ask himself, is this: Is not America worth being absorbed into?

Happily, many of the newer stocks are today asking themselves just that question and are answering that America is, indeed, profoundly worthwhile. None of our new-stock citizens have spoken so bravely and finely as has Gino Speranza, whose stirring words we will here quote.

Says Mr. Speranza: "There is a tendency in certain new-stock 'intellectuals,' aided and abetted by 'internationally minded' Americans, to theorize about a future amalgamated or mongrelized Americanism. Some of these look forward with satisfaction to a 'Synthetic America' or a federated United States composed of racial groups living side by side. . . . I, for one, am against all these. I am not, even remotely, of Anglo-Saxon or Nordic stock. But this is my country. And the test of service and devotion for the new stock may

---
5. Fairchild, Henry P.: *The Melting-Pot Mistake*, pp. 154-155.

be, after all, not how much we give of ourselves, but how much of ourselves we deny. The task and the call for us all—old stock and new—as I envision it, is to strive to keep America as it was, and, as I pray with all my mind and heart, as it may ever be."[6]

There speaks true Americanism! And any new-stock citizen who feels that way need not worry about his position in American life, because he is a real American and will be treated as such by all who are themselves good Americans. Snobbery and ignorant prejudice, of course, exist here, as elsewhere. Nevertheless, the fact remains that, generally speaking, the man or woman of foreign birth or descent whose attitude and conduct are genuinely American will be accorded equal opportunities and will not be discriminated against because of his or her national origin.

The persons who rail at our "snobbishness" and who complain that they are being treated as an inferior caste are, in practically every case, *alien-minded*. They are the persons who, whether born abroad or born here, are not mentally or spiritually part of us. They are the ones who are forever telling us what they think we should do, or they are those whose manners, standards, and business methods shock and offend our sensibilities.

Of course we don't like such people, and of course we hold them socially at arm's length. What else should they expect? If they gave the matter a little more thought, they might realize that their angry discontent merely shows that in their heart of hearts they want America to adjust itself to them, instead of trying to adjust themselves to America. And they might as well get that idea out of their heads, because America will do no such thing.

But when alien-minded critics assert that they are victims of caste, they assert what is not true. We have only one social division that can be termed "caste." That is the color line, drawn between the White and non-White elements of our population. The color bar, however, is no grievance for the European immigrant. It does not personally concern him. What he terms "caste" is, therefore, *class*—a very different matter, because individuals may cross class lines, if they can qualify.

Of course, class lines exist in America, as they do in every complex society. Furthermore, class lines are undoubtedly drawn more tightly than they once were, chiefly owing to the presence of alien elements. And, as we have already seen, this is a wise and necessary means of guarding our racial stock against too rapid intermixture and of protecting our national life and culture from the impact of alien, antagonistic forces.

However, now that immigration restriction has stopped the alien influx,

---

6. Speranza, Gino: *Race or Nation*, pp. 32-33.

the present rigidity of class lines should gradually relax as alienism wanes and the protective necessity thereby diminishes. It is really for the aliens to decide how soon our class lines shall be relaxed. The faster they assimilate, the quicker the relaxation will be. Meanwhile, it is always possible for any individual alien to outdistance his fellows, become fully Americanized, and be completely absorbed into the national life. Or, if training and tradition make this impossible for him, he can look forward to it for his children or grandchildren. Only those stocks that are mentally and temperamentally most remote from us need fear that they will never be absorbed. And that is obviously something for which neither we nor they are at fault. Persons who really feel that neither they nor their descendants will ever be one with us simply do not belong here. For their own sakes as well as ours, their wisest course would be to go elsewhere.

If unadapted, dissatisfied individuals could only realize that *nobody* is really to blame for the general situation, it would greatly diminish *personal* bitterness and hence ease social friction in many ways. We should all try as far as possible to take an objective attitude toward the problems that confront us. Men may differ profoundly as to how problems should be solved and may oppose one another strenuously in seeking to bring about their respective solutions. Yet they need not hate one another as individuals or regard opposition as a personal matter. By turning a public controversy into a private feud, they ulcerate their own souls with the venom of malice and rancor and so degrade themselves. Therefore, even those who most dislike America should not hate Americans. On the other hand, we Americans should not hate even those whom we may rightly regard as the most dangerously disaffected elements in the population. Plain speaking we must have. Drastic public action may be required. But personal abuse and hatred should be vigorously combated by sensible men of all parties. To many members of disaffected minorities, this may at first glance seem a counsel of perfection. Yet if they will consider the matter, they will see that it is in their own interest. For if blind hatred should hold sway, if popular passions should rage unrestrained, would not those minorities be the worst losers?

However, unless all signs fail, the fabric of our national life is too staunch to be rent by storms of passion and hatred. On the contrary, the omens point unmistakably to better times. The reawakening of the American people and the stabilization of the national life have already produced material and spiritual fruits that proclaim an abundant harvest. Never was the country more soundly prosperous, and never was our prosperity on a healthier basis. Not since the nation's youthful days have there appeared such hopeful signs of idealistic and cultural growth.

America is entering a new and better time. It is re-welding its nationhood, and on firm foundations it is erecting a majestic structure, spacious and ample for all who call it *home*. This new America is being built on the rock of sane idealism. Sentimental theories and short-sighted egoism are alike in giving way before patriotic devotion and enlightened common sense. America is becoming more and more a land where, within the bounds of the public good, every individual has his chance and is given a "square deal."

Despite the difficulties of our transition period, these are times of splendid opportunity, which promise a yet more splendid future. Let every man realize this. Even if he is dissatisfied with certain aspects of American life, let him see how he can help improve it by constructive effort, instead of wasting his energy in vain attempts to pull it down and build something different in its place. Such notions get him nowhere but merely lead to disillusionment and all-round failure.

The only wise course for the unadapted alien to pursue is to accept the fact of America, try to understand it, establish friendly relations with Americans, and seek by mutual cooperation to make America a worthy heritage for both his children and theirs. Such an attitude will give him a new vision and will bring him contentment through constructive effort. Even if he himself never becomes fully one with us, he can be reasonably sure that by rearing his children in such ideals, they will share in that better America that the future holds in store.

For only when America is reforged, only when it has once more become a true nation inhabited by a united, like-minded people, can it really achieve the high destiny of which it is capable. Think of the political, economic, and social problems, logically apart from alienism, that await solution! If we were today a people truly one in spirit, we could apply our entire thought and energy to the solution of those problems. As it is, they are all more or less crosscut and complicated by the vexatious issue of alienism, which handicaps us at every turn. That is why we are not progressing socially and culturally as fast as truly advanced peoples like those of Australia, New Zealand, and the Scandinavian nations. Those people do not compare with us in natural resources. Yet they are making far better use of the opportunities nature has given them, because they possess the precious treasure of true unity. They are like-minded folk, who think and feel basically in the same way. And not until we Americans are also a like-minded folk can we match their constructive progress in ways that are truly worthwhile.

There is the real challenge of the future! That is why every man and woman who loves America should strive unceasingly toward national reconstruction. For great as that task is, it is merely a stepping-stone to still higher destinies. To have done with our present dissensions, to emerge, through national unity, into a freer realm of spiritual concord and mutual understanding, should be the true inspiration for the reforging of America.

# List of Works Cited

*The American Commonwealth*, Bryce, James; vol. II, p. 498 (second ed. 1911).
*American Economic Review*, Supplement, vol. II, no. 1, March 1912.
*The American Negro*, Thomas, W. Hannibal. (1901)
*The American Negro of Today*, Washington, Booker T.; p. 67.
*Atlantic Monthly*, August, 1920. Rossiter, William S.: "Who Are Americans?"
*Atlantic Monthly*, August, 1926. Mitchell, Langdon.
*The Basis of Ascendancy*, Murphy, Edgar Gardner; p. 139 (1909).
*The Basis of Racial Readjustment*, Woofter, Thomas J.; p. 1 (1925).
*Century*, January, 1926. Thomson, C. A.: "The Man from Next Door."
*Congressional Record*, Vaile, William N., December 16, 1925.
*The Conquest of New England by the Immigrant*, Brewer, Daniel Chauncy; (1926).
*Culture and Democracy in America*, Kallen, Horace M.
*Current History*, March, 1924. Gregg, W. W.: "The Mulatto—Crux of the Negro Problem."
*Discussions in Economics and Statistics*, vol. II, p. 446. Walker, General Francis A.
*The Forum, September* 1892. Rood, H.: "The Mine Laborers in Pennsylvania."
*Journal of Heredity*, August 1926. Holmes, Professor S. J.: "The Nature of So-called Mixed Marriages among the Parents of College Students."
*The Literary Digest*, September 9, 1922, pp. 31-32, Quoted from.
*Literary Digest International Book Review*, August, 1924. Matthews, Brander: "Making America a Racial Crazy-Quilt."
*The Melting-Pot Mistake*, Fairchild, Henry P.; pp. 154-155.
*The Negro in American Life*, Dowd, Jerome; pp. 353, 517 (1926).
*The Negro Year-Book* for 1925-26, p. 76. Quoted from.
*The New Barbarians*, Abbott, Wilbur C.; (1925).
*The New Negro*, Locke, Alain; p. 134 (1925).
*A New England Girlhood*, Larcom, Lucy; (1889).
*North American Review*, January 1912. Hall, Prescott F.: "The Future of American Ideals."
*The Old World in the New*, Ross, E. A.; pp. 286-287 (1914).
*On New Shores*, Bercovici, Konrad pp. 15,17 (1925).
*The Passing of the Great Race*, Grant, Madison; (1916).
*Popular Science Monthly*, April, 1914. Doctor Frederick Adams Woods, "Racial Origins of Successful Americans."
*The Present Economic Revolution in the United States*, Carver, T. N.; p. 262 (1925).
*Race or Nation*, Speranza, Gino; pp. 14, 17, 20, 137-138 (1924).
*The Record of a City*, Kenngott, G. F.; (1912).
*Selective Immigration*, Davis, Hon. James J.; pp. 81, 27-29, 213-214, 208 (1925).
*Straight America*, Kellor, Frances; pp. 3-5 (1917).
*Studies in Evolution and Eugenics*, Holmes, S. J.; pp. 209-210 (1923).
*Thought, the Master of Things*. From the President's address, Coolidge, Calvin.
*When Africa Awakes*, Harrison, Hubert H.; p, 46 (1920).
*White America*, Cox, Earnest S. (1923).
*Why Europe Leaves Home*, Roberts, Kenneth L.; pp. 52-53 (1922).
*World's Work*, April 1923, pp. 602-610. Speranza, Gino.
*World's Work*, October, 1923. Strother, French: "The Immigration Peril."

*ff.: and following*
*n.: in footnote*

# INDEX

**Abbott**, Wilbur C., 199, 200; quoted, 143
**Abolitionists**, 48, belief of, in race equality, 21, 35, 36; *see also* Radicals
**Adams**, John, 111
**Agriculture** in America, 191, 192
**Africa**, limitation of slave trade from, 27 ff.; immigrants from, 54 n.
**Alienism**, revealed by Great War, 102; aggressive, 132 ff.; distinction between hyphenism and, 135, 136; need for effective policy toward, 142 ff.; Americans promoting, 190, 191; danger from, to Northeast, 196, 197; of new Americans, 201, 202; decrease in; 207, 208, 213; other problems overshadowed by, 379, 219
**Aliens**, immigration of, to America, 65, 66, 71 ff.; undesirable, 71, 89; effect of, on racial life, 94, 95; Ross' description of, 97; "colonies" or, 100, 101; aggressive, 103, 104, 131 ff.; 198, 199, 202-204 n.; separatist aspirations of, 131, 132; assimilability of individual, 131, 132; alliance of, against immigration, 136, 137, 142, 143, 198, 199; numerical claims of, 139; realization of alienism, 139, 140; American labor replaced by, 191; alliance between radicals and, 199, 202, 203; weakness due to small proportion of, 204-206; danger to, from anti-American activities, 206, 207; American social attitude toward, 213; unassimilated, 57, 190, 216, 217; concentration of, in North, 189; comparison of, to Southern extremists, 204; emigration of, 207, 214
**Alpines**, percentage of, among colonial immigrants, 4; in North Europe, 69; difference between East European, and Nordicized, 69, 70
**America**, importance of colonial period, 1 ff.; predominance of English in early, 2 ff.; Scotch migration to, 2, 3; German migration to, 3, 4; convicts shipped to, 5, 12; end of colonial period, 8, 9, 12; history of, affected by Revolution, 11, 18 ff.; population of, on eve of Revolution, 13, 14; independence declared by, 15, 16; emigration of Loyalists from, 16, 17; first racial loss of, 17; human cost to, of Revolution, 17; inevitability of separation of England and, 18; French influence in, 20, 151; Negro problem of, 6, 7, 21, 22, 149 ff.; immigration problem of, 21, 22, 53 ff.; 65 ff.; welding of national life of, 25 ff.; advantages from isolation, 25, 26, 212; growth of population from Revolution to 1860, 25, 26; two turning-points in race-life of, 29, 58, 59; emergence in, of a new culture, 31; great men produced by early, 31, 32; development of materialism in, 3, 39, 52, reconstruction in, 41 ff.; partisanship in, 51, 52; internationalism in, 56 ff.; national ideals of, 68, 69; Jewish problem in, 73, 74; industrial development, 77 ff.; predominance of

North Europeans in, 96, 142, 143; a prophecy concerning, 98; awakening of, caused by Great War, 99 ff.; "hyphenism" in, 102, 103; ideal of national conservation, 103, 104, 115, 117, 126, 127, 129 ff., 148, 149, 197; threatened mass immigration to, after Great War, 104 ff.; rise of modern immigration restriction in, 113 ff.; aggressive alienism in, 132 ff. 137 ff.; pluralistic, 142, 142; white population of, 189, 190; non-white population in, 190; benefit to, of restricted immigration, 195 ff.; danger to, from mass alienism, 198; prosperity of present-day, 209, 210, 218; homogeneity of old stock in, 210, 211; foreshadowings of cultural renaissance in, 211 ff.; architecture in, 212
**American** *Economic Review*, quotation from, 98
**Americans**, attitude of, toward British domination, 13; physical excellence of Native, 32; heritage bequeathed by Old, 32; national ideal of, 58 ff.; friction between Irish and, 62, 63; "social sterilization" of native, 80 ff.; historical thinking of, 125, 130; the new, 135, 136, 202 ff.; replaced by aliens, 191; social attitude toward aliens, 178 ff.; optimism of, 99, 100; ignorance of, concerning immigration conditions, 100 ff.
**Americanization**, of immigrants, 201, 202
**Amalgamation**, dislike of southern Negroes for, 171, 168; opposition to, based on race difference, 181
**Anglo-Saxons**, predominance of, in America, 2, 138; impossibility of Confederation, 18; Western pioneers from stock of, 27; immigration of, to America, 61, 62; similarity of, Scandinavians to, 63, 64; alien revolt against, 138
**Andaman Islanders**, 59
**Appomattox Court House**, 41
**Architecture**, national spirit revealed in, 212
**Armenians**, 69, 76
**Asiatics**, immigrant, 72, 76; restriction laws against, 76, 112, 113, 149, 150; bootlegged immigrants from, 120
**Ashkenazim Jews**, 73, 74
**Assimilation**, predisposition of North Europeans to, 60, 61; real meaning of, 61, 213-215; Anglo-Saxon power of, 61, 62; distinction between naturalization and, 61, 62; of Scandinavians, 63, 64; of Dutch, 63, 64; of old immigration, 64, 81, 82; lack of, among Poles, 72, 73; Letto-Lithuanians refractory to, 73; of Italians, 75; lack of, in Syrians and Armenians, 76; inability for, of new immigrants, 93, 94, 148; America's realization of shortcomings of, 101, 102 ff.; unfitness of Mexicans for, 122, 123; of individuals, 131, 132, 213, 214; early American power of, 132; intelligent immigrants temperamentally unadapted to, 140; possibilities of European

231

immigrant, 148; lack of, among French-Canadians, 189, 190
Atlanta, Booker Washington's address at, 167, 168; Commission on Inter-Racial Co-operation at, 177
Australia, immigration policy of, 67 n., 81, 112; true unity in, 219
Austria, political segregation in, 185
Azores Islands, immigrants from, 76

Balkans, immigrants from, 72, 73
"Barred zone," 112, 113, 115 n.
"Bauern," the, 63
Benson, Allan, quoted, 104
Bercovici, quoted, 139, 140
Biracialism, suggested policy of, 150, 179 ff.; distinction between caste and, 179, 180; benefit of, to Negroes, 181; from white man's point of view, 182 ff.; applied to politics, 185
Birth-rate, effect on native American, of immigration, 80, 86, 94, 95; normal in South and West, 95, 96; decline in Negro, 154, 155; decrease of, among new immigrants, 192-194
Blocs, alien, 126
Bohemians, the, 73
Bolshevik, Negro radicalism backed by, 176
Boone, Daniel, 29
Booth, 41
Brazil, 21, 170
Bristol, 12
Britain, *see* Great Britain
British, Scotch-Irish settled as loyalist garrison by, 2, 3 ; restriction of sending convicts to America overruled by, 5; attitude of, toward colonial America, 12 ff.; revolution followed by revulsion against customs of, 19, 20; Australia settled mainly by, 81; intermarriage between Americans and immigrant, 214, 215
"British America," possibilities of a, 13, 14
British Isles, Mediterraneans in, 69
British West Indies, migration of Loyalists to, 16, 17
Bryce, James, quoted, 84
Burke, 12, 14

Cajuns, the, 133
Calabria, delinquents from, 89, 90
Calhoun, John C., 19, 35, 204
California, Chinese influx into, 66, 67
Canada, Loyalist migration to, 17; immigrants from, 121
Canadians, intermarriage between Americans and, 214, 215
Cape Verde Islands, 54 n.; "Brava" Portuguese from, 76
Caribbean, instability of republics of, 149
Carolinas, the, non-English elements in early, 2, 3
Carpetbaggers, the, 49
Carver, T. N., 77

Caste, distinction between bi-racialism and, 180; distinction between class and, 217
Catherine, Czarina, 15
Charleston, (South Carolina), race-relations in, 166, 173
Chatham, 12, 14; *see also* William Pitt
Chicago, Negro quarters of, 176, 177
China, Tai-ping Rebellion in, 66
Chinese, influx of, into California, 66-68; unassimilability of, 68, 148; opposition of Americans to intermarriage with, 149
Chinese Exclusion Act, 67, 68, 112
Civil War, Negroes a cause of, 6, 7, 151; comparison of aftermath of Revolution and, 17, 18; not inevitable 18, 19; emotionally reinforced by Revolution 19; temporary sinking of immigration during, 26, 27, 53; high average physique of armies of, 30, 31; effect of, on national life, 33, 38, 39, 83, 199, 100; material and human costs of, 37, 38; reduction of birth-rate during, 38; racial impoverishment of, 38, 39; America's optimism intoxicated by, 99, 100; disaster of new immigration compared to, 93; materialism following, 77, 83, 99, 100, 209, 210
Class-lines, in America, 217, 218
Clay, 35
Climate, effect of American, on South Europeans, 194
Coins, "Liberty and Security," 22
Colonial Council, proposed by Franklin, 9, 12
Colonies, American, seemingly inevitability of separation of, from Great Britain, 11 ff.; grounds of, for dissatisfaction, 12 ff.; British attitude toward, 12; loyalty of, to England, 14; British attempts to subdue, 15; independence declared by, 15, 16
Colonies, foreign, 72, 75, 100, 139, 201
Colonists, American, predominance of English among, 2 ff.; national and racial origins of, 3, 4; high selection of, 4, 5, 29; primacy in development of America acquired by, 6; bonds of union among, 7 ff.; relations between motherland and, 8, 9; Loyalists among, 16; national aspirations founded on theoretical and cosmopolitan ideals, 20
Colonization, possible Negro, 186, 187
Color line, the, principle of national life, 149, 150; denounced by Northern radicals, 153, 156 ff.; 166; recognized foundation in South, 166 ff.; an advantage to the Negro, 169 ff.; in the North, 175; strengthening of, 176; applied to Orientals, 181; necessity for legal sanction of, 183; America's only caste, 217
Communists, distinction between humanitarian internationalists and, 57
Concord, 14
Confederates, possible proscription of, 17, 18; spirit of, 37
Congress of 1865, the, attitude of, toward

# INDEX

South, 45 ff.; Johnson's unpopularity with, 45 ff.
Congressional Committee on Immigration, bearings of, 93
*Conquest of New England by the Immigrant, The*, 95
Constitution, the American, 21; slave-trade prohibited by, 27, 28, 109
Convicts, sent to America, 5, 12; sent to Australia, 81
Coolidge, Calvin, quoted, 109, 129
Copperheads, 18, 44
Cotton-gin, invention of, 28
Cox, Earnest S., 187 n.
Crédit Mobilier, 52
Creoles, the, 133
Croley, 48
Cro-Magnons, the, 69 n.
Culloden, 3, 15
Cultural Pluralism, 141
*Culture and Democracy in the United States*, 140
Cumberland, "The Butcher," 15
Curran, Henry, 116, quoted, 118, 119
Czechs, immigrant, 73

Danes, character of immigrant, 64
Davis, James J., 115, quoted, 89, 120, 194, 200, 201; on immigration policy, 110
Davis, Jefferson, 36 n., 37
Death-rate, among aliens, 193; alien infant, in New York City, 193, 194
Declaration of Independence, 12, 15; interpretation of phrase in, 21
Delaware, included as slave soil, 27 n.
Democratic Party, 44-46, 50, 51
Denmark, a source of old immigration, 60
Deportation methods, proposed wholesale, 120
Diderot, 20
Disease, among emancipated Negroes, 154, 155
Dowd, quoted, 170, 184, 185
Dubois, Dr., 175
Dutch, the, 63, footholds in colonial America, 3, 4; immigration of, to America, 64

East, industrial development in, 25, 77 ff.; undesirable elements of old immigration in, 80; concentration of immigrants in, 87, 96, 130, 189, 191, 198; danger to, from alienism, 196, 197
Emigration, of the Loyalists, 16, 17; of unassimilable aliens, 207, 214
"Encyclopedist" school, the French ideas of, 20; consequences to America of ideas of, 21, 22
England, American attitude toward domination of, 13; population of, on eve of Revolution, 13; Florida ceded to, and recovered from 13 n.; inevitability of separation of America and, 18; *see also* Britain

English, the, predominance of, among early American colonists, 1, 2; convicts sent to America, 5, 12; colonists' loyalty to, 5; hostility of French for colonists, 8; relations between motherland and overseas, 8, 9; power of assimilation with Americans of, 59, 60, 61; *see also* British
Eskimos, 59
Europe, Eastern, complexity and instability of, 69, 70-72; Alpines in, 69; immigrants from, 72-75; Ashkenazic Jews in, 74; bootlegged immigrants from, 120
Europe, Northern, stability and basic unity of, 69, 70
Europe, Southern, racial and political conditions of, 70; varying degrees of culture in, 71, 72; bootlegged immigrants from, 120
Europeans, East, effect on industry, of immigrants, 82; present immigration quota of, 117, 118; percentage of, American white population, 148; radicalism among, 200; few Intermarriages between Americans and, 214, 215
Europeans, North, predominance of, in America, 2, 4, 96, 147, 148, 189, 190; favored by America's immigration policy, 58 ff.; racial mixtures among, 69; predominance of Nordics among, 69; immigration of, 80 ff., 117, 118; America founded by, 147, 148; became America farmers, 191, 192; intermarriage of Americans and, 214, 215
Europeans, South, immigrants from, 75, 81, 82; present immigration quota of, 117, 118; percentage of in American white population, 147, 148; effect of American climate on, 194; radicalism among, 196, 197; few Intermarriages between Americans and, 214, 215
Europeans, Western, present immigration quota of, 117, 118

Fairchild, Henry P., quoted, 215, 216
Famine, potato, in Ireland, 26
Federal Reserve banking system, 93
Filene, Edward A., quoted, 125
Fisk, Jim, 52
Flemings, immigration of, to America, 64
Florida, ceded to United States, 14 n.
Forests, stripped by lumber kings, 84
Forty-Eighters, the, 63
France, Jacobin rulers of, 21; immigrants from, 60, 64 n.; Cro-Magnons of, 69 n.
Franklin, Benjamin, 9, 10, 12, 14; immigration problems, forecast by, 110, 111
Frederick the Great, 15
Freedmen, 152 ff.
Freedman's Bureau, 49, 153
French, the, among early settlers in America, 1, 2; hostile pressure from, 1, 8; eminent men contributed to America by, 4, 5; influence of, in America, 20, 151

## 234  INDEX

French Revolution, Democratic tendencies stimulated by, 19, 20
French-Canadians, in United States, 190

Garvey, Marcus, 176, 187
George III, 13, 15
Georgia, non-English elements in early, 2; Loyalists in, 16; opposition of, to extinction of slavery, 22, 33, 34, 41
Germans, in colonial America, 2, 3; immigration of, 26, 62, 63; assimilability of, 131
Germany, a source of Old immigration, 60; Alpines in, 69
Gladstone, 37
Gould, Jay, 52
Gracchi, the, 88
Grant, Ulysses, 41, 42, 49
Grant, Madison, 196
Great Britain, relations of colonies and 8 ff.; loyalty of colonists to, 13, 14, 16; attempts of, to subdue America, 15; soldiers given by colonists to cause of, 16; a source of old immigration, 60; *see also* England
Great War, drop in immigration at out-break of, 54; mental and spiritual changes caused by, 99, 100, ff., 209; causes aliens' realization of alienism, 136, 137
Greece, Ancient, 11
"Gresham's Law," 186, 106, 107
Greeks, decrease of, in America, 193
Gregg, W. W., quoted, 172

Hall, Prescott F., 96, 113
Hanover, King George elector of, 15
Harding, Warren G., quoted, 117
Harlem, 162
Harrison, Hubert H., quoted, 176
Hartford Convention of 1814, the, 19 n.
Hayes, Rutherford B., President, 1877, 50
Hayne, 35
Hebrides, the, 69 n.
Henry, Patrick, 20
Hessians, hired by Britain, 15
Highlanders, Scotch, 2, 3
Hillquit, Morris, campaign slogan of, 104
"Hobos," of the nineties, 85
Hogarth, 85
Holland, a source of old immigration, 60
Holmes, S, J., quoted, 131
House of Commons, Franklin examined before, 14
Hrdlicka, Ales, 31, 210 n,
Hudson, the, Dutch settlements along, 3
Huguenots, French, In colonial America, 2, 4; rapid assimilation of, 4; eminent men contributed to America by, 5
Hungarians, immigrant, 73
"Hunkios," 73 n.
"Hyphenism," in America, 102, 132, 133; distinction between alien, ism and, 135, 136;

Doctor Kallen a champion of, 140 ff.

Iberian Peninsula, racial changes in, 70
Icelanders, the, immigration of, 63, 64
Immigration, origin of problem in Encyclopedists' ideas, 22; open policy of early America toward 22, 23, 53, 54; first great wave of, 26; low average of, up to 1820, 26, 27; Irish, 26, 62, 63; German, 26, 62, 63, 74; problem of, 52, 65, 71; importance of, 54, 56; America's present policy, 58 ff.; Scotch, 65; undesirable elements of, 64 ff.; 71, 89; alien, 65, 66, 71; Chinese, 66-68; East European, 72-75; of Jews, 73-75; South European, 75; Italian, 75, 76, 95; Anglo-Saxon, 61; Scandinavian, 63; Dutch, 64; Flemish, 64; Spanish, 76; Portuguese 76; Western Asiatic, 76; of North Europeans, 80 ff.; difference between New and Old, 93, 130, 131; Johnson Act, 118, 119, 109, 209; "bootlegged," 119 ff.; suggested alien-registration law, 120, 121; New World, 121 ff., from Canada, 121; from Mexico, 121 ff., 149; bearings of Congressional Committee on, 93; evils of mass, 104, 105, 133 ff.; threatened mass, 104, 105 ff.; unnecessary to efficient industry, 105, 106; high-water mark of, 105; perils of, seen by founders of nation, 110-112; slavery problem overshadows, 112; economic attitude toward, 114; report of Roosevelt Commission on, 114; apportionment of, 116 ff.; quota schedules of, 117, 118; effect of, on industry, 79 ff., 124; on native American birth-rate, 80, 94, 95; restriction of, opposition to, 56, 88, 90, 136, 137, 142, 143, 198, 199; law of 1882, 90; dignity of labor revived by, 92; Increase in advocates of, 102, 103; Asiatic, 112, 113, 149, 150; early European, 112, 113; rise of modern, 113 ff.; law of 1917, 115 n.; benefits from, 124, 192, 195 ff.; disasters averted by, 130, 204, 212
Immigration, New, 60, 61, 64-66, 68, 69, 71 ff.; four main groups of, 72; perils of, 81, 82, 94, 95, 96; alien character of, 81, 82, 86, 92, 101, 102; cessation of Old, because of, 86, 94, 95, 118, 119; effect on industry of New, 81, 82, 114; undesirable elements in, 89, 90, 93; unassimilability of, 92, 93; concentration of, in Northeast, 87; disaster of, compared to Civil War, 93; effect of, on racial life, 93-95
Immigration Restriction League, 96 n.
Immigrants, natural selection among early, 89; transatlantic rates for, 89; low-grade alien labor, compared to Negro slaves, 90; mental capacity of, 94 (East European, 114; South European, 114; from Western Asia, 114;) three attitudes among, 200 ff.; intermarriages within groups or, 214, 215
Immigrants, New, present stock of, in America, 96, 190; mental capacity of, 94; appeal of

# INDEX

Red movement to, 104, 200; concentration of, in Northeast, 191, 192; ill-adapted to agricultural life, 191, 192; decrease in birthrate of, 192-194; low infant death rate of, in New York City, 193, 194; psychological strains on, from adaptation to American life, 194; historic background of, 200; few intermarriages between Americans and, 213 ff.

**Immigrants, Old,** 60 ff.; non-alien character of, 64, 65; cessation of, because of New, 86, 94, 95, 118; migration to West, 80 ff.; assimilability of, 80, 81; raised to preeminence by restriction laws, 117, 118; present stock of, In America, 189, 190

**Independence,** distinction between inevitability of, 11, 13, 14, 18; fact of, and manner achieved, 11, 18; stimulation to Americans of, 18, 99, 100

**Indians,** a factor in uniting colonists, 7, 8; set by British Government on colonies, 15-17; joined by Loyalists, 17; perils to Pioneers from, 29; lack of national spirit in, 55; Mexican, 121-123; population, in United States, 190

**Industry,** development of, in East, 77 ff.; leaders of, 78, 83-85, 91; effect of immigration on, 79 ff., 92, 93, 105, 106, 104, 191; transformation of conditions In Pennsylvania, 82; based on Greenie labor, 91; immigration favored by, 121 ff.

**Internationalism,** to America, 56 ff.; difference between humanitarian and Communist, 57; humanitarian, 110

**Inter-Racial Co-operation,** Commission on, 177, 178

"**Invisible Empire,**" 50

**Ireland,** a source of Old immigration, 60; potato famine in, 62; "Old Black Breed" types of, 69 n.

**Irish,** Scotch in colonial America, 2, 3; Celtic, 3; immigration of, 26, 62, 63; Celtic distinguished from Scotch, 62 n.; friction between Americans and, 62

**Israel,** Ashkenazim descended from, 74

**Italians,** in New Amsterdam, 3; racial stocks of North and South, 70, 71, 75, 76; immigrant, 75, 76, 90; American attitude toward North and South, 131, 132

**Italy,** racial changes to, 70; delinquents from, 90

**Jackson, Andrew,** 35, 36
**Jamestown,** 5
**Japan,** 115 n.; Gentleman's Agreement with, 113
   **Japanese,** unassimilability of, 148; opposition of Americans to intermarriage with, 149
**Jefferson, Thomas,** 20, 27, 41, 110, 111, 131, 151, 187
**Jews,** in New Amsterdam, 3; American attitude toward, 132; immigrant, 193
**Jews, East European,** 69, 70; racial make-up of immigrant, 73-75; national life unknown to, 75, 200
**Johnson Immigration Act** of 1924, 29, 54, 64, 65, 93, 94, 96 n., 113, 114-119, 209; National Origins clause of, 115, 116
**Johnson, Andrew,** Lincoln's reconstruction policies continued by, 41-43; unpopularity of, 45; attempt to remove by impeachment, 46
**Johnson, Albert,** 109
**Johnson, Samuel,** quoted, 13
**Judaism,** In Southern Russia, 74

**Kallen, Horace M.,** 140 ff.
**Kellor, Frances,** quoted, 103
**Kenngott, G. F.,** quoted, 79
**Khazars, the,** 70, 74
**Kipling,** quoted, 31
"**Knights of the White Camellia,**" 50
"**Know-Nothing**" movement, 112, 114
**Ku Klux Klan,** 50

**Labor, Chinese,** 66, 67; East European, 72; replacement of native American by immigrant, 79 ff., 84, 88, 89, 90, 91, 92, 95, 96, 191; brokers in, 89; low-grade alien, compared to Negro slaves, 90; Industrial progress hindered by cheap, 91; benefited by immigration restriction, 92; organized, a restrictionist force, 114; Mexican, 121 ff.; relations of capital and, 124, 125

**Lapps,** Mongoloid, 120 n.
**Larcom, Lucy,** quoted, 78, 79
**Laughlin, H. H.** 94
**Lawrences, the,** 83
**Lee, Robert E.,** 36, 41, 43
**Letto-Lithuanians,** immigrant, 73
**Lexington,** 14, 15
**Liberia,** Republic of, 186, 187
"**Liberty and Security**" coins, 22
**Like-mindedness,** basis of nationality, 147, 148
**Lincoln, Abraham,** 45, 152, 153; election of, signal for secession, 36; his plan for reconciliation, 41, 42; a believer in Negro colonization, 186, 187
"**Lobbies,**" in Washington, 114, 125, 126
**Louisiana,** mass-alienage in, 133
**Lowell,** 83; Industrial conditions preceding Civil War, 78, 79
*Lowell Offering,* 78
**Lowlands,** Scotch, 2, 3
**Loyalists,** the, 16; feud between Patriots and, 16; expulsion of, 16, 17
**Lumber Kings,** 84

**Machinery,** labor-saving, achievement of, 124-126
**Madison,** 110, 111
**Magyars,** immigrant, 73

Malaysia, Chinese immigration to, 67, 68
Māori, the, 185
Maryland, English predominance in early, 2
Marx, 57
Mason, of Virginia, 28
Mason-Dixon Line, 27, 34, 36
Materialism, 88, 89, 97; following Civil War, 77, 83, 99, 100, 209
Matthews, Brander, quoted, 132, 142
Mayflower, the, 5
Mediterraneans, in North Europe, 69; in Italy and Spain, 70; difference between British and South European, 70
Melbourne, 81
Melting-Pot, a myth, 214-216
Mexicans, unassimilability of, 122, 123, 257; population of, in America, 148
Mexico, immigrants from, 121 ff., 149; instability of, 149
Migration, British, to America, 2,3; of Scotch to America, 3; German, to America, 3,4; of Loyalists from America, 16, 17; mass, to America, 53 ff.; America's gates closed to mass, 107; of Negroes to North, 176, 177, 182, 183
Miscegenation, decrease of, 171, 176; necessity of legal prohibition of, 183
Mitchell, Langdon, quoted, 203, 204
"Molly Maguires," the, 81
Montgomery (Alabama), first Confederate capital, 36
Moton, Doctor, 168, 179; quoted, 168, 169
Mountaineers, loyalty of, to Union, 36
Mulattoes, explosive element in race problem, 172 ff.; leaders of radical movement, 172, 174, 175; decrease of, 172, 173, 175, 176; increase of dark, 173; aristocracy of Negrodom in slavery, 173, 174; few radicals among southern, 174; discontent among northern, 175, 176
Murphy, Edgar Gardner, quoted, 167, 168

Nashville (Tenn,), settlement of, 29, 30
Nation, as distinguished from a government, 55
Natural selection, among American colonists, 4; among Pioneers, 30, 31; among immigrants, 89, 191, 194, 195; among races, 148, 149
Nationality, basic realities of, 147
National Origins Clause, the, 116, 117, 123, 124
Naturalization, distinguished from assimilation, 61, 62
Negroes, number of, at outbreak of Revolution, 7; national problem, 6, 7, 149 ff.; colonial opposition to importation of slaves, 12; origin of problem, in Encyclopedists' ideas, 21, 22; Abolitionists' belief in equality of, with white men, 21; attitude of radicals toward, 47 ff.; enfranchisement of, 49; West Indian immigrant, 123; unassimilability of, 148; basic cause of Civil War, 149-151; suggested solutions of problem, 149, 150; freedmen, 151; entitled to naturalization, 151 n.; effect of Reconstruction on, 151 ff.; change In feelings of masters for, 152 ff.; average physical fitness of, before and after emancipation, 152, 154, 155; proportionate increase of whites and, 154; decline of birth-rate of, 154; Harlem, a capital of, 162; belief of South in education of, 168; acceptance by intelligent, of race-separation, 169, 171; advantage to, of race-separation, 169 ff., 176 ff.; tendency to crowd-contagion, 172; proportion of mulattoes among, 172, 173; attitude of, toward northern mulattoes, 176; northern migration of, 176, 177, 182, 183; growth of radicalism among northern, 176, 177; comparison of attitudes of northern and southern whites toward, 178, 179; possible ultimate colonization of, 186, 187
New Amsterdam, a polyglot town, 3
*New Barbarians, The,* 96
New England, English predominance in early, 2; patriotism in, 9; earliest talk of secession occurred in, 19 n.; industrial development in, 77 ff., 81, 82; racially conquered by aliens, 95; "Little Polands" in, 192; replacement of natives in, 194, 195
New Jersey, non-English elements in early, 6; growth of Dutch element in, 3, 4
New Mexico, mass-alienage in, 133
New Orleans, mulatto society in, 173
*New Secession, The,* 204
New York, non-English elements in early, 2, 3; Scotch in, 2, 3; only cosmopolitan spot in colonial America, 3; Loyalists in, 16 emigration of Loyalists from, 16 17; alien masses in, 95; Negro quarter of, 176, 177; new immigrants in, replacing natives, 195
New York State, "Little Polands" in, 192
New Zealand, immigration policy of, 112; political segregation in, 185; true unity in, 219
Nordics, predominance of, in colonial America, 4; in Northern Europe, 69
North, the, slavery extinguished in, 27; growth of, 35; migration of Negroes to, 176, 177, 182, 183; radicalism in, 179, 190, 191
Northwest Ordinance, the, 27, 28
Northwest Territory, slavery prohibited in, 28
Norway, a source of Old immigration, 60; Mongoloid Lapp of, 69 n.
Norwegians, character of immigrant, 64

*Operatives' Magazine,* 78
Orientals, color-line applied to, 181
Orientals, in United States, 190

Padrone system, 90
Paine, Tom, quoted, 20, 21

# Index

Pan-African movement, 176, 187
*Passing of the Great Race, The,* 196
Patriots, feud between Loyalists and, 16
Paupers, 193
Peasants, East European, 72, 73; South European, 72; Italian, in America, 75, 82; Slav, 82; effect of immigrant, on economic conditions of, 82, 83
Penn, William, 3
Pennsylvania, non-English elements in early, 2, 3; Scotch migration to, 2, 3; Welsh migration to, 3; German migration to, 3, 4; Industrial development in, 78, 81; change in economic, conditions in, 82; aliens in, 95
"Pennsylvania Dutch," the, 3
Peonage, 90
Peons, Mexican, 121, 149
Petrosino, Lieutenant, quoted, 90
Phillips, Wendell, 48
Pilgrims, 5, 6
Pioneers, Anglo-Saxon origin of, 27; natural selection among, 29, 30; industrial, 78, 83, 84
Pipe-Line immigration, 89, 90
Pitt, William (Lord Chatham), 8, 9
Plymouth, 5
Poland, Jewish immigration to, 74
Poles, the, non-assimilability of, 73, 74; colonies of, in America, 191, 192
Politics, corruption of, 67, 38, 39, 52; condition of, in 1865, 43 ff.; and racial readjustment, 183 ff.
Population, percentage of, colonial stock in present-day American, 6, 210, 211; Negro, 6, 7, 149, 150, 154, 190; of colonies and England, 13; shown by first national census, 25, 26; growth of, to 1860, 25, 26, 38; rapid growth of in West, 30; increase of, in North and West over South, 37; Jewish in America, 75; present Italian, in America, 75; high-grade, of Australia, 81; present white American, 96, 189, 190; Anglo-Saxon predominance in American, 138; relative increase in Negro and white, 154, 155; non-white, in America, 190
Portugal, 11; racial make-up of, 70
Portuguese, the "Brava," 54 n., 133; immigrant, 76
Prosperity, temporary, due to New immigration, 87; due to immigration restriction, 91-93; Americans blinded by false, 93, 97, 98; present-day, 209, 219, 220
Puritans, the, prolificness of, 2; idealistic motives of, 4, 5; eminent men contributed to America by, 5

Quebec, defeat of French at, 8
Quota schedule, 117, 118

Race, origin of colonial population, 4; loss to American, by Loyalist expulsion, 17; amalgamation of white and Negro, favored by radicals, 22, 47 ff., 151; two turning points in life of American, 29; impoverishment of American, by Civil War, 38; national life dependent upon make-up of, 55, 56; bade realities of, 256; divisions of mankind into, 258; undesirable results of intermarriage between, 258, 259; difference in, 147, 148, 167, 168, 180, 181; separation, in the South, 165 ff., 176 ff.
Radicals, racial policy of, 47 ff.; *see also* Abolitionists; aggressive alienism sympathetically regarded by, 142; in North, 153, 184, 185, 198; publications of, 165; alliance between aliens and, 199, 202
Radicalism, revolutionary, in America, 104; essentially a mulatto movement, 172; growth of, among northern Negroes, 176; among new immigrants, 200
Reconstruction, Lincoln's plan for, 41, 42; response of southerners to, 42, 43; effect on, of Congress of 1865-66, 44 ff.; aim of Congressional, 47; Republican, 47 ff.; Southern, 49 ff.; Northern disapproval of, 50; collapse of, 50, 153; Negro worse sufferer from, 151 ff.; tragedy to South of, 153; effect on southern mulattoes of, 174; national, necessity for plain speaking, 205 ff.
Reed, David A., 115
Republican Party, 44, 49, 50
Republicans, Radical, 47 ff.
Revolution, total white population of America at outbreak of, 4; the, not inevitable, 11, 14, 18, 19; American's misunderstanding of, 11 ff.; course of American history affected by, 11, 12, 17 ff.; causes of, 5, 12, 13, 15, a twofold civil war, 16; human cost to America of, 17; comparison of aftermath of Civil War and, 17, 18; influence of, on national consciousness, 17 ff.; Civil War emotionally reinforced by, 19; followed by anti-British bias, 19, 20 French aid to Americans in, 20
Roberts, Kenneth L., quoted, 107
Rome, Old, 87, 88
Rood, H., quoted, 82
Roosevelt, Theodore, 76, 102, 114, 189
Ross, E. A., quoted, 91, 97
Rossiter, William S., 211 n.
Rousseau, 20, 23, 110
Russia, Soviet, 57; Jewish immigration to, 74
Russians, the, 69, 70
*R. U. R.,* 67

Sardinia, delinquents from, 90
Savannah, social caste of light mulattoes in, 173
Scalawags, the, 49
Scandinavia, a source of Old immigration, 60; true unity in, 219
Scandinavians, the, assimilability of, 59, 131; immigration of, to America, 63, 64; similari-

ty of, to Anglo-Saxons, 64
Scotch, lowland, 2, 3; Highland, 2, 3; assimilability of, 59, 60; immigration of, 65
Scotch-Irish, in colonial America, 2, 3
Sectionalism, 33; decline or, 30
Sephardim Jews, 73- 75
Ships, immigrant, 5
Sicily, delinquents from, 89
Slavery, colonial opposition to, 12; limitation of, 27; southern attitudes toward, 27, 33, 34; prohibition of trade in, 27, 28, 109; spread of, in South, 28, 35; distinction between race-problem and, 150, 151
Slaves, emancipation of, demanded by Abolitionists, 21, 22; strength of holders, 37
Slavs, in Eastern Europe, 69, 70; decrease of Balkan, in America, 193
Slums, absence of, before 1840, 79; absence of, in West, 79; in Australia, 80, 81; In East, 92; Improvement in conditions of, with reduced immigration, 105, 106
Smithsonian Institute, 31 n., 210 n.
Socialist Party, 104
South, the, Loyalists in, 16; Negro rule imposed on, 22; attitude toward slavery of, 27, 33, 34-36; spread of slavery in, 28, 35; possible result to, from unprohibited slave-trade, 29; "cotton belt" of, 35; expansion of *far*, 35; proportion of slave-owners among white population of, 37; competition between free farmer and slave-owners, 37; response of, to reconstruction policies, 42, 43; attitude toward, of Congress of 1865-66, 44 ff.; divided into military districts, 49; secret societies in, 50; battle-ground of political and racial warfare, 50 ff.; creation of a Solid, 50, 51; race-segregation in, 166 ff.; 176 ff.; belief of, in education of Negroes, 168; political situation in, 183 ff.; increase or colonial stock in, 195, 196
South Africa, decrease of miscegenation in, 171
South Carolina, Loyalists in, 16; opposition of, to extinction of slavery, 27, 33, 34; nullification of tariff by, 34, 35; first shots of Civil War fired by troops of, 36 n.
Southern Sociological Congress, 177
Spain, Florida ceded to England and recovered by, 14 n.; racial make-up of, 70, 71
Spaniards, the, among early settlers In America, 1, 2; effect on English colonists of hostile pressure from, 1, 2, 8; immigrant, 76
Speranza, Gino, 134, 135; quoted, 216, 217
Steamship Lobby, the, 88
Stephens, Alexander H., 36 n.
Stevens, Thaddeus, 22, 47, 48
Strikes, In nineties, 85; post-war outlaw, 104
Strother, French, quoted, 101
Sugar Islands, 87, 88
Sumner, Charles, 22, 47, 48
Supreme Court, emasculation of, threatened by Congress, 47
Sweat-shop system, 90
Sweden, a source of Old immigration, 60
Swedes, the, footholds In colonial America, 1; character of immigrant, 63, 64
Switzerland, immigrants from, 63, 64 n.; Alpines in, 69
Sybilline Books, the, 110
Sydney (Australia), 81
Syrians, 126; immigrant, 72

Tai-ping Rebellion, the, 66
Thomas, W. Hannibal, 175 n.
Thomson, C. A., quoted, 122
Tolerance, distinguished from indifference, 203, 204
Toombs, Robert, 36 n.
Tories, the, see Loyalists
Tunis, 90
Tuskegee Institute, 168
Tweed, Boss, 52

Ukraine, Jewish immigration to, 74
Ulster, mass-migration from, 2, 3
Unemployment, previous to 1914, 91
Unionists, Southern, 39, 34, 36, 37
"United Empire Loyalists," 17
United States, Gentleman's agreement with Japan, 112, 113
University Commission on Southern Race-Problems, 177

Vaile, of Colorado, 116, 117
Virginia, English predominance in early, 2; patriotism in, 9, 33, 35, 36; split of, over loyalty to Union, 36
Voting, curial, 185

Walker, Francis, A., quoted, 82, 86
War of 1812, the, 19, 20, 25
Washington, "lobbies" in, 114, 115, 125-127
Washington, Booker, 167, 168, 174; quoted, 170
Washington, George, 19, 27, 34; quoted, 26, 110, 111
Webster, 35
Welsh, migration of, 3
Wendell, Barrett, dedication to memory of, 140
West, the, growth of, 20, 25, 26, 35, 30, 35, 77, 78; Anglo-Saxon stock of pioneers to, 27; German migration to middle, 63; increase of colonial stock in, 195, 196
West Indies, immigration from, 123
West Virginia, formation of, 36
Whiskey Ring, the, 52
Whitney, Eli, 28
Women, work of southern, for better race-relations, 178
Woods, Frederick Adams, 210 n.
Woofter, Thomas J., quoted, 168

Y. M. C. A., study groups of, 177

www.ingramcontent.com/pod-product-compliance
Lightning Source LLC
Chambersburg PA
CBHW032106090426
42743CB00007B/249